£90.00

Economics of Sustainable Tourism

Tourism is one of the world's largest industries and one of its fastest-growing economic sectors, helping to generate income and employment for local people. At the same time, it has many negative outsourced effects on the environment and local culture. Achieving a more sustainable pattern of tourism development is high on the global agenda, aiming to meet human needs while preserving the environment now and for the future.

Economics of Sustainable Tourism aims to critically explore how tourism economic development can move closer to a sustainable ideal from a firm economic analytical anchor. Grounded in economic theory and application, it analyses tourists' satisfaction and impacts of tourism on the host community, investigates the productivity of the industry and identifies factors that could increase economic and sustainable development, such as trade relationships. It offers further insight into how destinations' sustainability can be measured and the economic benefits of more sustainable destinations, and sets the agenda for future research. The book includes a range of theoretical and empirical perspectives and includes cutting-edge research from international scholars.

This significant volume provides a new perspective on the sustainable tourism debate and will be valuable reading for students, researchers and academics in the fields of tourism and economics.

Fabio Cerina is Lecturer in Economic Policy at the Department of Social and Economic Research, University of Cagliari, and Research Fellow at the Center for North South Economic Research (CRENoS).

Anil Markandya is Professor of Economics at the University of Bath, UK and Scientific Director of the Basque Centre for Climate Change in Bilbao, Spain.

Michael McAleer is Distinguished Professor, Department of Quantitative Economics, Complutense University of Madrid, Spain.

Routledge critical studies in tourism, business and management

Series editors: Tim Coles

University of Exeter, UK,

and

Michael Hall

University of Canterbury, New Zealand.

This ground-breaking monograph series deals directly with theoretical and conceptual issues at the interface between business, management and tourism studies. It incorporates research-generated, highly specialized cutting-edge studies of new and emergent themes, such as knowledge management and innovation, that affect the future business and management of tourism. The books in this series are conceptually challenging, empirically rigorous, creative and, above all, capable of driving current thinking and unfolding debate in the business and management of tourism. This monograph series will appeal to researchers, academics and practitioners in the fields of tourism, business and management, and the social sciences.

Published titles:

Commercial Homes in Tourism
An international perspective (2009)
Edited by Lynch, McIntosh and Tucker

Sustainable Marketing of Cultural and Heritage Tourism
Chhabra

Economics of Sustainable Tourism
Edited by Cerina, Makandya and McAleer

The Routledge Critical Studies in Tourism, Business and Management monograph series builds on core concepts explored in the corresponding Routledge International Studies of Tourism, Business and Management book series. Series editors: Tim Coles, University of Exeter, UK and Michael Hall, University of Canterbury, New Zealand.

Books in the series offer upper-level undergraduates and master's students comprehensive, thought-provoking yet accessible books that combine essential theory and international best practice on issues in the business and management of tourism such as HRM, entrepreneurship, service quality management, leadership, CSR, strategy, operations, branding and marketing.
Published titles:

International Business and Tourism (2008)
Coles and Hall

Economics of Sustainable Tourism

Edited by Fabio Cerina,
Anil Markandya and
Michael McAleer

Routledge
Taylor & Francis Group

LONDON AND NEW YORK

First published 2011
by Routledge
2 Park Square, Milton Park, Abingdon, Oxon OX14 4RN

Simultaneously published in the USA and Canada
by Routledge
270 Madison Avenue, New York, NY 10016

Routledge is an imprint of the Taylor & Francis Group, an informa business

© 2011 Fabio Cerina, Anil Markandya and Michael McAleer

The right of Fabio Cerina, Anil Markandya and Michael McAleer to be
identified as editors of this work has been asserted by them in accordance
with the Copyright, Designs and Patent Act 1988.

Typeset in Times New Roman by Wearset Ltd, Boldon, Tyne and Wear

British Library Cataloguing in Publication Data
A catalogue record for this book is available from the British Library

Library of Congress Cataloguing in Publication Data
Economics of sustainable tourism / edited Fabio Cerina, Anil Markandya,
and Michael McAleer.
p. cm.
Includes bibliographical references and indexes.
1. Sustainable tourism. I. Cerina, Fabio. II. Markandya, Anil, 1945–
III. McAleer, Michael.
G156.5.S87E26 2010
338.4′791–dc22

2010013214

ISBN: 978-0-415-58385-5 (hbk)
ISBN: 978-0-203-84233-1 (ebk)

Contents

Figures

Tables

Contributors

Eugeni Aguiló Pérez is Professor at the Department of Applied Economics in the University of the Balearic Islands, Palma de Mallorca. His interests are in the field of tourism economics, especially the application of quantitative economic techniques to the tourism phenomenon. He mainly publishes in specialized journals as *Annals of Tourism Research*, *Tourism Management*, *Tourism Economics* and the *Journal of Travel Research*.

Joaquín Alegre Martín is Professor at the Department of Applied Economics, University of the Balearic Islands, Palma de Mallorca. His research interests are in the microeconomic analysis of tourist demand, tourism destination competitiveness and the tour operator industry.

Giovanni Bella has been Lecturer at the University of Cagliari since January 2004, where he teaches undergraduate macroeconomics and postgraduate environmental economics. His research interests are in environmental economics, economic development and endogenous growth, macroeconomics, economics of transition and regional convergence, and mathematics.

Fabio Cerina is Lecturer in Economic Policy at the Deparment of Social and Economic Research, University of Cagliari, and Research Fellow at the Centre for North South Economic Research (CRENoS). His research interests are in tourism, the environment and growth, and economic geography.

Yaovarate Chaovanapoonphol is Assistant Professor at the Department of Agricultural Economics and Agricultural Extension, Faculty of Agriculture, Chiang Mai University. Her research interests are in rural economics, applied econometrics in agriculture, and economics and agribusiness.

Jaume Garau Taberner is Lecturer of the Department of Applied Economics at the University of the Balearic Islands, Palma de Mallorca. His PhD thesis was on tourist satisfaction, dissatisfaction and place attachment at sun and sand mass tourism destinations. His research interests are in tourism demand, tourist loyalty and tourism destination competitiveness, particularly in the case of mass mature destinations.

Sauveur Giannoniis is Lecturer in Economics at the University of Corsica (France). He completed his PhD in Economics in 2007, with an emphasis on the relationship between tourism development and growth. His main research fields are tourism and environmental economics.

Francisco J. Ledesma Rodríguez is Reader at the Department of Economic Analysis, University of La Laguna, Tenerife. His fields of research include tourism economics, international trade and exchange rates.

Christine Lim is Professor of Tourism Manaegement at the Waikato Management School, University of Waikato, New Zealand. Her research is of an applied nature in tourism demand modelling, which combines time series modelling, tourism economics and management.

Michael McAleer is Distinguished Professor, Department of Quantitative Economics, Complutense University of Madrid, Spain. He has published in a wide range of leading international journals, and his research interests include theoretical and applied econometrics, theoretical and applied statistics, time series analysis, financial econometrics, modelling environmental systems, intellectual property, methodology, tourism research and tourism management.

Anil Markandya is Professor of Economics at the University of Bath in the United Kingdom and Scientific Director of the Basque Centre for Climate Change in Bilbao, Spain. His research interests lie in the areas of microeconomics, quantitative economics, including econometrics, and environmental economics. It is the last of these that has been the focus of his research over the past 20 years and he is an acknowledged international authority in the field. Anil has published a textbook entitled *Environmental Economics for Sustainable Growth* (Edward Elgar, 2002).

Ståle Navrud is Professor of Economics at the Department of Economics and Resource Management, Norwegian University of Life Sciences, Ås, Norway. He has a solid international reputation in the area of environmental and non-market valuation, primarily for his focus on the environmental impacts of renewable energy, health effects of environmental exposure, recreational values, water quality, biodiversity, and historic and cultural heritage sites.

Yasuo Ohe is Professor of Rural Economics at the Department of Food and Resource Economics, Chiba University, Japan. His research topics are rural tourism and farm diversification.

Jorge V. Pérez Rodríguez is Head of the Department of Quantitative Methods in Economics and Business Administration at the University of Las Palmas de Gran Canaria. His research interests are in financial econometrics, time series analysis, in particular non-linear time series modelling and forecasting, artificial neural networks, and applied econometrics, in particular microeconometrics and panel data analysis.

Juan Ignacio Pulido Fernández is Lecturer in Applied Economics in the Department of Economics at the University of Jaén (Spain). His main research interests focus on destination management and economic development, sustainability, tourism impacts and innovation. He has published in journals such as *Tourism Economics* and the *Journal of Cultural Economics.*

Jaume Rosselló Nadal is Associate Professor at the the Department of Applied Economics in the University of the Balearic Islands, Palma de Mallorca. His interests are in the field of tourism economics, especially the application of quantitative economic techniques to the tourism phenomenon. He mainly publishes in specialized journals such as *Annals of Tourism Research, Tourism Management, Tourism Economics* and the *Journal of Travel Research.*

Marcelino Sánchez Rivero is Tenured Professor of Economic Statistics at the Department of Economics, University of Extremadura, Spain. His research interests are in tourism sustainability, tourism competitiveness, tourism demand, latent structure models, analysis of contingency tables and item response theory.

María Santana Gallego is Research Fellow at the Department of Economic Analysis, University of La Laguna, Tenerife. Her research interests are in tourism economics, international trade and exchange rates.

Vania Statzu is Postdoctoral Researcher at the Department of Economic and Social Research, University of Cagliari. Her research interests are in environmental economics and sustainability, water and energy economics, and social capital analysis.

Elisabetta Strazzera is Associate Professor of Economics at the Department of Economic and Social Research, University of Cagliari. Her research interests are in microeconomics, microeconometrics, environmental and resource economics.

Tran Huu Tuan is Lecturer at the College of Economics, Hue University, Vietnam. He holds both MSc and PhD degrees in Environmental and Resource Economics. His research specializes in economic valuation using both stated-preference and revealed-preference approaches, climate change adaptation, economic impact assessments of natural disasters. He has a number of publications in the field of economic valuation of natural and cultural resources and economic impact assessments of natural disasters.

Nguyen Van Phat is PhD holder in the field of Economics. He is Senior Lecturer in the Faculty of Business Administration with a major in tourism and marketing for small and micro enterprises. He has intensive experience in this area as he conducted, and was involved in, many studies in Vietnam. Currently, Dr Nguyen is Rector of the College of Economics, Hue University, Vietnam.

Aree Wiboonpongse is Professor at the Department of Agriculture Economics and Agricultural Extension, Faculty of Agriculture, Chiang Mai University. Her research interests are in community enterprise, including tourism, rural economics and applied econometrics.

The economics of sustainable tourism

An overview

Fabio Cerina, Anil Markandya and Michael McAleer

This volume is based on ten theoretical and empirical chapters that cover several topics on tourism economics, with special emphasis on sustainability, productivity, tourism demand and the impact of tourism on the host community. It brings together selected papers from the First Conference of the International Association for Tourism Economics (IATE), held in Palma de Mallorca, Spain, from 25 to 27 October 2007 and jointly organized by the University of the Balearic Islands, Spain; the Fondazione Eni Enrico Mattei (FEEM), Italy; the Centre for North South Economic Research (CRENoS), Italy; and the Tourism and Travel Research Institute, Nottingham University, United Kingdom.

The book is divided into three parts, entitled 'Tourism demand and the host community', 'Tourism and productivity' and 'Sustainable tourism: environment and cultural heritage conservation'.

Part I presents four chapters that are concerned with the analysis of tourist satisfaction and the impacts of tourists on the host community. The first two chapters develop a rigorous analysis of the determinants of tourism demand, while the last two reverse this perspective and deal with the effects of tourism demand on residents' attitudes and residential water demand, respectively. Each of these chapters comprises a case study whose relevance makes it particularly useful for general policy suggestions and guidelines.

The purpose of the first chapter, 'Time series modelling of tourism demand from the United States, Japan and Malaysia to Thailand', by Yaovarate Chaovanapoonphol, Christine Lim, Michael McAleer and Aree Wiboonpongse, is to investigate the major determinants of the demand for international tourism to Thailand. In particular, the chapter focuses on the impact of changes in the consumer price index on tourism demand from the United States, which represents the long-haul inbound market; Japan as the most important medium-haul inbound market; and Malaysia as the most important short-haul inbound market. Accordingly, the authors analyse the monthly tourist arrivals and economic determinants from 1971 to 2005, using ARIMA with exogenous variables (ARMAX) models to analyse the relationships between tourist arrivals from these three countries to Thailand. The economic determinants and ARMA models are used to predict the effects of the economic, financial and political determinants on the numbers of international tourists to Thailand. A major conclusion of this chapter is that the consumer price index has a significant impact on the number of tourist arrivals only for long-haul tourism from the United States, and not on medium- and short-haul international tourist arrivals.

The second chapter, 'Determinants of tourist satisfaction at sun and sand mass destinations' by Joaquín Alegre Martín and Jaume Garau Taberner, is also concerned with tourist demand, but the focus is on the analysis of tourist preferences. Using data from a survey conducted in 2007 at one of the Mediterranean's leading sun and sand destinations, namely the Balearic Islands, this chapter analyses the factor structure of tourist satisfaction and shows that certain threshold levels of delivery of key services are essential for satisfaction. Among this group of key services we find accommodation, easy access to information (or being an easy holiday to arrange), cleanliness and hygiene, safety, tranquillity, scenery, and prices in line with budgets. Interestingly, climate and beaches do not appear in this group. This result should have important policy implications for local policy-makers.

As we have noted, Chapter 3 reverses the perspective and analyses the impact of tourism on the host community. In 'Determinant attitudes to tourism in a mass tourist destination: a comparative-static analysis', Eugeni Aguiló Pérez and Jaume Rosselló Nadal investigate how residents in the Balearic Islands, Spain, regard tourism as affecting their community. This case study is important in providing a framework for research into attitudes towards this industry in a mature Mediterranean tourist destination. By means of a two-period survey, and using ordered logit models, this chapter shows that the host population of a mature tourist destination, such as the Balearics, generally tends to acknowledge the economic benefits of tourism. The cultural and social benefits are also perceived to be an advantage by residents of the Balearics, but to a lesser degree. At the same time, it is recognized that tourism creates various different problems, including over-saturation of the community's services, traffic congestion and high prices. However, local residents conclude that there is a positive balance between revenue from tourism and the necessary costs that are incurred.

In Chapter 4, 'A panel data analysis of residential water demand in a Mediterranean tourist region: the case of Sardinia', Vania Statzu and Elisabetta Strazzera focus on the impact of tourism on the host community and, in particular, on residential water demand. The aim of the chapter is to estimate the effect of the presence of tourists on unofficial structures on the demand of water in the domestic sector, together with other factors influencing the residential demand for water. By analysing a data set concerning water consumption in Sardinia, the authors show that in regions where an important share of tourism is accommodated in holiday homes, the average level of residential water consumption is significantly inflated by the presence of tourists. This is an element that should be taken into account when comparing regional or district consumption levels. Higher average consumption levels may be due to less responsible consumption behaviour, or lower efficiency in the maintenance of water infrastructures.

Part II of the book deals with the productivity of the tourism sector. This issue is investigated, from both empirical and theoretical perspectives, by three chapters that analyse how different factors (environmental resources, trade relationships, rural areas and labour) may contribute to increasing the productivity of an economy that specializes in tourism.

The first chapter of this part, 'Pollution-averse tourists and growth' by Fabio Cerina and Sauveur Giannoni (Chapter 5), is a theoretical investigation of the long-run relationship between growth and environmental sustainability in a small economy that specializes in tourism based on natural resources. The authors present two versions of a growth model in which tourism development generates pollution, while tourists are pollution-averse. They establish that long-run positive economic growth exists only for a particular value of tourists' aversion to pollution. Furthermore, they show that an intensive use of facilities is associated with a lower growth rate for destinations specializing in green tourism. They also show that if the destination can choose the degree of utilization of facilities, tourism will generate positive growth only if tourists are not too heavily pollution-averse. In this case, the growth rate of the economy will be a negative function of tourists' aversion to pollution, so that the 'greener' the destination, the slower is growth. The results of the analysis might be of assistance to policymakers in many developing countries that are endowed with environmental and cultural amenities. The choice to be faced is between addressing economic effort towards the development of an attractive tourist sector, or investing resources in more traditional industrial sectors that are characterized by higher technological intensity. It is an open question as to which might be more suitable to contribute to the growth of the economy as a whole.

Chapter 6 is dedicated to an empirical investigation of the relationship between tourism and trade. In this chapter, entitled 'On the relationship between tourism and trade' by María Santana Gallego, Francisco Ledesma Rodríguez and Jorge Pérez Rodríguez, the authors use UK data to provide convincing empirical evidence of a bidirectional relationship between tourism and trade. More precisely, when the short-run nexus is analysed using Granger causality tests, such a relationship is found to be unidirectional, specifically from trade to tourism (i.e. an increase in trade leading to more tourism). However, when the long-run nexus is tested by means of co-integration analysis, the authors find that tourism also causes trade. They point out that, as growth theory suggests that trade (and tourism, as a source of trade in services) promotes growth via increased market size, this effect can be encouraged by a virtuous complementary relationship between international flows of tourists and international trade.

Chapter 7 analyses the role of rural areas in the productivity of the tourism sector. More precisely, 'Evaluating labour productivity of diversifying rural tourism: evidence from Japan' by Yasuo Ohe first compares rural tourism activity with past farm products resulting from rural resource use, and develops a basic framework to conduct an empirical evaluation of the state of market formation of rural tourism activity in Japan. Second, the chapter examines the relationship between the utilization of rural resources and rural tourism. Third, it estimates the marginal labour productivity of rural tourism activities, and examines the formation of the market for rural tourism in connection with the utilization of rural resources. Finally, the chapter also considers policy implications for the development of rural tourism. The main findings are that providing tourism services is a more viable form of employment than farming-related services and that rural tourism remains an undersupplied service that needs more favourable institutional conditions if it is to flourish.

Part III focuses on the sustainability of tourism development. While sustainable tourism is a key word in the other chapters of this book, it represents the core of the analysis in the three chapters that make up this part. This issue is investigated from three different perspectives, namely: (1) methodological, through the construction of an index that is able to measure sustainability of tourist destinations; (2) theoretical, through a growth model that analyses the dynamic properties of an economy specializing in tourism based on environmental resources; and (3) empirical, by means of an analysis of the economic benefits derived from a proposal designed to preserve and restore a cultural heritage site.

The first task is accomplished in Chapter 8, 'Clustering tourism destinations by means of composite indices of sustainability' by Juan Ignacio Pulido Fernández and Marcelino Sánchez Rivero. This chapter establishes the methodological base for the design of a global composite index for the measurement of sustainable tourism development. Its calculation responds to the fourfold dimension of sustainability, namely economic, social, environmental and institutional, and facilitates the monitoring and control of results of development policies of sustainable tourism. At the same time, it also serves as an element for the measurement of convergence among different tourism destinations in order to obtain a deeper knowledge about the elements that condition market competitiveness. The use of different weights ensures that the composite sustainable-tourism index fulfils its main purpose of ranking tourism sustainability, so that the progress of tourism destinations towards sustainability can be determined and compared. Such a tourism-sustainability ranking will encourage destinations to make their own choices concerning sustainability, to set policies and to establish support programmes with well-defined targets and monitoring procedures. Moreover, the decision-makers involved will have more information with which to evaluate the performance of these programmes.

The second issue is faced by Giovanni Bella in Chapter 9, 'Equilibrium dynamics and local indeterminacy in a model of sustainable tourism'. The chapter presents a theoretical model where the representative agent faces a tourism-oriented economic scenario. In this framework, tourism is based on the use of the existing environmental resources. This leads to an inevitable trade-off as both positive effects (in terms of new output) and negative impacts (in terms of environmental degradation) are generated. The problem, then, is to choose the optimal number of tourists to be hosted in this economy, as well as the long-run level of both consumption and natural resource extraction that maximizes aggregate social welfare. An important result of this chapter is that when externalities are taken into account, indeterminacy and multiple equilibria issues arise. It is then important for the policy-maker to find a way to 'select' the appropriate equilibrium, possibly based on cost–benefit analysis. This chapter is complementary to that of Cerina and Giannoni (Chapter 5), where indeterminacy is ruled out. However, as in Bella's analysis, environmental and natural resources pose important constraints on the development of a tourism sector.

A relevant empirical issue that is related to the analysis of sustainability is raised by Tran Huu Tuan, Nguyen Van Phat and Ståle Navrud in Chapter 10, 'How tourism can help preserve cultural heritage sites: constructing optimal entrance fee schemes to collect visitors' WTP for the World Heritage Site My Son in Vietnam'. The authors apply the contingent valuation (CV) method to estimate the economic benefits that would be created by a proposed plan to preserve and restore the site. By estimating the magnitude of the benefits and showing the respondents' willingness to pay (WTP) to preserve and restore the site, the chapter is also useful in informing decisions on designing pricing strategies (specifically, entrance fees) for cultural tourist destinations that are similar to My Son. Determining the demand for cultural assets, and particularly the price elasticity of the WTP for this site with different visitor groups, can help policymakers to generate a pricing policy that will regulate visitor flows and maximize visitor revenues for this tourist destination. The empirical results suggest that the adoption of the optimal price regime would both increase revenues and reduce congestion at the site. However, this pricing regime would not reduce the congestion problem due to Vietnamese visitors. The idea of imposing a pricing structure with seasonal differentiation to reduce the number of Vietnamese visitors in the high season is one way of addressing this problem.

The book concludes with a final chapter that summarizes the issues raised, evaluates the main findings and messages of the ten main chapters, and discusses some future developments in this exciting area of research in tourism economics.

Part I

Tourism demand and the host community

1 Time series modelling of tourism demand from the United States, Japan and Malaysia to Thailand

Yaovarate Chaovanapoonphol, Christine Lim, Michael McAleer and Aree Wiboonpongse

1.1 Introduction

Thailand is one of the most important tourism destinations in Asia. The numbers of tourist arrivals from different countries of origin has been increasing continuously over the past few decades. The United States, Japan and Malaysia are Thailand's major tourist source markets, respectively representing long-haul, medium-haul and short-haul tourism markets for Thailand, with market shares of 7.21 per cent, 10.35 per cent and 11.88 per cent of total international tourist arrivals to Thailand in 2005, respectively (Tourism Authority of Thailand, 2005). The average annual growth rates during the period 1971–2005 were 4.74 per cent, 10.42 per cent and 8.03 per cent, respectively, for the United States, Japan and Malaysia.

The United States is the most important long-haul inbound tourism market for Thailand and is considered to be one of the highest-potential growth markets for tourism in Thailand. This market has shown strong growth since 1996, driven by strong economic growth. However, the market slowed, and faced a serious decrease in 2003 because of the Iraq conflict as well as the SARS outbreak, but resumed its normal growth pattern in 2004. In 2005, there were 639,658 American visitors, or 7.21 per cent of international visitor arrivals. Most Americans visited Thailand in non-group tours and consider Thailand a holiday destination. The average length of stay of American visitors to Thailand was 11.46 days, and the average amount spent was 3,804.64 baht per person per day, which earned Thai tourism income of 25,257.39 million baht (Tourism Authority of Thailand, 2005).

Japan is the most crucial medium-haul inbound market to Thailand. This market had a strong growth rate during 1994–1996 because of the strong economy and the strength of the Japanese yen. The market continuously slowed after 2001 because of 9/11, the SARS outbreak and Japan's economic crisis of 2003, but returned to its normal growth trend in 2004. In 2005, there were 1,196,654 Japanese visitors to Thailand, making up 10.35 per cent of total international visitor arrivals. Most Japanese tourists travelled to Thailand in non-group tours, and consider Thailand a holiday destination. The average length of stay of Japanese visitors to Thailand was 8.09 days, and the average amount spent was 4,205.25 baht per person per day, which earned Thai tourism an income of 40,209.18 million baht, the highest for all source countries (Tourism Authority of Thailand, 2005).

Malaysia is the most crucial short-haul inbound market for Thailand. The Malaysian tourist market is a high-sharing market, and the growth rate is always encouraging as the Malaysian border is connected to southern Thailand, and transportation can be by air, land or sea. During 1996–1997, the market slowed, and then faced a serious decrease in 1998 because of the Malaysian economic crisis. In 1999, the Malaysian economy recovered, and the Malaysian tourist market subsequently prospered. In 2003, SARS caused a decrease in the number of Malaysian tourists, but the problem was soon resolved. In 2005, there were 1,373,946 Malaysian visitors to Thailand, making up 11.88 per cent of total international visitor arrivals. Most Malaysian tourists were on non-group tours, and considered Thailand a holiday destination. The average length of stay of Malaysian visitors in Thailand was 3.68 days and the average amount they spent was 3,666.72 baht per person per day, which generated an income of 18,102.07 million baht for Thai tourism (Tourism Authority of Thailand, 2005).

The purpose of this chapter is to investigate the relationship between the demand for international tourism to Thailand and economic determinants, specifically the consumer price index. Autoregressive moving average with exogenous variables (ARMAX) models are used to analyse the relationships between tourist arrivals from the different countries to Thailand and the consumer price index, and to examine the effects of economic variables on the numbers of tourists to Thailand. We examine monthly tourist arrivals from three major countries of origin, namely the United States, Japan and Malaysia, which represent Thailand's largest long-haul, medium-haul and short-haul tourism markets, respectively.

The structure of the remainder of the chapter is as follows. Section 1.2 gives the methodologies used in the chapter. Section 1.3 provides the empirical results

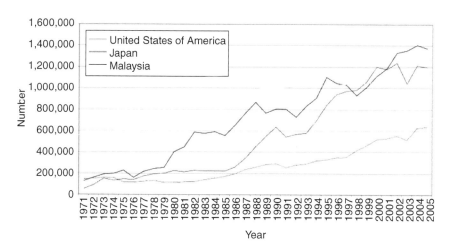

Figure 1.1 Numbers of tourist arrivals from the United States, Japan and Malaysia to Thailand, 1971–2005.

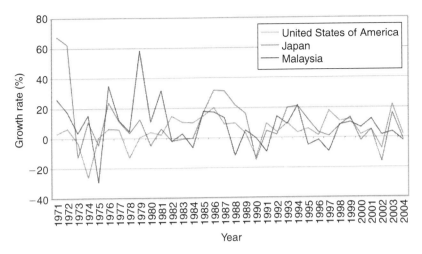

Figure 1.2 Annual growth rate of tourist arrivals from the United States, Japan and Malaysia to Thailand, 1971–2005.

from seasonal unit root tests and ARIMA/ARIMAX models. Some concluding remarks are presented in Section 1.4.

1.2 Methodology

1.2.1 Seasonal unit root test

As the monthly data series demonstrate varying seasonal patterns, before estimating the tourism demand of Thailand model it is necessary to test for the presence of seasonal unit roots. In this section, the seasonal unit root test (see Franses, 1991, and Beaulieu and Miron, 1993) is applied for seasonal and non-seasonal unit roots in the logarithm of tourist arrivals from three different destinations. The differencing operator, Δ_{12}, will have 12 roots on the unit circle, as follows (see, for example, Maddala and Kim, 1998):

$$
\begin{aligned}
1 - L^{12} = &(1-L)(1+L)(1-iL)(1+iL) \\
&\times \left[1+\left(\sqrt{3}+i\right)L/2\right]\left[1+\left(\sqrt{3}-i\right)L/2\right] \\
&\times \left[1-\left(\sqrt{3}+i\right)L/2\right]\left[1-\left(\sqrt{3}-i\right)L/2\right] \\
&\times \left[1+\left(\sqrt{3}+i\right)L/2\right]\left[1-\left(\sqrt{3}-i\right)L/2\right] \\
&\times \left[1-\left(\sqrt{3}+i\right)L/2\right]\left[1+\left(\sqrt{3}-i\right)L/2\right]
\end{aligned}
\tag{1.1}
$$

where all terms other than $(1 - L)$ denote seasonal unit roots.

Testing for unit roots in monthly time series is equivalent to testing for the significance of the parameters in the auxiliary regression model estimated by ordinary least squares (OLS):

$$\varphi^*(L)y_{8,t} = \pi_1 y_{1,t-1} + \pi_2 y_{2,t-1} + \pi_3 y_{3,t-2} + \pi_4 y_{3,t-1} + \pi_5 y_{4,t-2}$$
$$+ \pi_6 y_{4,t-1} + \pi_7 y_{5,t-2} + \pi_8 y_{5,t-1} + \pi_9 y_{6,t-2} + \pi_{10} y_{6,t-1} \qquad (1.2)$$
$$+ \pi_{11} y_{7,t-2} + \pi_{12} y_{7,t-1} + \mu_t + \varepsilon_t$$

where μ_t, the determinantal part, consists of a constant, a time trend and 11 seasonal dummy variables. Applying OLS to Equation 1.2 gives estimates of the π_i parameters. The null hypothesis of unit roots is tested by a t-test of the separate π's in $\pi_3 \dots \pi_{12}$. If the null hypothesis is rejected, one can treat the variable of interest as seasonally stationary. The tests involve the use of the t-test for the first twelve hypotheses and an F-test for the last six hypotheses, as follows:

1   H_0: $\pi_1 = 0$, H_1: $\pi_1 < 0$ (if this hypothesis is not rejected, there is a unit root at the zero frequency);
2   H_0: $\pi_1 = 0$, H_1: $\pi_1 < 0$, $i = 2, 3, \dots, 12$ (if these hypotheses are not rejected, there are no seasonal unit roots);
3   H_0: $\pi_i = \pi_{i+1} = 0$, H_1: $\pi_i \neq 0$ and/or $\pi_{i+1} \neq 0$, $i = 3, 5, 7, 9, 11$ (if pairs of π's are equal to zero, it allows for all pairs of conjugate complex roots (see Aguirre, 2000), and H_0: $\pi_3 \dots \pi_{12} = 0$, H_1: $\pi_3 \dots \pi_{12} \neq 0$ (if the joint hypothesis is not rejected, unit roots are present at all the seasonal frequencies).

If all the estimated coefficients in the auxiliary test regression are statistically different from zero, the series presents a stationary seasonal pattern and the appropriate procedure to model the series would use seasonal dummies. If there are no seasonal unit roots, first differences are applied to the data. On the other hand, when seasonal unit roots are found to be present, the Δ_{12} filter is applied to the data (see Maddala and Kim, 1998).

1.2.2 ARMAX model

The ARMAX model is an extension of the autoregressive moving average (ARMA) model with explanatory variables (X). It has been applied to analyse the dynamic correlation between variables in economics, marketing and other areas in the physical and social sciences (see, for example, Lim *et al.*, 2008). This approach is based on Box–Jenkins (1970) models, which comprise two models for representing the behaviour of observed time series processes, namely the autoregressive (AR) and moving average (MA) models. Lim *et al.* (2008) showed that the AR and MA processes can be applied to capture the current pattern of tourist arrivals from particular tourism markets based on its own past arrivals and the random error from previous periods – that is, AR and MA processes of orders p and q, respectively, which are given by:

$$A_t = \sum_{i=1}^{p} \varphi_i A_{t-1} + \varepsilon_t \qquad (1.3)$$

and

$$A_t = \varepsilon_t - \sum_{j-1}^{q} \theta_j \varepsilon_{t-j}. \qquad (1.4)$$

The general formulation of an ARIMA (p,d,q) model can be written as:

$$\left(1 - \varphi_1 L - \dots - \varphi_p L^p\right) A_t = C + \left(1 - \theta_1 L - \dots - \theta_q L^q\right) \varepsilon_t, \; t = 1, \dots, n \qquad (1.5)$$

and

$$C = \left(1 - \varphi_1 - \dots - \varphi_p\right) \mu$$

where A_t=number of tourist arrivals from one of the three countries to Thailand at time t; μ=constant mean; φ_i=autoregressive parameter $(i=1,\dots,\; p)$; θ_j=moving average parameter $(j=1,\dots,\; q)$; L=backward shift operator; and ε_t is a normally and independently distributed random error term.

The ARMA model is based on stationary time series processes. A tourist arrivals series is stationary if the mean, variance and covariance of the series remain constant over time. The unit root test is a formal method of testing for the stationarity of a series. If a time series, A_t, is not stationary, it can be transformed into a stationary series by taking first differences to obtain autoregressive integrated moving average models (ARIMA). The formulation of ARIMA (p, d, q) models can be written as:

$$\left(1 - \varphi_1 L - \dots - \varphi_p L^{p+q}\right) A_t = C + \left(1 - \theta_1 L - \dots - \theta_q L^q\right) \varepsilon_t, t = 1, \dots, n \qquad (1.6)$$

or

$$A_t = C + \varphi_1 A_{t-1} + \dots + \varphi_{t-p} A_{t-p-d} + \varepsilon_t - \theta_1 \varepsilon_{t-1} - \theta_2 \varepsilon_{t-2} - \theta_q \varepsilon_{t-q}. \qquad (1.7)$$

where

$$1 - \varphi_1 L - \dots - \varphi_{p+d} = \left(1 - \varphi_1 L - \dots - \varphi_p L^p\right)\left(1 - L\right)^d$$

and d is the number of times the data are differenced to obtain stationarity, p is the lag length of the autoregressive error term, and q is the lag length of the moving-average error term. The ARMAX model is an extension of ARIMA modelling, which contains lagged dependent and explanatory variables, and a moving average disturbance.

An extension of Equation 1.7 to include a single explanatory, such as consumer price index (CPI) variable, results in the following single-equation ARMAX model:

$$A_t = C + \varphi_1 A_{t-1} + \dots + \varphi_{t-p} A_{t-p-d} + \beta_0 x_t + \beta_1 x_{t-1} + \varepsilon_t - \theta_1 \varepsilon_{t-1} - \theta_2 \varepsilon_{t-2} - \theta_q \varepsilon_{t-q}, \qquad (1.8)$$

where x_t and x_{t-1} are the current and one-period-lagged CPI in the original country, respectively. This model also assumes that the errors are independently and identically distributed, with zero mean, constant variance and zero covariance.

The most commonly used explanatory variables included in a model of international tourism demand are income, population, relative prices, exchange rates and transportation costs (see, for example, Muñoz, 2007; Chang and McAleer, 2009; Chang *et al.*, 2009). In this chapter, the consumer price index is considered to be the appropriate explanatory variable as it reflects the purchasing power of a particular country. Higher consumer price indexes tend to lower the purchasing power of people, which leads to a decrease in tourism demand. The other reason is that other variables, such as gross domestic product and income, are unavailable as monthly data series.

In the analysis of international tourism demand from the United States, Japan and Malaysia to Thailand, the logarithm of tourist arrivals and CPI are selected as proxies for international travel demand and purchasing power, respectively. The sample period for each country is different, owing to the limited availability of monthly CPI data. The data used here comprise monthly international tourist arrivals and the CPI for different time periods because of the limited availability of monthly data series, namely 1971–2005 for the United States, 1978–2005 for Japan and 1972–2005 for Malaysia. Tourism demand data for Thailand are obtained from the Tourism Authority of Thailand (TOT), and CPI data are obtained from the Reuters 2007 database. The data series are tested for the existence of seasonal unit roots and are expressed and analysed in terms of the logarithmic first differences (log differences) and logarithmic annual differences.

1.3 Empirical results

1.3.1 Seasonal unit root test

Before the ARMAX model is used to estimate the relationship between tourist arrivals from the United States, Japan and Malaysia and CPI, tourist arrivals and the CPI are tested for stationarity. Tests of the null hypothesis that monthly international tourist arrivals and the CPI have seasonal unit roots are given in Tables 1.1 and 1.2. Testing for seasonal unit roots involves an intercept, seasonal dummies, trend and the lag length of the series. The empirical results are compared with the 5 per cent critical values given by Franses (1991). The Wald test is applied for the first 12 hypotheses to obtain the calculated t statistics, and the last 6 hypotheses are used to obtain the calculated F statistic. It appears there is evidence for the presence of seasonal unit roots in tourist arrivals from some countries, and in the CPI of some countries.

The empirical results of the unit root tests of tourist arrivals, as given in Table 1.1, reveal that the joint null hypothesis, H_0: $\pi_3 \ldots \pi_{12}=0$, indicating that the presence of a unit root at all the seasonal frequencies of tourist arrivals from Japan, cannot be rejected at the 5 per cent significance level. The seasonal unit root null hypotheses of tourist arrivals from the United States and Malaysia are both rejected, implying that a non-seasonal unit root is present in the series.

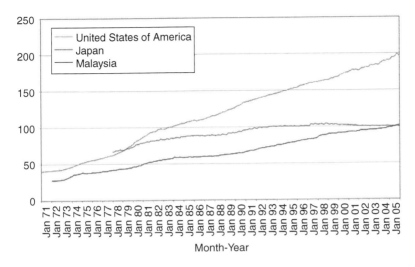

Figure 1.3 Consumer price index of the United States, Japan and Malaysia, 1971–2005.

Table 1.1 Estimates of seasonal unit roots testing of tourist arrivals from three major source countries to Thailand

Null hypotheses	USA (2)	Japan (12)	Malaysia (2)
$\pi_1 = 0$	−2.58	−1.86	−2.27
$\pi_2 = 0$	−4.77**	0.08	−6.20**
$\pi_3 = 0$	−5.19**	0.14	−4.70**
$\pi_4 = 0$	−0.35	−1.02	−0.91
$\pi_5 = 0$	0.33**	0.51**	−7.02**
$\pi_6 = 0$	0.21**	−0.13	−6.15**
$\pi_7 = 0$	0.38	−1.48**	−3.33**
$\pi_8 = 0$	−0.36	1.74**	1.13**
$\pi_9 = 0$	−0.15	−0.57	−5.46**
$\pi_{10} = 0$	−0.27	−0.48	−2.98
$\pi_{11} = 0$	0.58	−0.76	−5.71**
$\pi_{12} = 0$	−0.34	1.01**	1.04**
$\pi_3 = \pi_4 = 0$	13.53**	0.21	11.54**
$\pi_5 = \pi_6 = 0$	0.06	0.81	24.68**
$\pi_7 = \pi_8 = 0$	0.10	1.42	12.18**
$\pi_9 = \pi_{10} = 0$	0.04	0.21	16.14**
$\pi_{11} = \pi_{12} = 0$	0.17	0.57	18.44**
$\pi_3 = \ldots = \pi_{12} = 0$	5.01**	0.71	18.62**

Notes
1 ** denotes that the seasonal unit root null hypothesis is rejected at the 5% significance level.
2 Numbers in parentheses denote the number of lagged values of the dependent variable.

Table 1.2 Estimates of seasonal unit root tests of the consumer price index

Null hypotheses	USA (2)	Japan (2)	Malaysia(1)
$\pi_1 = 0$	−3.42**	−2.49	−2.28
$\pi_2 = 0$	−4.86**	−3.07**	−4.51**
$\pi_3 = 0$	−3.75**	−2.43**	−4.54**
$\pi_4 = 0$	−5.78**	−3.82**	−4.92**
$\pi_5 = 0$	−1.25	−1.38	2.37**
$\pi_6 = 0$	0.43**	−0.56	0.09**
$\pi_7 = 0$	−0.21**	−0.80**	−0.29**
$\pi_8 = 0$	−0.77	−0.28	−1.43
$\pi_9 = 0$	1.34**	1.15**	0.33
$\pi_{10} = 0$	1.90**	1.58**	−1.11
$\pi_{11} = 0$	0.14	−2.25**	−1.01
$\pi_{12} = 0$	0.53**	0.65**	−1.86
$\pi_3 = \pi_4 = 0$	25.13**	10.53**	22.48**
$\pi_5 = \pi_6 = 0$	1.10	0.97	2.95
$\pi_7 = \pi_8 = 0$	0.45	0.53	1.09
$\pi_9 = \pi_{10} = 0$	2.40	1.67	0.77
$\pi_{11} = \pi_{12} = 0$	0.25	2.68	2.65
$\pi_3 = \ldots = \pi_{12} = 0$	6.28**	3.01	7.90**

Notes
1 ** denotes that the seasonal unit root null hypothesis is rejected at the 5% significance level.
2 Numbers in parentheses denote the number of lagged values of the dependent variable.

Taking first differences of the logarithm of CPI, and applying the seasonal unit root tests, is also considered. In Table 2.2, the estimates reveal that the joint null hypothesis, H_0: $\pi_3 \ldots \pi_{12}=0$, indicating the presence of a unit root at all the seasonal frequencies for the CPI of Japan, cannot be rejected at the 5 per cent significance level. The seasonal unit root null hypotheses of CPI in the United States and Malaysia are both rejected at the 5 per cent significance level, implying that a non-seasonal unit root appears in the series for both countries. These results suggest that the seasonal filter, $(1 - L^{12})$, and differencing operation, Δ_{12}, should be applied for the Japanese tourist arrivals series, while the non-seasonal filter, $(1 - L)$, is used for American and Malaysian tourist arrivals data.

1.3.2 ARIMA models for tourist arrivals

Monthly tourist arrivals data (in logarithms) from the three major countries, namely the United States, Japan and Malaysia, are used to capture the patterns in the data series. Various autoregressive (AR), moving average (MA) and autoregressive integrated moving average (ARIMA) models have been estimated using OLS to determine whether the tourist arrivals series can be described by AR, MA or ARIMA processes. The appropriate models are selected for tourist arrivals based on significant *t*-statistics at the 5 per cent significance level for the AR and MR coefficients, with no serial correlation at the 5 per cent level, using the Lagrange Multiplier (LM) test for serial correlation. In particular, the estimated models are tested for serial correlation as serial correlation leads to bias in the estimates, and invalid inferences. Diagnostic checking of the residuals, based on the correlograms of the estimated residuals of the ARIMA models, provides further support for the results of LM tests for serial correlation, which means there is no serial correlation in the residuals. In addition, the models are selected using model selection criteria, including the Akaike information criterion (AIC) and the Schwarz Bayesian criterion (SBC), whereby smaller values are preferred.

In the ARIMA process, the tourist arrivals variables for the United States and Malaysia use the non-seasonal filter, $(1 - L)$, while the seasonal filter, $(1 - L^{12})$, is applied to tourist arrivals from Japan. Table 1.3 presents the results of the various fitted ARIMA models for the logarithm of tourist arrivals from the three major source countries to Thailand using the EViews 4.1 econometric software package. The fitted models in this chapter show the ARIMA models and seasonal patterns for seasonal ARIMA (SARIMA) models. Additionally, the best-fitting ARIMA model for each country is chosen to have the lowest values of AIC and SBC. After empirical examination, the most appropriate ARIMA models are determined to be the ARIMA(1,1,1) (12,1,12)$_{12}$, ARIMA(1,1,12) and ARIMA(12,1,12) models for the United States, Japan and Malaysia, respectively.

The empirical specification for tourist arrivals from the United States for the period 1971–2005 is given as follows:

$$\Delta y_t = 0.01 + u_t$$

$$(1 - 0.27L)(1 - 0.96L^{12})\, u_t = (1 - 0.85L^1)\,(1 - 0.74L^{12})\varepsilon_t$$

$$(4.31)\ (59.64)\ (-25.67)\ (-18.26)$$

The best-fitting ARIMA model for the relationship between the logarithm of tourist arrivals from the United States is determined as having significant estimates but with no serial correlation at the 5 per cent significance level (with Durbin–Watson value of 2.02).

For the Japanese tourist arrivals series during 1978–2005, the appropriate ARIMA model, in which the estimated parameters are significant and with no serial correlation at the 5 per cent significance level, is the ARIMA(1,1,12) model. The best-fitting model for tourist arrivals from Japan can be expressed as follows:

$$\Delta_{12}\, y_t = 0.07 + u_t$$

$$(1 - 0.85L^1)\, u_t = (1 - 0.60L^{12})\varepsilon_t$$

$$(28.33)\ (-13.12)$$

The selected model indicates that the autocorrelations are within the 95 per cent confidence interval (with Durbin–Watson value of 2.06), which implies that there are no significant residual autocorrelations.

Table 1.3 Estimates of the best-fitting ARIMA models for inbound tourists from the United States, Japan and Malaysia to Thailand

Variable	Coefficient	t-Statistics	AIC/SBC	LM(SC)
United States of America				
C	0.01	0.94	AIC = −1.08	F = 148.60
AR(1)	0.27	4.31	SC = −1.03	P = 0.00
SAR(12)	0.96	59.64		
MA(1)	−0.85	−25.67		
SMA(12)	−0.74	−18.26		
Japan				
C	0.07	4.72	AIC = −1.79	F = 344.44
AR(1)	0.85	28.33	SC = −1.76	P = 0.00
MA(12)	−0.60	−13.12		
Malaysia				
C	0.01	2.39	AIC = −0.39	F = 70.88
AR(6)	−0.10	−2.62	SC = −0.33	P = 0.00
AR(7)	−0.11	−2.66		
AR(12)	0.57	11.53		
MA(1)	−0.65	−17.32		
MA(12)	−0.21	−4.78		

Notes
1 AIC and SBC are the Akaike information criterion and Schwarz Bayesian criterion, respectively.
2 LM(SC) refers to the Lagrange multiplier test for serial correlation.

For the Malaysian tourist arrivals series during 1972–2005, the ARIMA models are presented in Table 1.6, in which the estimated parameters are significant and with no serial correlation at the 5 per cent significance level, which is ARIMA(12,1,12). The empirical results show that ARIMA(12,1,12) is the most appropriate model to describe tourist arrival patterns from Malaysia as it has the smallest AIC and SBC values. The best-fitting model for tourist arrivals from Malaysia can be expressed as follows:

$$\Delta y_t = 0.01 + u_t$$

$$\left(1 + 0.10L^6\right)\left(1 + 0.11L^7\right)\left(1 - 0.57L^{12}\right)u_t = \left(1 - 0.65L^1\right)\left(1 - 0.21L^{12}\right)\varepsilon_t$$

(−2.62) (−2.66) (11.53) (−17.32) (−4.78)

The selected model indicates that the autocorrelations are within the 95 per cent confidence interval (with Durbin–Watson value of 2.00), which implies that there are no significant residual autocorrelations in the appropriate model.

1.3.3 ARIMAX models

According to the results from the seasonal unit roots tests for each variable in the ARMAX process, the tourist arrivals variables for the United States and

Malaysia are used in the non-seasonal filter, $(1 - L)$, while the seasonal filter, $(1 - L^{12})$, is applied for tourist arrivals from Japan. For the consumer price index (CPI), the non-seasonal filter, $(1 - L)$, is applied for tourist arrivals from the United States and Malaysia, and the seasonal filter, $(1 - L^{12})$, is used for tourist arrivals from Japan.

The initial regressions of the ARMAX models for the United States, Japan and Malaysia are given in Tables 1.4–1.6. The empirical results reveal that the explanatory variable considered, namely the logarithm of CPI, does not have a significant impact on international tourist arrivals from Japan and Malaysia at the 5 per cent significance level. Moreover, the constant term was not different from zero for the initial ARMAX models for tourist arrivals from the United States and Malaysia. The CPI indicates the negative and significant impact on tourist arrivals from the United States to Thailand, with a coefficient of −1.99, while the constant term has a significant impact only on tourist arrivals from Japan to Thailand, with a coefficient of 0.079. Additionally, the Lagrange multiplier test, LM(SC), indicates that the errors are not serially correlated at the 5 per cent significance level for all the ARMAX models. After we had estimated the initial models, the ARMAX models for the three countries were re-estimated, and the results of the final models are presented in Tables 1.7–1.9.

The empirical results obtained for the final ARMAX models for the United States, Japan and Malaysia, as presented in Tables 1.7–1.9, indicate that the insignificant variables at the 5 per cent level of the initial models (as shown in Tables 1.4–1.6) are excluded from the final models. In other words, it is possible to obtain more parsimonious models by excluding the exogenous variables which are not significant. The empirical estimates show that the ARMAX model for the United States confirms that changes in the consumer price index (CPI) have a negative and significant impact on tourist arrivals

Table 1.4 ARMAX model of log difference of tourist arrivals from the United States, 1971–2005

Sample (adjusted): 1972(3)–2005(12) and 406 after adjusting endpoints

Variable	Coefficient	Std error	t-Statistic	Prob.
C	0.011489	0.007242	1.586357	0.1134
DLOG(CPIUSA)	−1.992614	0.641219	−3.107542	0.0020
AR(1)	0.292335	0.059673	4.898931	0.0000
SAR(12)	0.956943	0.015971	59.91766	0.0000
MA(1)	−0.889082	0.028954	−30.70683	0.0000
SMA(12)	−0.742024	0.040583	−18.28418	0.0000
R-squared	0.605011	Mean dependent var.		0.004713
Adjusted R-squared	0.600074	SD dependent var.		0.219612
SE of regression	0.138882	Akaike info criterion		−1.095713
Sum squared resid.	7.715310	Schwarz criterion		−1.036506
Log likelihood	228.4297	F-statistic		122.5375
Durbin–Watson stat.	2.027509	Prob(F-statistic)		0.000000

Table 1.5 ARMAX model of log seasonal difference of tourist arrivals from Japan, 1978–2005

Sample (adjusted): 1979(2)–2005(12) and 323 after adjusting endpoints

Variable	Coefficient	Std error	t-Statistic	Prob.
C	0.078776	0.019088	4.127020	0.0000
DLOG(CPIJP,0,12)	−0.535034	0.968870	−0.552225	0.5812
AR(1)	0.849038	0.030262	28.05649	0.0000
MA(12)	−0.598050	0.046419	−12.88368	0.0000
R-squared	0.683118	Mean dependent var.		0.068149
Adjusted R-squared	0.680138	SD dependent var.		0.173833
SE of regression	0.098314	Akaike info criterion		−1.788999
Sum squared resid.	3.083325	Schwarz criterion		−1.742217
Log likelihood	292.9233	F-statistic		229.2280
Durbin–Watson stat.	2.062109	Prob(F-statistic)		0.000000

Table 1.6 ARMAX model of log difference of tourist arrivals from Malaysia, 1972–2005

Sample (adjusted): 1973(2)–2005(12) and 395 after adjusting endpoints

Variable	Coefficient	Std error	t-Statistic	Prob.
C	6.63E-05	0.003515	0.018869	0.9850
DLOG(CPIMY)	1.950104	1.078522	1.808126	0.0714
AR(6)	−0.108329	0.040140	−2.698789	0.0073
AR(7)	−0.109425	0.039692	−2.756850	0.0061
AR(12)	0.563050	0.048748	11.55033	0.0000
MA(1)	−0.672224	0.036407	−18.46415	0.0000
MA(12)	−0.213958	0.042986	−4.977372	0.0000
R-squared	0.480666	Mean dependent var.		0.005792
Adjusted R-squared	0.472635	SD dependent var.		0.271161
SE of regression	0.196917	Akaike info criterion		−0.394504
Sum squared resid.	15.04524	Schwarz criterion		−0.323992
Log likelihood	84.91448	F-statistic		59.85167
Durbin–Watson stat.	1.978456	Prob(F-statistic)		0.000000

from the United States to Thailand, with a coefficient of −1.99. This implies that increases in the CPI in the United States lead to decreases in the numbers of tourist arrivals from that country to Thailand. The reason for this outcome is that the United States is a long-haul travel market for Thailand, so the purchasing power of Americans is likely to affect their travel demand to Thailand. However, Japan and Malaysia are medium-haul and short-haul tourism markets for Thailand, respectively, so the CPI in these countries has little or no effect on the numbers of tourist arrivals from these countries to Thailand. In short, the empirical results are consistent with the fact that travelling from Japan and Malaysia to Thailand is not expensive as regards the cost of travel and living allowances.

According to these results, the CPI is important in explaining the US demand for tourism to Thailand. The estimated eaffect of this variable is negative and greater than 1, implying that changes in the cost of living in the United States affect demand for tourism to Thailand. The major implication of this finding for the tourism industry is that provision of high-quality services is important for earning a strong reputation and for attracting new and repeat tourists, as tourists from the United States tend to be high-income and repeat tourists. For Japanese and Malaysian tourists, the cost of living in each country does not have a statistically significant impact on the demand for tourism to Thailand as these two countries are not sufficiently far from Thailand. However, developed infrastructure, such as roads, quality of hotels and quality of cuisine, should be considered, as tourists from these countries, and particularly from Japan, are high-income tourists.

1.4 Concluding remarks

This chapter has analysed the impact of changes in the consumer price index on tourism demand from the United States, Japan and Malaysia to Thailand using an ARMAX model. Tourist arrivals and the consumer price index of these three countries, which represent long-haul, medium-haul and short-haul inbound tourism markets for Thailand, respectively, were tested and transformed to obtain a stationary process. The sample periods under consideration for each country were 1971–2005 for the United States, 1978–2005 for Japan and 1972–2005 for Malaysia. The differences are due to the limited data availability in the monthly consumer price index from the Reuters database. After we had tested for seasonal unit roots, the ARIMA model was estimated to capture the time series behaviour of tourist arrivals based on historical data. The empirical results indicated that the best-fitting models to explain tourist arrivals of the three major countries were ARIMA and seasonal ARIMA models.

Table 1.7 ARMAX model of log difference of tourist arrivals from the United States, 1971–2005

Sample (adjusted): 1972(3)–2005(12) and 406 after adjusting endpoints

Variable	Coefficient	Std error	t-Statistic	Prob.
DLOG(CPIUSA)	−1.987887	0.685126	−2.901493	0.0039
AR(1)	0.282228	0.061150	4.615319	0.0000
SAR(12)	0.966194	0.013457	71.79885	0.0000
MA(1)	−0.877621	0.030976	−28.33214	0.0000
SMA(12)	−0.749281	0.038262	−19.58289	0.0000
R-squared	0.603219	Mean dependent var.		0.004713
Adjusted R-squared	0.599261	SD dependent var.		0.219612
SE of regression	0.139023	Akaike info criterion		−1.096111
Sum squared resid.	7.750322	Schwarz criterion		−1.046772
Log likelihood	227.5106	Durbin–Watson stat.		2.024894

Table 1.8 ARMAX model of log seasonal difference of tourist arrivals from Japan, 1978–2005

Sample (adjusted): 1979(2)–2005(12) and 323 after adjusting endpoints

Variable	Coefficient	Std error	t-Statistic	Prob.
C	0.072730	0.015405	4.721119	0.0000
AR(1)	0.848784	0.029963	28.32766	0.0000
MA(12)	−0.601763	0.045850	−13.12473	0.0000
R-squared	0.682814	Mean dependent var.		0.068149
Adjusted R-squared	0.680832	SD dependent var.		0.173833
SE of regression	0.098207	Akaike info criterion		−1.794233
Sum squared resid.	3.086279	Schwarz criterion		−1.759147
Log likelihood	292.7687	F-statistic		344.4366
Durbin–Watson stat.	2.062039	Prob(F-statistic)		0.000000

Table 1.9 ARMAX model of log difference of tourist arrivals from Malaysia, 1972–2005

Method: least squares
Sample (adjusted): 1973(02)–2005(12) and 395 after adjusting endpoints

Variable	Coefficient	Std error	t-Statistic	Prob.
AR(6)	−0.092477	0.039787	−2.324305	0.0206
AR(7)	−0.091011	0.039367	−2.311872	0.0213
AR(12)	0.582046	0.050658	11.48969	0.0000
MA(1)	−0.621270	0.038623	−16.08541	0.0000
MA(12)	−0.202207	0.047616	−4.246609	0.0000
R-squared	0.471270	Mean dependent var.		0.005792
Adjusted R-squared	0.465847	SD dependent var.		0.271161
SE of regression	0.198180	Akaike info criterion		−0.386700
Sum squared resid.	15.31744	Schwarz criterion		−0.336334
Log likelihood	81.37327	Durbin–Watson stat.		2.030710

The initial ARMAX models were estimated for the three countries to test for the existence of appropriate variables and models. The consumer price index was found to have a significant impact on the number of tourist arrivals only for long-haul tourism from the United States. Alternative ARMAX models were estimated in order to obtain the best-fitting models to explain the factors affecting tourism demand from the three different countries of origin.

Acknowledgements

The first and last authors thank the Thailand Research Fund (TRF) for financial support. The third author thanks the Australian Research Council and National Science Council, Taiwan, for financial support. Special thanks are extended to Pawitporn Wongsak for excellent research assistance.

References

Aguirre, A. (2000) 'Testing for seasonal unit roots using monthly data'. Online, available at: www.cedeplar.ufmg.br/pesquisas/td/TD%20139.doc (accessed 27 February 2005).

Beaulieu, J. J. and Miron, J. A. (1993) 'Seasonal unit roots in aggregate U.S. data', *Journal of Econometrics*, 55: 305–328.

Chang, C.-L. and McAleer, M. (2009) 'Daily tourist arrivals, exchange rates and volatility for Korea and Taiwan', *Korean Economic Review*, 25 (2): 241–267.

Chang, C.-L., McAleer, M. and Slottje, D. (2009) 'Modelling international tourist arrivals and volatility: an application to Taiwan', in D. Slottje (ed.), *Quantifying Consumer Preferences*, Bingley, UK: Emerald Group Publishing, pp. 303–320.

Franses, P. H. (1991) 'Seasonality, nonstationarity and the forecasting of monthly time series', *International Journal of Forecasting*, 7: 199–208.

Lim, C., Min, J. C. H. and McAleer, M. (2008) 'Modelling income effects on long and shot haul international travel from Japan', *Tourism Management*, 29: 1099–1109.

Maddala, G. S. and Kim, I. M. (1998) *Unit Roots, Cointegration and Structural Change*, Cambridge: Cambridge University Press.

Muñoz, T. G. (2007) 'German demand for tourism in Spain', *Tourism Management*, 28: 12–22.

Tourism Authority of Thailand (1971–2005) *Thailand Statistical Report* (various years), Bangkok, Thailand.

Tourism Authority of Thailand (2005) 'Situation 2005'.

2 Determinants of tourist satisfaction at sun and sand mass destinations

Joaquín Alegre Martín and Jaume Garau Taberner

2.1 Introduction

Tourist satisfaction is acknowledged to be an indicator of a destination's capacity to succeed (Go and Grovers, 2000; Kozak, 2002, 2004; Yüksel and Rimmington, 1998). Fuchs and Weiermair (2004) argue that tourist satisfaction is one of the main competitive edges for a destination. Further, tourist satisfaction is an antecedent of loyalty and positive word of mouth. Thus, understanding tourist satisfaction is essential to define a positioning strategy for a tourist destination. Tourist satisfaction with a destination is dependent on a wide set of different factors. The complexity of the tourist experience is attributable to the different products and services that combine to form a holiday (Murphy *et al.*, 2000; Buhalis, 2000). Correspondingly, it is necessary not only that the specific attributes that satisfy the tourist should be identified, but also that how their performance impacts on tourist satisfaction should be detected (Pizam and Taylor, 1999).

European second-generation mass tourist resorts (i.e. those that emerged in the Mediterranean in the 1960s) are currently undergoing a period of stagnation (Farsari *et al.*, 2007; Manera and Garau, 2010). European consumers' new habits and new demands might have a critical effect on these classic sun and sand destinations, with a decrease in classic desire for sun and sand, and a reduction of the importance of the destination's climate or beaches as a key to competitive advantage (Knowles and Curtis, 1999; Moutinho, 2000; Poon, 1993). Accordingly, mature destinations should seek to fulfil the current requirements of the demand. This means they need to study the existing factor structure of tourist satisfaction at these destinations.

In the literature, it has been established that the factors that define tourist services can be classified into three types, depending on the impact they make on tourist satisfaction (Deng, 2007; Erto and Vanacore, 2002; Fuchs and Weiermair, 2003, 2004; Füller and Matzler, 2007; Füller *et al.*, 2006; Matzler *et al.*, 2006; Pawitra and Tan, 2003; Tan and Pawitra, 2001). A distinction is made between those factors that increase tourist satisfaction, those that only prevent the tourist from feeling dissatisfied and those factors that can work both ways. In a scenario in which there is strong competition among rival destinations, it is essential to know which attributes generate the greatest satisfaction with a destination. To do this, basically two methods have been used. The first, proposed by Vavra (1997), is based on the importance grid. This author distinguishes between the explicit importance that a consumer attaches to an attribute (the self-stated importance) and the implicit importance (the effect the attribute has on an objective variable such as overall satisfaction). The basic idea of this approach is to display the mean importance scores for service attributes (explicitly rated by consumers), and the implicit importance scores. The implicit importance scores may be derived by regressing performance scores for the attributes on scores for overall satisfaction (the stronger the relationship, the more important the attribute). By analysing explicit and implicit levels of importance, three types of factors can be identified: basic or must-be factors (very high-rated in terms of explicit importance by consumers, even though they have no, or very little, influence on total customer satisfaction; with a low implicit importance and a high explicit one), excitement factors (with very low importance scores yet a very high implicit influence on overall satisfaction) and performance or one-dimensional factors (with either a low explicit and implicit importance or high explicit and implicit importance). The second method is the penalty–reward contrast analysis proposed by Brandt (1987). Using a regression model, an analysis was made of the impact that satisfaction with a certain factor has on overall satisfaction with the service. The main hypothesis behind Brandt's model is that, for some factors, this effect acts asymmetrically. Satisfaction with a factor can have a much greater positive effect on overall satisfaction than the negative effect of dissatisfaction. Basic factors are defined as those for which dissatisfaction with an attribute has a greater penalty effect on overall satisfaction than the possible reward effect. In the case of excitement factors, the reward exceeds the penalty. When the reward and penalty effects are equal, the factors are considered to be performance factors. In analyses of tourism services, these two methods have been used and compared by Fuchs and Weiermair (2004), Matzler *et al.* (2006) and Füller and Matzler (2007). However, there does not seem to be a consensus on the best method to use to identify the three types of factors (Bartikowski and Llosa, 2004; Fuchs and Weiermair, 2004; Matzler and Sauerwein, 2002; Oh, 2001).

This chapter is aimed at analysing the factor structure that determines the satisfaction of European tourists at a series of rival sun and sand destinations. As Enright and Newton (2004, 2005) point out, tourist destinations are not competitive or uncompetitive in abstract terms but competitive or uncompetitive in relation to other destinations. In this chapter, an analysis is made of a series of destinations that compete for the same segment of the market. More specifically, the data is taken from a survey conducted in the Balearic Islands in the high season of 2006. The tourists who were interviewed belong to the three main nationalities who visit the destination: Germans, Britons and Spaniards. In 2006, these nationalities accounted for about 81 per cent of all tourism to the Balearics (Govern de les Illes Balears, 2007). The tourists who were interviewed were asked for information about the sun and sand destinations where they had spent their summer holidays over the previous three years. As a result, the analysis presented here is focused not solely on the Balearic Islands but on a group of sun and sand destinations that compete with the Balearics for the same segment of European tourism. The attributes or factors that characterize sun and sand destinations were selected by reviewing some proposed models of destination competitiveness (Crouch and Ritchie, 1999; Dwyer and Kim, 2003), and empirical analyses of tourist satisfaction (Alegre and Cladera, 2006; Baker and Crompton, 2000; Crompton and Love, 1995; Kozak, 2002; Kozak and Rimmington, 1999; Yoon and Uysal, 2005).

In the first section of the chapter, the literature on the subject of tourist satisfaction is reviewed and an outline of factor classification methods proposed by Vavra (1997) and Brandt (1987) is given. These methods are applied and their results are examined from an empirical point of view. It is show that the penalty–reward analysis prevails over the importance grid analysis, from both a methodological and an empirical perspective. The results obtained allow for the identification of the factor structure of satisfaction at sun and sand tourist destinations. The chapter ends with a brief discussion of the managerial implications of the research. Placing attributes of the sun and sand product in terms of the proposed three groups should allow destinations to identify key drivers of satisfaction, and to formulate improvement priorities (Füller and Matzler, 2007; Sauerwein *et al.*, 1996; Matzler *et al.*, 2004a).

2.2 Literature review

2.2.1 Satisfaction and multiple attributes

Consumer satisfaction is associated with different aspects of a product or service (Swan and Combs, 1976; Johnston, 1995; Sampson and Showalter, 1999; Bartikowski and Llosa, 2004). Mittal *et al.* (1998: 33–34) summarize some of the reasons why it is advisable to take a multi-attribute approach when dealing with consumer satisfaction. First, consumers judge their consumer experiences not only globally but also by rating different attributes. Second, consumers can have mixed impressions of a product or service, so that different aspects of a product can be judged in different ways. Third, an attribute-based analysis gives a better diagnosis of how a product or service works. Fourth, suppliers need to know how overall satisfaction is generated and how different attributes influence it. Lastly, overall satisfaction and satisfaction with attributes are two qualitatively different concepts.

In the case of a tourist destination, consumer satisfaction is clearly a multidimensional concept. Tourist satisfaction is based on tourists' perceptions of different aspects of the destination. Each plays a different role in the determination of overall satisfaction (Danaher and Arweiler, 1996; Kozak and Rimmington, 2000; Murphy *et al.*, 2000).

Enright and Newton (2004, 2005) uphold the idea that a destination is competitive if it can attract and satisfy potential tourists and that this ability to compete is determined not only by specific tourist-related factors but also by a broader range of factors. In the literature on sun and sand tourism products, the climate, beaches, scenery, quality of hotels and safety are included as destination-specific attributes. In this study, most of the factors that have been used previously to describe this type of destination were included (Kozak, 2001; Mangion *et al.*, 2005; Aguiló *et al.*, 2005; Yoon and Uysal, 2005; Alegre and Cladera, 2006). According to the classification system used by Enright and Newton (2005), most of them are specifically tourist related, not including business factors. Some attributes related to pull factors (e.g. familiarity with the destination and the presence of friends or relatives) were also included.

2.2.2 The factor structure of tourist satisfaction

In their review of the literature, Matzler and Sauerwein (2002: 318–319) define the following factor structure for satisfaction:

1 *Basic factors.* Consumers regard these factors as being guaranteed by the service provider, with no need to request them specifically. They are factors that determine certain minimum requirements. If they are not fulfilled, they generate a high level of customer dissatisfaction, although they do not increase satisfaction if they are fulfilled. These factors determine a minimum threshold for penetrating a market.

2 *Performance factors.* These are factors that increase satisfaction levels if they are fulfilled and reduce them if not. Their effect on overall satisfaction is therefore symmetrical. They are designed to meet consumers' needs and desires, and the service provider must offer them in a competitive way.

3 *Excitement factors.* These are factors that increase consumer satisfaction if they are fulfilled but do not cause dissatisfaction if they are not. A service supplier must try to rise above its rivals in these respects.

The two methods that are used in this chapter to identify the factor structure of tourist satisfaction – the importance grid and the penalty–reward analysis – will now be outlined.

1 *Importance grid* (Vavra, 1997). The explicit importance of an attribute or factor can be defined as the stated importance it is given by a consumer when he or she is asked for a direct assessment. This information can be obtained about a series of attributes or factors by conducting a consumer survey. The interviewee must judge how important each attribute is using a scale based on ordinal numbers. The implicit importance of an attribute can be calculated by correlating satisfaction with that attribute with another external criterion like overall satisfaction. Implicit importance measures the impact that satisfaction with a particular factor has on overall satisfaction. Underlying both concepts is the hypothesis that the two variables offer different information. While a consumer might rate certain factors as being

very important, if they are basic factors their impact on overall satisfaction can be low. Vavra's (1997: 383) proposal is aimed at identifying factors by combining their explicit and implicit importance values:

- Factors with a high explicit importance and low implicit one are *basic factors*. Although consumers might regard them as being very important, their influence on overall satisfaction is very low.
- Factors with a low explicit importance and high implicit one are *excitement factors*. Consumers regard them as not being very important. However, when they achieve positive satisfaction levels, they have a big influence on overall satisfaction.
- Factors with a high (low) explicit importance and high (low) implicit one are *performance factors*. If the factor is given a high importance in both cases, it is something to be taken into account in improving performance. If, in contrast, it is given a low importance in both cases, the service provider can pay it less attention.

2   *Penalty–reward analysis* (Brandt, 1987). Brandt (1987, 1988), Mittal *et al.* (1998) and Anderson and Mittal (2000) have studied the relationship between overall satisfaction and the performance of different attributes under the assumption that the effects of their performance on overall satisfaction are asymmetrical. A high level of satisfaction with an attribute might not have any effect on overall satisfaction, while a low level of satisfaction might be detrimental to it. This asymmetric response can be analysed using a regression model whose endogenous variable is overall satisfaction and whose exogenous variables are dummy ones which indicate whether an attribute is judged as performing positively or negatively. More specifically, for each attribute two dummy variables are defined. One of them indicates whether the consumer's assessment was positive (or very positive) and the other indicates whether it was negative (or very negative). A midway assessment is therefore used as the reference category. The estimated parameters of each of these dummy variables should have a positive sign (*reward*) and a negative one (*penalty*), respectively. The constant of this regression can be interpreted as the mean level of overall satisfaction for all consumers expressing indifference towards all the attributes. From the results of the regression, the set of attributes can be classified according to the following criteria:

- If, for an attribute, the penalty is greater than the reward, it is a *basic factor*.
- If the reward is higher than the penalty, it is an *excitement factor*.
- If both coefficients are the same, it is a *performance factor*.

Although both methods (i.e. the importance grid and the penalty–reward analysis) use a similar classification system with three types of factors, their empirical application does not yield equivalent results (Matzler and Sauerwein,

2002; Bartikowski and Llosa, 2004; Fuchs and Weiermair, 2004; Busacca and Padula, 2005). The main reason for this discrepancy is the hypothesis of linearity on which the importance grid is based. According to the linear hypothesis, the relationship between satisfaction with an attribute and overall satisfaction is symmetrical (Matzler *et al.*, 2004b; Busacca and Padula, 2005). Under this assumption, the value of the estimated partial correlation coefficient (or beta coefficient) between satisfaction with an attribute and overall satisfaction is the same whatever the level of satisfaction with the attribute. For example, with the importance grid, an attribute with a low partial correlation coefficient (when it performs well, it scarcely influences overall satisfaction) and a high stated importance is defined as a *basic factor*. However, if the same attribute performs badly (i.e. if satisfaction with the attribute is low), it is very likely that, given its importance, the level of overall satisfaction will be reduced (Matzler and Sauerwein, 2002; Matzler *et al.*, 2004b). This asymmetry can be interpreted as being attributable to the fact that satisfaction with an attribute and its stated importance are not independent variables (Matzler *et al.*, 2004b). That is, a change in satisfaction with an attribute can lead to a change in its importance.

Following Busacca and Padiula (2005: 557), these relationships can be illustrated graphically. In Figure 2.1, the hypothetical relationship between the performance of an attribute and a consumer's overall satisfaction is shown if this attribute can be considered to be a *basic factor*. When the factor performs well, possible improvements will tend to have a low influence on overall satisfaction. However, if the performance of the factor tends to worsen, because it is a *basic factor* its impact on overall satisfaction will be high. In Figure 2.2, the same hypothetical relationship is shown in the case of an *excitement factor*. In this case, if the factor performs well it has a big impact on overall satisfaction, whereas poor performance has a low impact. That is, as the performance of an

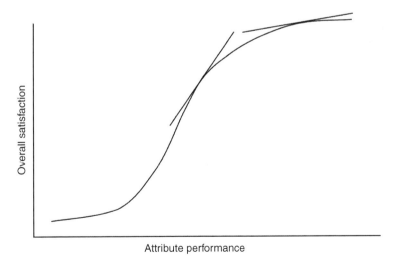

Figure 2.1 Relationship between the performance of a basic factor and overall satisfaction.

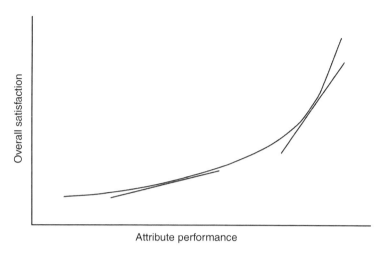

Attribute performance

Figure 2.2 Relationship between the performance of an excitement factor and overall satisfaction.

attribute worsens, its impact on overall satisfaction lessens. As Matzler and Sauerwein (2002) indicate, the presence of this type of non-linear relationship makes it necessary to estimate the impact of each attribute, whether it has a high performance or not.

2.3 Empirical analysis

Information about the destinations was obtained from a survey in which tourists from the three main nationalities visiting the Balearics (Germans, Britons and Spaniards) were interviewed at the end of their holiday. As was noted earlier, these three nationalities account for 81 per cent of tourism to the Balearics (Govern de les Illes Balears, 2007). The survey was conducted at Palma Airport between 15 July and 25 August 2006. To perform the following analyses, the database was previously filtered, first to eliminate those tourists who own a villa or apartment in the Balearics, since their answers might be heavily conditioned. Likewise, to avoid other atypical types of tourism, tourists with a very low declared per capita daily expenditure (<0.5th percentile) or very high one (>99.5th percentile) were excluded. The final sample comprised a total of 1,786 tourists.

   In the survey, information was requested about the tourists' motivations in choosing the sun and sand destinations they had visited during the previous three years. The interviewee was asked to indicate how important a total of 24 (tangible and intangible) attributes that are characteristics of sun and sand destinations were in motivating them to choose a destination. Their importance was rated using a five-point Likert scale ranging from 1 ('not at all important') to 5 ('very important'). In the second part of the survey, the interviewee was asked to rate the same 24 attributes for their latest holiday in the Balearics and for each of the sun and sand destinations they had visited during the previous two summers. The 24 factors were rated on a scale ranging from 1 ('not at all satisfied') to 5 ('very satisfied'). Using the same scale, the interviewee was also asked to rate their overall satisfaction with the destinations they had visited.

The attributes that were used in the survey were chosen following a review of leading analyses of the attributes of sun and sand destinations (Kozak and Rimmington, 1999; Kozak, 2002; Alegre and Cladera, 2006; Aguiló *et al.*, 2005; Yoon and Uysal, 2005). Additionally, two pilot surveys were conducted during the months of March and June 2006 to test the suitability of the attributes that had been chosen. The results of the tests were presented at three international conferences on tourism: the 15th International Leisure and Tourism Symposium ESADE (Barcelona, 2006), the Second International Conference on Tourism Economics (Palma, 2006) and the International Conference of Trends, Impacts and Policies on Tourism Development (Crete, 2006). The list of attributes that was finally included is as follows: the quality of accommodation, cultural activities (museums, festivals, exhibitions, etc.), nightlife, tourist attractions (leisure parks, etc.), the climate, local cuisine, a cheap destination, contact with nature (hiking, etc.), the local lifestyle, easy access from the country of origin, facilities for the elderly and/or children, easy access to information and/or ease of arranging the holiday, cleanliness and hygiene, scenery, beaches, sports activities, the presence of friends and/or relatives, familiarity with the destination, interesting towns or cities, getting to know other tourists, safety, tranquillity, prices in line with budgets and, finally, historic sites.

As for the destinations that were finally included, a decision was made to analyse information when a destination was rated by at least 3 per cent of the interviewees. Table 2.1 shows the main coastal destinations that were visited by tourists from the sample (in addition to the Balearic Islands).

Table 2.1 Destinations visited in the summer holidays of 2004–2006 (excluding the Balearic Islands)

	%
Mainland Spain Mediterranean coastal areas	22.90
Canary Islands	20.73
Italian coast	11.52
Greek coast	10.70
Mediterranean coast of France	10.03
Caribbean	7.28
Turkish coast	6.12
Tunisian coast	2.94
Egyptian coast	2.51
Bulgarian coast	2.56
Croatian coast	2.22
Moroccan coast	0.48

2.4 Results

2.4.1 The importance grid

To create an importance grid, first the mean value of the stated importance values from the tourist survey for each of the attributes was estimated. The values that were obtained determine the coordinates of each attribute on the horizontal axis. Second, to obtain the implicit importance values the partial correlation coefficients between overall satisfaction and stated satisfaction were estimated for all the attributes. These coefficients were obtained using the results of a regression model where overall satisfaction is the endogenous variable. From an empirical point of view, the main drawback in the estimation of this model is when negative coefficients are obtained. This kind of result is not easy to interpret because it indicates that an increase in satisfaction with this attribute is associated with a reduction in overall satisfaction. In our analysis, this result was obtained for the following attributes: a cheap destination, contact with nature, easy access to information and/or ease of the holiday to arrange, and the presence of friends or relatives at the destination. In previous empirical literature, negative coefficients are attributed to the presence of multicollinearity, justifying the use of a factor or principal components analysis to group the attributes. Nonetheless, this procedure does not necessarily avoid the appearance of negative coefficients (see, for instance, Chu, 2002). One alternative is to eliminate attributes whose coefficient has initially taken a negative value when the model is estimated. With the data from the sample, both alternatives were put into practice. A similar factor structure was identified in both cases. As a result, a presentation will be made of the results of the model only when attributes with a negative coefficient were eliminated.

Figure 2.3 shows the importance grid. For each attribute, the horizontal axis shows the mean values of the stated importance (explicit importance) of the attributes. The vertical axis shows the partial correlation coefficients between overall satisfaction and stated satisfaction with each attribute (the implicit importance). The lines that divide the figure into four sections represent the mean values of both variables. With Vavra's classification system (1997), almost all the factors are located in the first and third quadrants. They are therefore *performance factors*. The most important factors include the quality of the accommodation, scenery, beaches, prices in line with budgets, cleanliness, safety and the climate. Those that are least important include the local cuisine, nightlife, interesting towns and cities, getting to know other tourists, familiarity with the destination, cultural activities, the local lifestyle and historic sites. The method did not detect any *excitement factors* and situated tranquillity and ease of access on the threshold of *basic factors*.

2.4.2 The penalty–reward analysis

The dummy variables that were needed for the penalty–reward analysis were defined using the satisfaction ratings for each attribute. To capture the negative effect of an attribute's bad performance on overall satisfaction, a dummy

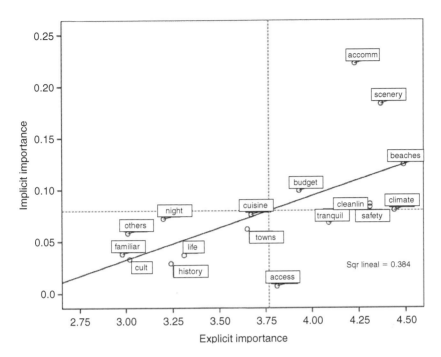

Figure 2.3 Importance grid of factors at sun and sand destinations. (Only those attributes that give positive partial correlation coefficients are shown.)

variable was codified that takes a value of 1 when the level of satisfaction corresponds to categories 1 ('not at all satisfied') or 2 ('not very satisfied') and 0 otherwise. To capture the positive effect of an attribute that performs well, a second dummy variable was defined with a value of 1 if the tourist's declared rating was 'very satisfied' and a value of 0 if not. The results of the estimated regression between overall satisfaction and the 48 dummy variables (2 for each of the 24 attributes) led to some statistically non-significant coefficients. In a second estimation, only those coefficients that were statistically significant were included (see Table 2.2). The regression model has a coefficient of determination equal to 0.458. For six factors, none of the dummy variables was significant. They were the tourist attractions, cheapness of the destination, contact with nature, ease of access, facilities for the elderly or children, and the presence of friends or relatives.

To classify the factors in accordance with the criteria used by Brandt (1987), the hypothesis of symmetric effects was tested for those factors with significant positive and negative effects. For each factor, a Wald test was performed to test for the hypothetical equality (in absolute values) of coefficients (β_{j+} and β_{j-}) which corresponded to the two dummy variables. The test was performed for 11 factors, with the hypothesis of symmetric effects being rejected in 5 cases.

Table 2.2 Estimated coefficients for the penalty–reward analysis

	Coefficients of the dummy variables and significance of the tests				
	High satisfaction β_{j+}	Sig. H_0 $\beta_{j+}=0$	Low satisfaction β_{j-}	Sig. H_0 $\beta_{j-}=0$	Sig. H_0 $\beta_{j+}+\beta_{j-}=0$
Accommodation	0.228	0.000	−0.337	0.000	0.052
Cultural activities	0.108	0.000	−0.068	0.047	0.373
Nightlife	0.089	0.000	−0.098	0.006	0.843
Climate	0.074	0.000	−0.109	0.081	0.607
Local cuisine	0.098	0.000	−0.096	0.023	0.969
Local lifestyle	0.072	0.016	−0.106	0.008	0.510
Easy access to info/easy holiday to arrange			−0.113	0.024	
Cleanliness and hygiene	0.060	0.007	−0.275	0.000	0.000
Scenery	0.152	0.000	−0.363	0.000	0.002
Beaches	0.158	0.000	−0.169	0.000	0.844
Doing sports	0.075	0.017			
Familiar destination	0.130	0.000			
Interesting towns/cities	0.110	0.000			
Getting to know other tourists	0.121	0.000			
Safety			−0.335	0.000	
Tranquillity	0.063	0.003	−0.187	0.000	0.016
Prices in line with budgets	0.066	0.006	−0.169	0.001	0.083
Historic sites	0.077	0.008			
Constant	3.809	0.000			
$R^2 = 0.458$					

Note
Only coefficients with a relevant level of significance were estimated.

Consequently, for all 18 attributes that were finally included in the regression, the hypothesis was only not rejected in 6 cases. The results of the estimations and the significance of the tests (null hypothesis: $\beta_{j+}=0$, $\beta_{j-}=0$, $\beta_{j+}+\beta_{j-}=0$) are shown in Table 2.2. Figure 2.4 shows the estimated coefficients. The main conclusion we can draw from the aforementioned results is that the attributes cannot generally be assumed to have symmetric effects. That is, the impact of each factor on overall satisfaction is not symmetric: it takes different values depending on whether the factor has been rated positively or negatively.

To identify the *basic factors*, the coefficient of the dummy variable for low satisfaction had to be higher than the coefficient of the dummy for a high level of satisfaction. This occurred with seven factors: accommodation, ease of access to information/ease of arranging the holiday, cleanliness, the scenery, safety, tranquillity and prices in line with budgets. The *excitement factors* had to have a 'reward' coefficient that was higher than the 'penalty' one. Five factors were detected: doing sports, interesting towns or cities, familiarity of the destination, historic sites and getting to know other tourists. The remaining six factors are *performance factors*: cultural activities, nightlife, the climate, local cuisine, local lifestyle and beaches. Notice that the way in which the factors are classified differs from the classification that was achieved with the importance grid. The main difference is that in this case, in addition to *performance factors*, *basic factors* and *excitement factors* were identified (Table 2.3).

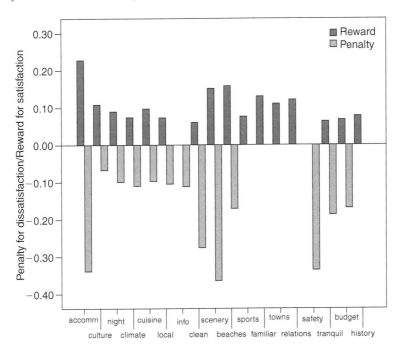

Figure 2.4 Penalty–reward analysis.

Note: Coefficients of the dummy variables for the factors included in the regression model.

Table 2.3 The determinants of competitiveness at sun and sand destinations

DESTINATION COMPETITIVENESS

TOURIST SATISFACTION

PERFORMANCE FACTORS

Beaches   Climate   Nightlife   Cultural activities
Local life style   Local cuisine

EXCITEMENT FACTORS

Interesting towns/cities   Doing sports   Historic sites
Familiarity of destination   Getting to know other tourists

BASIC FACTORS

Accommodation   Ease of access to info/ease of arranging the holiday
Cleanliness and hygiene   Scenery
Safety   Tranquillity   Prices in line with budgets

2.5 Conclusions

Tourist satisfaction is acknowledged to be an indicator of a destination's capacity to succeed. Several other authors (Yüksel and Rimmington, 1998; Thomason *et al.*, 1999; Go and Grovers, 2000; Kozak, 2002, 2004; Fuchs and Weiermair, 2004) argue that tourist satisfaction is one of the main competitive edges for a destination. Literature on tourism has proposed two methods of analysing the factor structure of tourist satisfaction at a destination: the importance grid and the penalty–reward analysis. However, previous work on empirical evidence does not reach a clear consensus on the best method to use. In this chapter, we have used both methods in analysing satisfaction with Mediterranean sun and sand mass tourism destinations.

The two methods that were used to identify the factor structure of satisfaction with sun and sand destinations give different results. Two hypotheses underlie the use of the importance grid for explicit and derived importance. First, the method assumes that the information that is obtained from the explicit importance and derived importance values does not coincide. Second, the derived importance values are obtained on the assumption that there is a linear relationship between how the attributes perform and overall satisfaction. With our data, neither of the two hypotheses seems valid. The results of the importance grid show that the explicit importance that tourists lend the different factors is strongly correlated with the derived importance that is obtained by calculating its influence on overall satisfaction. As a result, the factors tend to be identified as *performance factors*. Additionally, with the *penalty–reward* method it was detected that tourists use a different value to reward or penalize the factors' good or bad performance. The main explanation for this is the existence of an asymmetrical relationship between satisfaction with the attributes and overall satisfaction. This asymmetric relationship in some factors makes it possible to identify *basic* and *excitement factors*, as well as *performance* ones. In consequence, from a methodological point of view the penalty–reward analysis seems more appropriate since it enables the factor structure of satisfaction with sun and sand tourism to be identified.

As for the results that were obtained, the way in which the penalty–reward analysis classifies the factors into three types shows decision-makers at tourist destinations what aspects of the destination should be given more attention in order to improve its competitive edge. The factors that the analysis detected as being basic define an essential part of the sun and sand product (accommodation, ease of access to information/ease of arranging the holiday, cleanliness and hygiene, safety, tranquillity, scenery, prices in line with budgets). With these factors, decision-makers should make sure that certain minimum performance levels are guaranteed, since satisfaction ratings that are below a certain threshold will seriously penalize the destination. Interestingly, neither the climate nor beaches figure among this set of factors. According to the results of the analysis, both factors should be considered to be *performance factors*. Among the latter, the most important factor is the beaches since their effect on overall satisfaction is the highest, in both a positive and a negative sense. This is therefore one of the main factors to be taken into account by decision-makers. The remaining *performance factors* are associated with cultural activities, the nightlife, lifestyle and local cuisine. As for *excitement factors*, some of the factors identified were not formerly considered to be essential attributes at sun and sand destinations. From the results that were obtained, it should be understood that managing these attributes properly will provide a competitive edge over other rival destinations. Giving tourists easy access to information about the destination and increasing their knowledge about places or towns of historic interest can have a substantial impact on overall satisfaction. Similarly, being able to complement a sun and sand holiday with sporting or social activities may have a positive effect on assessments.

In addition to the aforementioned classification, we must not overlook the direct information provided by the estimated coefficients of the penalty–reward model. The values of the coefficients indicate which factors have the greatest impact on overall satisfaction. In the analysis we performed, the three top factors with a positive effect are the accommodation, beaches and scenery. These last two factors also carry the highest penalty coefficients. These results highlight the importance of some of the factors that are considered to be *basic*. Although it is important to understand that certain minimum standards are required for these factors if a destination is to compete, it is equally important to take into account that if these factors are well managed, they can also have a crucial effect on overall satisfaction.

Acknowledgements

Joaquín Alegre and Jaume Garau acknowledge financial support from SEJ2007-65255 and SEJ2004-06649 projects, respectively. The authors thank Dr Carles Manera and Dr Llorenç Pou for their helpful comments.

References

Aguiló, E., Alegre, J. and Sard, M. (2005) 'The persistence of the sun and sand tourism model', *Tourism Management*, 26 (2): 219–223.

Alegre, J. and Cladera, M. (2006) 'Repeat visitation in mature sun and sand holiday destinations', *Journal of Travel Research*, 44: 288–297.

Anderson, E. W. and Mittal, V. (2000) 'Strengthening the satisfaction–profit chain', *Journal of Service Research*, 3 (2): 107–120.

Baker, D. and Crompton, J. (2000) 'Quality, satisfaction and behavioral intentions', *Annals of Tourism Research*, 27 (3): 785–804.

Bartikowski, B. and Llosa, S. (2004) 'Customer satisfaction measurement: comparing four methods of attribute categorisations', *Service Industries Journal*, 24 (4): 67–82.

Brandt, R. D. (1987) 'A procedure for identifying value-enhancing service components using customer satisfaction survey data', in C. Suprenant (ed.) *Add Value to Your Service*, Chicago: American Marketing Association, pp. 61–65.

Brandt, R. D. (1988) 'How service marketers can identify value-enhancing service elements', *Journal of Services Marketing*, 2 (3): 35–41.

Buhalis, D. (2000) 'Marketing the competitive destination of the future', *Tourism Management*, 21 (1): 97–116.

Busacca, B. and Padula, G. (2005) 'Understanding the relationship between attribute performance and overall satisfaction', *Marketing Intelligence and Planning*, 23 (6): 543–561.

Chu, R. (2002) 'Stated-importance versus derived-importance customer satisfaction measurement', *Journal of Services Marketing*, 16 (4): 285–301.

Crompton, J. L. and Love, L. L. (1995) 'The predictive validity of alternative approaches to evaluating the quality of a festival', *Journal of Travel Research*, 34 (1): 11–24.

Crouch, G. I. and Ritchie, J. R. B. (1999) 'Tourism, competitiveness, and social prosperity', *Journal of Business Research*, 44: 137–152.

Danaher, P. J. and Arweiler, N. (1996) 'Customer satisfaction in the tourist industry: a case study of visitors to New Zealand', *Journal of Travel Research*, 34 (1): 89–93.

Deng, W. (2007) 'Using a revised importance–performance analysis approach: the case of the Taiwanese hot spring tourism', *Tourism Management*, 28: 1274–1284.

Dwyer, L. and Kim, C. (2003) 'Destination competitiveness: determinants and indicators', *Current Issues in Tourism*, 6 (5): 369–414.

Enright, M. and Newton, J. (2004) 'Tourism destination competitiveness: a quantitative approach', *Tourism Management*, 25: 777–788.

Enright, M. and Newton, J. (2005) 'Determinants of tourism destination competitiveness in Asia Pacific: comprehensiveness and universality', *Journal of Travel Research*, 43: 339–350.

Erto, P. and Vanacore, A. (2002) 'A probabilistic approach to measure hotel service quality', *Total Quality Management*, 13 (2): 165–174.

Farsari, Y., Butler, R., and Prastacos, P. (2007) 'Sustainable tourism policy for Mediterranean destinations: issues and interrelationships', *International Journal of Tourism Policy*, 1 (1): 58–78.

Fuchs, M. and Weiermair, K. (2003) 'New perspectives of satisfaction research in tourism destinations', *Tourism Review*, 58 (3): 6–14.

Fuchs, M. and Weiermair, K. (2004) 'Destination benchmarking: an indicator-system potential for exploring guest satisfaction', *Journal of Travel Research*, 43, February: 212–225.

Füller, J., and Matzler, K. (2007) 'Customer delight and market segmentation: An application of the three-factor theory of customer satisfaction on life style groups' *Tourism Management*, 29 (1): 116–126.

Füller, J., Matzler, K. and Faullant, R. (2006) 'Asymmetric effects in customer satisfaction', *Annals of Tourism Research*, 33 (4): 1159–1163.

Go, F. M. and Grovers, R. (2000) 'Integrated quality management for tourist destinations: a European perspective of achieving competitiveness', *Tourism Management*, 21: 79–88.

Govern de les Illes Balears (2007) 'El turisme a les Illes Balears. Dades informatives 2006', www.inestur.es.

Johnston, R. (1995) 'The determinants of service quality: satisfiers and dissatisfiers', *International Journal of Service Industry Management*, 6 (5): 53–71.

Knowles, T. and Curtis, S. (1999) 'The market viability of European mass tourist destinations. a post-stagnation life-cycle analysis', *International Journal of Tourism Research*, 1: 87–96.

Kozak, M. (2001) 'Repeaters' behavior at two distinct destinations', *Annals of Tourism Research*, 28 (3): 784–807.

Kozak, M. (2002) 'Destination benchmarking', *Annals of Tourism Research*, 29 (2): 497–519.

Kozak, M. (2004) *Destination Benchmarking: Concepts, Practices and Operations*, Wallingford, UK: CAB International.

Kozak, M. and Rimmington, M. (1999) 'Measuring tourist destination competitiveness: conceptual considerations and empirical findings', *International Journal of Hospitality Management*, 18: 273–283.

Kozak, M. and Rimmington, M. (2000) 'Tourist satisfaction with Mallorca, Spain, as an off-season holiday destination', *Journal of Travel Research*, 38 (3): 260–269.

Manera, C. and Garau, J. (2010) 'Economic growth, tourism, and insularity: the case of the Mediterranean', in C. Manera and J. Garau (eds) *Insularity in the Mediterranean: Economic and Environmental Challenges*, Madrid: Pirámide, pp. 49–80.

Mangion, M.-L., Durbarry, R. and Sinclair, M. T. (2005) 'Tourism competitiveness: price and quality', *Tourism Economics*, 11 (1): 45–68.

Matzler, K. and Sauerwein, E. (2002) 'The factor structure of customer satisfaction: An empirical test of the importance grid and the penalty-reward-contrast analysis', *International Journal of Service Industry Management*, 13 (4): 314–332.

Matzler, K., Bailom, F., Hinterhuber, B., Renzl, B. and Pichler, J. (2004a) 'The asymmetric relationship between attribute-level performance and overall customer satisfaction: a reconsideration of the importance–performance analysis', *Industrial Marketing Management*, 33 (4): 271–277.

Matzler, K., Fuchs, M. and Schubert, A. K. (2004b) 'Employee satisfaction: does Kano's model apply?', *Total Quality Management*, 15 (9–10): 1179–1198.

Matzler, K., Renzl, B. and Rothenberger, S. (2006) 'Measuring the relative importance of service dimensions in the formation of price satisfaction and service satisfaction: a case study in the hotel industry', *Scandinavian Journal of Hospitality and Tourism*, 6 (3): 179–196.

Mittal, V., Ross, W. T. and Baldasare, P. M. (1998) 'The asymmetric impact of negative and positive attribute-level performance on overall satisfaction and repurchase intentions', *Journal of Marketing*, 62 (1): 33–47.

Moutinho, L. (2000) 'Trends in tourism', in L. Moutinho (ed.) *Strategic Management in Tourism*, Wallingford, UK: CAB International, pp. 3–16.

Murphy, P., Pritchard, M. P. and Smith, B. (2000) 'The destination product and its impact on traveller perceptions', *Tourism Management*, 21 (1): 43–52.

Oh, C.-O. H. (2001) 'Revisiting importance-performance analysis', *Tourism Management*, 22 (6): 617–627.

Pawitra, T. A. and Tan, K. C. (2003) 'Tourist satisfaction in Singapore: a perspective from Indonesian tourists', *Managing Service Quality*, 13 (5): 399–411.

Pizam, A. and Taylor, E. (1999) 'Customer satisfaction and its measurement in hospitality enterprises', *International Journal of Contemporary Hospitality Measurement*, 11 (7): 326–339.

Poon, A. (1993) *Tourism, Technology and Competitive Strategies*, Wallingford, UK: CAB International.

Sampson, S. E. and Showalter, M. J. (1999) 'The performance–importance response function: observations and implications', *The Service Industries Journal*, 19 (3): 1–25.

Sauerwein, E., Bailom, F., Matzler, K. and Hinterhuber, H. H. (1996) 'The Kano model: how to delight your customers', preprints Volume I of the IX International Working Seminar on Productions Economics, Innsbruck, Austria.

Swan, J. and Combs, J. (1976) 'Product performance and consumer satisfaction: a new concept', *Journal of Marketing*, 40 (2): 25–33.

Tan, K. C. and Pawitra, T. A. (2001) 'Integrating SERVQUAL and Kano's model into QFD for service excellence development', *Managing Service Quality*, 11 (6): 418–430.

Thomason, L., Colling, P. and Wyatt, C. (1999) 'Benchmarking: an essential tool in destination management and the achievement of the best value', *Insights*, 23 (January): 111–117.

Vavra, T. G. (1997) *Improving Your Measurement of Customer Satisfaction: A Guide to Creating, Conducting, Analyzing, and Reporting Customer Satisfaction Measurement Programs*, Milwaukee, WI: ASQ Quality Press.

Yoon, Y. and Uysal, M. (2005) 'An examination of the effects of motivation and satisfaction on destination loyalty: a structural model', *Tourism Management*, 26 (1): 45–56.

Yüksel, A. and Rimmington, M. (1998) 'Customer-satisfaction measurement', *Cornell Hotel and Restaurant Administration Quarterly*, 39 (6): 60–70.

3 Determinant attitudes to tourism in a mass tourist destination

A comparative-static analysis

Eugeni Aguiló-Pérez and Jaume Rosselló-Nadal

3.1 Introduction

Tourism activities influence host communities and give rise to highly controversial beliefs. They have certainly exerted a considerable economic, productive and cultural influence, but it is also evident that they have been a source of social conflict for different groups and movements (Aguiló and Rosselló, 2005; Ap and Crompton, 1993; Davis *et al.*, 1988; Floyd and Johnson, 2002; Fredline and Faulkner, 2000; Williams and Lawson, 2001). Turner and Ash (1975) support the view that tourism contributes towards Third World development, although it tends to incorporate the negative cultural aspects of the industrialized countries that act as the destinations' source markets, thus hindering their progress and development. On the other hand, Britton and Clarke (1987) point out that mass tourism may have collaborated in hindering the permanency of local cultures and in spreading processes such as prostitution or delinquency. In spite of this, the majority of local residents see tourism as a tool for economic development (Gursoy *et al.*, 2002), and consequently it is not surprising that the findings of most studies on resident attitudes to tourism suggest that, overall, residents have positive attitudes to it (Andereck and Vogt, 2000; Korça, 1998), while only a few studies reported negative ones (Cheng, 1980, Johnson *et al.*, 1994; Pizam, 1978).

According to the *social exchange theory*, local residents are likely to participate in an exchange with tourists if they believe that they are likely to gain benefits without incurring unacceptable costs. If residents perceive that the positive impacts of tourism are greater than the negative ones, they are inclined to favour an exchange and, therefore, to endorse future tourism development in their community (Allen *et al.*, 1993; Getz, 1994; Gursoy *et al.*, 2002; Jurowski *et al.*, 1997; Perdue *et al.*, 1990; Pizam, 1978).

The relationship between resident attitudes to the effects of tourism and their support for, or opposition to, it is further corroborated by the *theory of reasoned action* (Ajzen and Fishbein, 1980; Fishbein and Ajzen, 1975, Dyer *et al.*, 2007; Stodolska, 2005). The theory of reasoned action indicates that individuals are rational, they make use of all available information and they evaluate the possible implications of their action before they decide to engage or not engage in a particular decision. The critical issue in forecasting behaviour is an individual's intentions, while these, in turn, are an antecedent to actual behaviour. Behavioural intentions have been defined as the subjective probability that an individual will engage in a specific behaviour (Fishbein and Ajzen, 1975). Intentions are made up of all the motivation-related factors that affect a certain type of behaviour, and they indicate the extent to which an individual will engage in a given behaviour. According to this theory, if an individual assesses a certain behaviour favourably, then they are more likely to intend to engage in that behaviour, as suggested by the social exchange theory.

When these theories were applied, the results brought to light differences in attitudes depending on a region's level of tourism development (Long *et al.*, 1990), the tourist industry's relationship with economics (Smith and Krannich, 1998; Williams and Lawson, 2001), high concentrations of tourism in specific places (Madrigal, 1995), the concentration of hotels (Bujosa and Rosselló, 2007), longer lengths of time living in the local community and native-born status (Sheldon and Var, 1984), a relation with jobs that are directly linked to tourism (Korça, 1998), the degree of familiarity with tourism and the local industry (Lankford, 1994), the degree of contact with tourists (Akis *et al.*, 1996), the perceived impact of leisure time (Lankford, 1994), a destination's level of development (Sheldon and Abenoja, 2001), a country's level of development (Teye *et al.*, 2002) and the type of tourism (Carlsen, 1999).

Consequently, research over the past two decades has demonstrated that attitudes to tourism can be related to a wide set of variables that characterize individuals and their perceptions. However, none of these studies has evaluated which of these variables predominate over the rest and how attitudes change with the passing of time. The purpose of this study, therefore, is to pinpoint the most decisive socio-economic characteristics that can be tied in with local resident attitudes to tourism in a mature destination like the Balearic Islands (Spain), using an ordered logit specification to filter the variables that are most influential in determining the answers to a large set of tourism-related questions. In addition, the influence of time is analysed by including a dummy variable that controls the period when the questionnaire was answered, thus determining how attitudes might have changed. Consequently, our aim is to contribute to debate by offering for the first time a dynamic view of resident attitudes.

3.2 Methodology

Over the years, one of the most frequently used tools in capturing individual opinions and perceptions has been the Likert scale. The Likert scale asks individuals to rate their support for/opposition to (agreement/disagreement with) different aspects related to a certain research area using whole numbers. For instance, using a five-point Likert scale, 1 can represent strong opposition, 2 opposition, 3 neither opposition nor support, 4 support and 5 strong support. In this context, it can be argued that an individual's choice is determined by a set of variables such as personal income, nationality or origin, age, or residence. Analytically,

$$L_k = f(x_i) \tag{3.1}$$

where L_k represents the possible answer that an individual might give, depending on their level of agreement with a proposed statement, using a k-point Likert scale, and x_i represents the individual's set of influential variables.

Because opinions are expressed in the form of a discrete ordered variable, it is not advisable to use a simple regression model with an ordinary least squares procedure to determine and quantify the type of relationship with the independent variables (Borooah, 2002; Greene, 2003; O'Connell, 2006), since the difference between the first two alternatives (1 and 2, for example) would be deemed the same as the difference between subsequent alternatives (3 and 4, for example) when in fact the value that each alternative takes simply indicates its sequential order. Nevertheless, using ordered logit (or probit) models it is possible to construct models that link the observed outcome to the values of determining variables (Borooah, 2002). The initial hypothesis that is implicit in an ordered model is the existence of a latent variable of opinion that is a linear function of the set of explanatory variables. Thus, analytically,

$$OP = x_i\beta + \varepsilon \tag{3.2}$$

where OP is the latent variable of opinion, x_i are i influential variables related to the individual, β is an i-dimensional vector to be determined and ε is the random error. Thus, the link between L_k and OP can be established through the following rule:

$$L_k = \begin{cases} 1 & \text{if} & P(OP) \leq \gamma_1 \\ 2 & \text{if} & \gamma_1 < P(OP) \leq \gamma_2 \\ 3 & \text{if} & \gamma_2 < P(OP) \leq \gamma_3 \\ \vdots & & \\ k & \text{if} & \gamma_{k-1} < P(OP) \end{cases} \tag{3.4}$$

where γ is a set of $k-1$ parameters to be estimated whose function it is to establish the correspondence between the probability function of the latent variable of opinion $P(OP)$ and L_k. Consequently, ordered models can easily be estimated and the relationship between responses and personal characteristics determined.

However, when a large set of personal determining variables are used in a regression analysis, the problem of multicollinearity can arise. Although attempts can be made to reduce this problem using principal component analysis techniques in order to obtain artificial variables (factors) that are not intercorrelated, later incorporating these factors into the regression analysis, the results of this procedure are more difficult to interpret and it has been proved that it is more inefficient than including the variables separately (Lubotsky and Wittenberg, 2001). As a result, the concept of general-to-specific modelling, highlighted by Krolzig and Hendry (2001: 832), was adopted, where starting from a general dynamic statistical model that captures the essential characteristics of the underlying data set, standard testing procedures are used to reduce its complexity by eliminating statistically insignificant variables, checking the validity of the reductions at every stage to ensure the congruence of the selected model.

Hence, only statistically significant variables remain in the final specification, while the significance of the whole model is retained.

3.3 Study area and data

3.3.1 The Balearic Islands

To illustrate how the above procedure can be applied, a survey on the host population of the Balearic Islands was used. The Balearic Islands are one of Spain's most internationally important tourist destinations. Located in the Western Mediterranean (Figure 3.1), with a surface area of 4,968.36 square kilometres and 955,045 inhabitants in 2004, they are considered to be an exceptional tourism centre and one of the world's top-ranking regions in terms of affluence, with a volume of 9.3 million international tourists in 2005 – a 1.2 per cent share of the total world market. At the same time, the importance of tourism for the region's economy can be ascertained by observing the Balearic Islands' own statistics, with estimated revenue of €46,060 million in 2005. Given these data, it is not surprising that tourism holds pride of place, accounting for a figure of between 30 per cent and 60 per cent of the total regional GDP, depending on how tourism is defined (Aguiló and Bardolet, 2002).

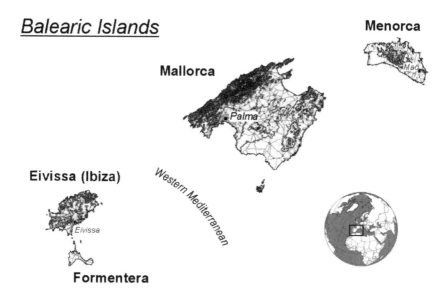

Figure 3.1 The Balearic Islands (Spain).

Foreign visitors to the Balearics first started to arrive in the early twentieth century, but it was in the 1960s that mass tourism took off. The number of arrivals rose from 0.4 million in 1960 to 3.5 million in 1973. After the first oil crisis, between 1981 and 1989, the number of tourists once again grew spectacularly, rising from 3.8 million to 7.1 million. Later, following the economic crisis of the early 1990s, arrival figures grew more moderately, a trend that has continued to the present day. However, this high level of tourism has also involved substantial immigration, with an estimated 18 per cent of the region's current residents not having been born in Spain (Mateu and Riera, 2006). On the other hand, it is often argued that the islands' expansion has gone hand in hand with the consumption of the archipelago's environmental resources (Buswell, 1996), and this could be a big obstacle to any future growth in tourism, or even to the maintenance of current levels of tourism revenue. As a result, over the past few years heavy restrictions on further tourism have been introduced through local laws, together with policies of different kinds, opening up debate on the controversial issue of continued growth versus environmental protection. Thus, an additional aim of this study is to quantify local resident perceptions in a mature destination where the dilemma of further tourism growth and environmental protection has not yet been solved.

3.3.2 Instrument

The survey developed for this study was based on previous work by Guyson *et al.* (2002) and Williams and Lawson (2001), who kindly provided the questionnaires used in their respective studies. However, a number of modifications had to be included, given the special characteristics of the study area. For instance, items on special environmental consequences, the expansion of local tourism enterprises to the Caribbean, or the tourist tax applied from the spring of 2002 to the autumn of 2003 were included.

Thus, a 12-page questionnaire was designed, comprising five main parts, to obtain the relevant sample data. The first and second parts included 22 statements on the positive and negative repercussions that tourism has for the islands, together with general hypothetical tourism policies where the respondents were asked to indicate their level of agreement, using a five-point scale. The third part explored the respondents' perceptions of general problems, such as crime, the environment or unemployment, and their sense of belonging to the Balearics. The fourth part contained 28 statements on tourism and its consequences for local welfare. In this part, the interviewees were asked to assess the tourist tax that was introduced, the need to reduce arrival numbers, their opinion of tourism entrepreneurs and the role of immigration. The final part comprised different questions on the respondents' demographic background and their links with revenue from tourism. Thus, the 50 survey statements from parts 1, 2 and 4 were the central core that was used to define local residents' personal attitudes to tourism, shown in Table 3.1.

Table 3.1 Statements about resident attitudes to tourism

Feelings about tourism	Attitude[a]
Q1. Tourism is likely to create more jobs for the community.	A–D
Q2. Tourism is likely to attract more investment for the community.	A–D
Q3. Tourism is likely to provide more business for local people and small businesses.	A–D
Q4. Tourism is likely to change the traditional culture.	A–D
Q5. Tourism is likely to put more pressure on local services such as the police, public safety or refuse collection.	A–D
Q6. Tourism is likely to result in traffic congestion.	A–D
Q7. The prices of goods and services are higher than in the rest of Spain because of tourism.	A–D
Q8. The price of land is higher than in the rest of Spain because of tourism.	A–D
Q9. Tourism is likely to create more leisure opportunities for the community.	A–D
Q10. Tourism is likely to have a positive impact on the cultural identity of the community.	A–D
Q11. Tourism is likely to destroy some natural resources.	A–D
Q12. Tourism is likely to provide an incentive for the conservation of historic heritage.	A–D
Q13. Tourism is likely to provide an incentive for the conservation of natural resources.	A–D
Q14. The overall results of tourism are positive.	A–D
How much you would oppose or support …?	
Q15. Nature-based tourism.	O–S
Q16. Attractions designed for large numbers of tourists such as theme parks.	O–S
Q17. Big new accommodation establishments (over 50 beds).	O–S
Q18. New rural accommodation establishments.	O–S
Q19. Cultural or historic-based attractions (visitor centres, museums…).	O–S
Q20. New tourist services (excluding accommodation).	O–S
Q21. Cultural and folk events (concerts, art and crafts, dance or festivals…).	O–S
Q22. The promotion of tourism in the Balearics should be increased.	O–S
Statements about tourism	
Q23. The economic situation in the Balearics is worrying.	A–D
Q24. I am prepared to pay more taxes in order to promote public policies related to the natural environment.	A–D
Q25. Tourists should pay for the environmental damage caused by tourism.	A–D

Q26.	Central government should pay for the environmental damage caused by tourism.	A–D
Q27.	The environment of the Balearic Islands has been destroyed, mainly by tourism.	A–D
Q28.	There would have been less environmental degradation if economic development had not been based on tourism.	A–D
Q29.	Due to the deterioration of natural resources, further tourism development is more difficult to implement.	A–D
Q30.	Tourism has led to the congestion of some natural areas.	A–D
Q31.	New tourism programs must be developed if the residents' welfare is to improve.	A–D
Q32.	The number of tourists must be reduced if the residents' welfare is to improve.	A–D
Q33.	(In reference to policies to reduce seasonality) The government must do nothing. As it is now, we have some months with a lot of work and others to rest.	A–D
Q34.	A reduction in the number of tourists during the summertime is desirable. This would reduce the annual number of tourists.	A–D
Q35.	An increase in the number of tourists during the wintertime is desirable. This would increase the annual number of tourists.	A–D
Q36.	An increase in the number of tourists during the spring and autumn is desirable. This would increase the annual number of tourists.	A–D
Q37.	An increase in the number of tourists during the wintertime but a reduction in summertime is desirable. This would help maintain the annual number of tourists.	A–D
Q38.	It is a good policy for tourists to pay an ecotax.	A–D
Q39.	Residents should pay an ecotax too.	A–D
Q40.	I agree with the fact that the ecotax should be paid only by tourists staying at hotels.	A–D
Q41.	I think that the ecotax should be paid at the airport and not at hotels.	A–D
Q42.	I agree with hoteliers when they say that they end up by paying the ecotax.	A–D
Q43.	Hoteliers have improved the welfare of Balearic residents.	A–D
Q44.	Hoteliers in the Balearic Islands are some of the best in the world.	A–D
Q45.	Investments by local hotel companies in the Caribbean can be rated as positive.	A–D
Q46.	Subsidies for more environmentally friendly tourist companies are a good policy.	A–D
Q47.	Residents' welfare is better now than twenty years ago.	A–D
Q48.	Residents' welfare is better now than fifty years ago.	A–D
Q49.	Immigration from the rest of Spain, which was characteristic of past decades, has been positive for the residents' welfare.	A–D
Q50.	Current immigration from abroad is positive for the residents' welfare.	A–D

Note

a Residents were asked to state their level of agreement–disagreement (A–D) or level of opposition–support (O–S) using a five-point Likert scale.

The data were collected via ordinary mail in a prepaid envelope, with the questionnaire having been randomly mailed to selected addresses taken from the telephone directory in two rounds. In the first round, 4,500 letters were sent out during the winter of 2002/2003, generating 791 usable replies. The second round took place during the winter of 2006/2007, when 3,000 residents were sent the questionnaire, resulting in 536 usable answers. Consequently, there was a response rate of 17.7 per cent, a percentage that can be regarded as low. However, for about one-third of the letters that went unanswered, the lack of response can be attributed to incorrect addresses given in the telephone directory and so the 'real' response rate can be said to be 28 per cent, a percentage closer to that found in other comparable studies.

Although the initial intention was to carry out a one-round survey, the incentive for carrying out a second round during the winter of 2006/2007 was the possibility that circumstances might have changed significantly, leading to slight changes in the opinions of the islands' inhabitants. Three main reasons have been suggested: first, the changing dynamics of the population, with quite large numbers of immigrants from abroad having settled in recent years; second, the changing situation vis-à-vis tourism and the economy, with a negative situation during the first round and an optimistic one during the second, probably because of the dynamics of European economies; and finally, a new regional government following elections in mid-2003, which led to a significant change in tourism, environmental and infrastructure-related policies.

3.3.3 Resident attitudes

Before we examine the main determinants of resident attitudes and opinions to tourism, it is important to highlight some general results for the total sample, given the special characteristics of a mature destination like the Balearics, while also pointing out the differences between the two rounds.

Results relating to the economic impact of tourism reflect a clearly positive opinion of the benefits that the industry represents for the economy of the Balearics. For instance, in both rounds more than 85 per cent of the sample agreed or strongly agreed that tourism generated employment, that it attracted investment and that it generated business opportunities for local residents. In contrast with this opinion, there was a general perception that the pressure of tourism was responsible for high price levels. Another significant result was the fact that about 60 per cent of the sample believed their income would fall if the local tourist industry were to face a hypothetical setback.

An analysis of current policies and potential proposals shows that there is only slight opposition to the introduction of new theme parks or general attractions that might lead to higher numbers of tourists. As expected, strong opposition was shown to the further creation of hotels with over 50 beds. However, this opposition was less intense in the second round. On the other hand, when an analysis was made of the respondents' attitudes to the creation of new rural hotels, there was a significant change of opinion, with widespread support for the idea that intensified during the second round. As for the promotion of tourism, a clear majority (65 per cent in both rounds) stated that more promotion is needed. Finally, what can also be inferred is their recognition of the problem that seasonality represents.

At the same time, the majority of the respondents believe that tourism leads to the over-saturation of the community's services and to traffic congestion. However, residents recognize that, thanks to tourism, considerable leisure opportunities are available. In summary, there is a general perception that local residents' welfare is better now than it was twenty or fifty years ago. As for cultural policies, most local residents support proposals for new cultural attractions, such as museums or auditoriums, and they are also in favour of the organization of yearly cultural events. There was changing opinion over a possible improvement to local residents' welfare if the number of arrivals were reduced. While in the first round 35 per cent believed that there should be a reduction in tourist numbers, with another 35 per cent disagreeing, in the second the corresponding percentages were 24 per cent and 57 per cent.

As for environmental problems, local residents seem to be conscious of the fact that tourism leads to the deterioration of natural resources. However, there is some ambiguity concerning the possibility that tourism might have contributed towards the conservation of some natural resources. When asked to identify where the responsibility lies for the destruction of the Balearic Islands' local environment, the respondents once again point to tourism as a key factor. Furthermore, most think that it has led to congestion in some natural parks.

As to the balance between the revenue obtained from tourism and the incurred costs, when local opinions are summarized, most of the respondents consider that the balance is positive, with this belief intensifying in the second round. Nevertheless, they do not constitute an overwhelming majority, since 15 per cent think that the balance is negative.

3.4 Results

In order to provide evidence of the relationship between attitudes to tourism and the socio-economic characteristics of the residents, the 50 survey statements from parts 1, 2 and 4 with information on local resident opinions (Table 3.1) were modelled according to the methodology described earlier. Information regarding the interviewees' socio-economic characteristics was also collected during the survey in part 5 of the questionnaire, and the corresponding abbreviations for these are shown in Table 3.2.

The final results of the estimation process can be seen in Table 3.3, where the 50 ordered logit models are presented. It is important to note that although, initially, ordered logit and ordered probit models were both used, given the lack of significant differences between the two models only the ordered logit models are shown. At the same time, it is important to highlight that the reference group for the estimated results is a woman with no children interviewed during the winter of 2002/2003, who was born in the Balearics and lives in the islands' capital,

Table 3.2 Influential variables

Name	Description
IRCD	Sense of belonging to the town/city where the interviewee lives, measured directly.
IRCI	Sense of belonging to the town/city where the interviewee lives, measured indirectly.
IRM	Sense of belonging to the municipality.
IRI	Sense of belonging to the island.
AGE	Age of the interviewee in years.
GEND	A dummy variable that takes the value 1 if the interviewee was a man.
NHOU	Number of members in the household.
CHOU	Number of children in the household.
BSPA	A dummy variable that takes the value 1 if the interviewee was born in Spain (but not in the Balearic Islands).
BNOR	A dummy variable that takes the value 1 if the interviewee was born in the rest of Europe (EU-15).
BSOU	A dummy variable that takes the value 1 if the interviewee was born in a country outside the rest of Europe (EU-15).
LMAL	A dummy variable that takes the value 1 if the interviewee is living in Mallorca but not in Palma (the capital).
LMEN	A dummy variable that takes the value 1 if the interviewee is living in Minorca.
LEIV	A dummy variable that takes the value 1 if the interviewee is living in Ibiza or Formentera.
INC	Level of income measured on a scale from 1 to 5, where 1 = low income; 5 = high income.
INCR	Extent to which the family's income is dependent on tourism measured on a scale from 1 to 4, where 1 = high level of dependence; 4 = no relationship.
A2007	A dummy variable that takes the value 1 if the interview was conducted during the second round (winter 2006/2007).

Palma. Thus, all the coefficients must be interpreted in relation to these individual characteristics. The results can be regarded as satisfactory in terms of the LR chi-square tests, in the sense that all the estimated models include a set of variables that were jointly significant. Nevertheless, in all cases, a low value for the pseudo R^2 was obtained, showing the models' low explanatory power. Although this circumstance can be a problem in forecasting individual attitudes, it does not constitute a problem when trying to find significant relationships between objective variables.

In the case of the independent variables, the most relevant one was to have been interviewed during the winter of 2006/2007 (A2007), and it was finally included in 37 of the 50 models. Indeed, it seems clear that the survey stage (the round when the survey was conducted) is statistically significant and, consequently, despite the destination's maturity, a four-year gap was sufficient to bring about a notable change in residents' perceptions and attitudes to tourism. As expected, the extent to which a family's income is dependent on tourism (INCR) is also one of the most important factors in determining resident attitudes, featuring in 70 per cent of the estimated models. The level of personal income (INC) – whatever the origin and whether related to tourism or not – is present in half the models that were analysed, emphasizing the influence of this socio-economic characteristic. Meanwhile, other socio-economic characteristics such as age (AGE), gender (GEND), the number of household members (NHOU), being born outside the Balearic Islands (BSPA, BNOR and BSOU) and living in the smaller islands of Minorca (LMEN) or Ibiza and Formentera (LEIV) play a lesser yet significant role in determining host attitudes, with a presence in the estimated models of 30 per cent or more for each of the variables.

As for measures of individuals' sense of belonging, it is important to highlight that only seven models did not include any of the four variables that were used to measure this characteristic. Individuals' sense of belonging to the town or city where they live, measured indirectly through a question about the importance of the local news, was the most relevant variable, appearing in 22 of the 50 models. In contrast, when it was measured directly, it was the least present variable. At the bottom of the list of significant variables, living in the biggest island but not in the main city (LMAL) was significant in 22 per cent of the estimated models, while the number of children in the household (CHOU) was only significant in 12 per cent of them.

But just as it is important to know what the main factors are, it is equally essential to know whether these determinants influence tourist perceptions and attitudes positively or negatively. In this context, when a comparison is made of the two rounds of interviews separated by a four-year period, resident perceptions of job and business opportunities clearly seem to become less categorical in the second round, although they have a stronger perception of the negative impact of congestion, public services, traffic congestion and the high level of prices. However, residents who were interviewed during the second round give more recognition to some of the constructive effects of tourism, such as its

Table 3.3 Estimated ordered logit models

	IRCD	IRC1	IRM	IRI	AGE	GEND	NHOU	CHOU	BSPA	BNOR	BSOU	LMAL	LMEN	LEIV	INC	INCR	A2007	N	LR	Psdo R²
Q1	–	–	–	–	–	-0.264	–	–	–	–	–	–	–	–	0.322	-0.409	-0.546	1195	95.83	0.0395
Q2	–	–	–	–	0.009	-0.422	–	0.137*	–	–	–	–	-0.432	–	0.199	-0.247	–	1152	55.70	0.0226
Q3	–	–	–	0.129	–	-0.461	–	–	0.284	–	–	–	–	–	0.290	-0.294	-0.207*	1170	78.94	0.0312
Q4	–	0.283	–	–	-0.007*	-0.332	-0.170	0.231	–	-0.649	–	-0.198*	-0.973	–	0.133	–	–	1133	73.79	0.0249
Q5	0.249	–	–	–	–	–	-0.102	–	–	-0.624	-0.578	–	-0.733	0.506	–	–	-0.291	1255	67.49	0.0206
Q6	–	0.132	–	–	–	-0.212	-0.078*	–	–	-0.580*	-0.649	–	0.682	0.865	–	–	-0.314	1261	53.19	0.0177
Q7	–	–	–	–	–	–	-0.112	–	–	-1.002	–	–	–	–	–	–	-0.333	1255	20.13	0.0067
Q8	0.224	–	–	–	–	–	–	–	0.257*	–	–	–	–	–	-0.168	–	–	1157	18.84	0.0065
Q9	0.276	–	-0.117*	–	–	-0.267	–	–	–	–	–	-0.254	-0.361	-0.420	–	-0.363*	–	1235	59.45	0.0182
Q10	–	–	–	–	–	–	–	–	0.441	–	0.856	–	-0.621	-0.585	–	-0.131	0.471	1235	62.78	0.0187
Q11	–	0.147	–	0.097*	-0.013	–	–	–	–	-0.859	-0.934	–	–	–	-0.099*	0.302	-0.531	1164	66.28	0.0217
Q12	–	0.195	–	–	0.011	–	–	–	0.263	–	0.735	–	–	–	–	-0.185	–	1241	32.57	0.0099
Q13	0.089*	–	–	-0.091*	0.010	–	–	–	–	–	–	–	-0.313*	–	–	-0.259	0.715	1231	72.45	0.0196
Q14	–	0.162	–	–	0.010	–	0.127	–	0.414	–	0.664	–	–	–	0.129	-0.375	0.342	1134	59.97	0.0194
Q15	-0.106*	–	–	–	0.009	–	–	–	-0.244*	–	0.613	–	–	-0.724	-0.105*	0.172	0.299	1169	45.28	0.0153
Q16	–	0.178	–	–	–	–	-0.100*	-0.142*	–	–	–	–	0.897	–	0.253	0.406	-0.261	1159	106.66	0.0294
Q17	–	0.231	–	–	–	–	-0.098	–	-0.222*	–	–	–	–	–	0.217	0.239	-0.791	1133	90.19	0.0277
Q18	–	0.101*	–	0.142	–	–	–	–	-0.314	–	–	–	–	–	–	0.217	-0.193*	1243	50.26	0.0133
Q19	–	-0.164	0.157	–	–	–	0.198	-0.210	–	–	–	0.41	–	-0.581	-0.154	0.151	0.363	1158	54.61	0.0188
Q20	–	0.098*	–	0.115*	–	-0.198*	0.111	–	-0.247	-0.563*	–	–	0.403	–	–	–	-1.110	1267	120.05	0.0306
Q21	–	-0.199	0.186	–	–	–	–	–	–	–	–	–	-0.431	-0.814	-0.213	0.137*	0.050	1170	78.55	0.0279
Q22	–	0.152	0.126*	–	–	–	–	-0.167	–	–	-0.616	–	–	-0.817	–	0.572	–	1241	111.38	0.0313
Q23	–	-0.158	-0.139	–	0.009	0.493	–	–	-0.342	0.788	-0.537*	-0.379	-0.795	–	-0.217	-0.318	–	1138	91.59	0.0274
Q24	–	–	–	–	–	-0.287	–	–	–	1.384	–	–	–	–	0.107	–	–	1173	34.26	0.0104
Q25	–	–	-0.215	0.439	–	–	–	–	–	–	–	0.210	–	–	0.232	0.232	–	1237	67.05	0.0185

	(1)	(2)	(3)	(4)	(5)	(6)	(7)	(8)	(9)	(10)	(11)	(12)	(13)	(14)	(15)	N	χ²	
Q26	—	—	—	-0.008	—	—	-0.241*	—	—	—	—	-0.343*	-0.177	0.261	0.656	1123	62.60	0.0188
Q27	0.122*	—	0.093*	-0.011	—	—	—	-0.695	-0.971	—	—	—	-0.144	0.205	-0.360	1162	47.53	0.0143
Q28	—	-0.145*	0.193	—	—	—	—	-0.897	-0.985	—	—	—	-0.217	0.164	-0.399	1146	55.38	0.0177
Q29	0.183	—	0.167	—	-0.130	—	0.399	—	-0.630	—	-0.346*	—	—	0.252	0.857	1199	94.38	0.0288
Q30	0.176	-0.160	0.206	—	—	—	—	—	—	0.297	-0.397	—	—	—	-0.235	1220	50.27	0.0173
Q31	0.269	—	0.201	—	-0.180*	—	0.297	—	—	—	—	—	—	0.582	0.407	1241	52.76	0.017
Q32	-0.280	-0.229	—	—	—	—	—	—	-0.766	—	—	—	—	—	-0.817	1230	169.22	0.0443
Q33	—	0.137	0.211	—	—	—	—	0.895	0.711	-0.223	—	—	—	—	-0.232	1248	25.11	0.0070
Q34	—	—	—	0.007	—	—	—	—	—	—	—	0.467	-0.123	0.267	—	1170	39.24	0.0119
Q35	-0.157	—	—	—	-0.080*	—	—	—	—	—	—	—	—	0.600	-0.580	1241	116.74	0.0331
Q36	0.130	—	0.148	—	0.091*	—	—	—	—	—	—	0.789	-0.142	-0.446	—	1158	78.35	0.0233
Q37	0.211	—	—	—	—	—	-0.327	—	-0.662	—	-0.349	—	—	—	0.266	1260	29.05	0.0078
Q38	0.143	—	0.123	—	—	—	—	1.014	—	—	0.414	—	—	0.223	—	1247	44.40	0.0136
Q39	-0.130	-0.245	-0.109*	—	—	—	—	—	—	—	-0.370	—	-0.273	0.177	0.594	1256	75.94	0.0239
Q40	—	0.159	-0.132	—	0.194*	—	—	—	—	—	-0.678	—	0.138	-0.185	0.963	1144	140.95	0.0409
Q41	0.210	—	—	—	—	0.190*	-0.286	—	—	—	—	—	0.110*	-0.410	-0.589	1114	60.44	0.0183
Q42	—	—	—	—	0.090*	—	—	—	—	—	-0.455	—	0.120	—	0.481	1048	60.27	0.0189
Q43	0.274	-0.227	0.196	0.014	0.100*	—	0.364	0.777	1.175	-0.321	0.574	-0.849	—	-0.332	0.992	1093	160.48	0.0528
Q44	0.143	0.114*	—	0.019	—	—	—	0.827	—	-0.357	-1.079	-1.641	—	-0.266	0.493	1150	139.32	0.0420
Q45	—	—	—	-0.007*	0.152	0.246	-0.211	0.653*	0.533*	-0.421	-0.536	-1.165	—	—	0.813	1099	105.17	0.0333
Q46	0.116*	—	0.137	-0.012	—	-0.383	0.489	—	—	0.222*	-0.351*	—	0.175	—	0.244	1155	43.94	0.0161
Q47	-0.194	—	0.171	0.012	0.101	-0.266	0.461	—	—	—	—	—	—	-0.297	0.726	1150	100.41	0.0309
Q48	0.116	—	—	0.013	—	—	1.361	—	—	—	—	—	—	-0.318	—	979	42.66	0.0167
Q49	—	—	—	0.008	—	-0.236	—	—	—	—	—	-0.405	—	—	0.638	1205	152.24	0.0460
Q50	0.245	-0.305	—	—	—	—	0.632	1.328	1.216	—	—	—	—	-0.272	0.947	1232	168.62	0.0458

Note

* Denotes significance only at the 10% level. The rest of the parameters are significant at 5%. Ancillary parameters are not reported here, for simplicity.

positive impact on the cultural identity of the community and the incentives it provides to conserve natural resources. In general, over the four years there was some increase in support for further tourism development based on more accommodation, restaurants and shops and, by extension, more tourists. Support for hoteliers and immigration also increased between the two rounds.

As expected, the extent to which a family's income is dependent on tourism plays a significant role because the higher the dependence, the more the positive effects of tourism are valued and the less the negative ones are taken into account. At the same time, the higher the level of dependency, the greater the support there is for further tourism development. On the other hand, very similar results are achieved within certain income brackets (irrespective of the source), with the exception of new attractions aimed at large numbers of tourists, new big accommodation centres, assessments of the economic situation in the Balearics, and the prospect of increasing yearly visitor numbers through more arrivals during the winter months. For all these four issues, people with a high level of income are more conservative and less concerned about the economic situation than residents with a high level of income that is dependent on tourism.

As for other socio-economic characteristics and their relationship with resident attitudes, it should be emphasized that, in general, men are less categorical in expressing their attitudes to both the opportunities brought by and the costs of tourism than women, although globally speaking they do not differ from the opposite sex. On the other hand, the older the interviewee, the more they believe that tourism acts as an incentive in helping to conserve natural resources and historic centres. It is also shown that older people tend to be very categorical in asserting that residents' welfare now is better than twenty or fifty years ago. When the number of household members is high, the interviewee tends to be more tolerant toward the negative consequences of tourism (the change in the local culture, congestion and high prices). This circumstance is also detected when people have been born in a foreign country.

When variables associated with individuals' sense of belonging are analysed, it is shown that the more integrated they are, the more emphatic their attitudes are to both the opportunities brought by and the costs of tourism, although individuals who are most integrated generally have a more positive approach to tourism. Generally speaking, however, people who are well integrated are strongly opposed to further tourism development, although they agree with an increase in the total number of visitors to the archipelago. They are also more emphatic in believing that tourists should pay an ecotax and that residents should not have to pay for the costs of tourism.

3.5 Conclusions

A growing number of research studies have recently appeared that analyse local resident perceptions and attitudes to tourism with the excuse of helping planners to manage development strategies while minimizing the potential negative effects and maximizing the overall population's support for such alternatives. As previous literature has shown, a large set of variables can be used to try to account for residents' perceptions and attitudes. The results of this study have shown which of these variables are the most decisive, highlighting the relevance of the time factor.

Because the survey for this study was carried out in two rounds, it showed that, although a period of four years can be perceived as too short to provide significant differences in the responses of residents living in a mature tourist destination like the Balearics, attitudes to tourism changed significantly over this period of time. In general, residents who were interviewed during the second round were observed to have a stronger recognition of some of the positive effects (e.g. the cultural repercussions and incentives for the conservation of the environment) and some of the negative effects (e.g. congestion and the overexploitation of natural resources), with some increase in support for further tourism development. It seems clear that because the Balearics are a small group of islands (with a fragile environment) that have seen a high level of economic development, this has generated a substantial number of people who reject the tourist industry and tourism entrepreneurs, although this opposition lessened in the second round of the survey. Given the variables that were used in the model to explain attitudes, changes in attitudes to tourism between rounds 1 and 2 of the survey cannot be attributed to changes in the socio-demographic profile of the host population (since this was captured by the model), but rather should be attributed to variations in the economic and tourism scenario and changes derived from the application of new policies.

Thus, through the application of the methodology described in this chapter, the key socio-economic determinants of residents' attitudes were identified, bringing to light the importance of certain variables such as a sense of belonging, the extent to which family incomes depend on tourism, and the level of family income. It also showed that other socio-economic characteristics influence opinions, but to a lesser extent. These results could be useful in programming new research into the field of residents' attitudes to tourism.

To sum up, the results of this study show that the host population of a mature tourist destination such as the Balearics generally tends to acknowledge the economic benefits of tourism. The cultural and social benefits are also perceived to be an advantage by residents of the Balearics, but to a low degree. At the same time, it is recognized that tourism creates various different problems, including the oversaturation of the community's services, traffic congestion and high price levels, although local residents conclude that there is a positive balance between revenue from tourism and the costs that are incurred.

References

Aguiló, E. and Bardolet, E. (2002) 'La economía balear en el 2001', *Cuadernos de Información Económica*, 167: 86–90.

Aguiló, E. and Rosselló, J. (2005) 'Host community perceptions: a cluster analysis', *Annals of Tourism Research*, 32: 925–941.

Ajzen, I., and Fishbein, M. (1980) *Understanding Attitudes and Predicting Social Behavior*, Englewood Cliffs, NJ: Prentice-Hall.

Akis, S., Peristianis, N. and Warner, J. (1996) 'Residents' attitudes to tourism development: the case of Cyprus', *Tourism Management*, 17: 481–494.

Allen, L. R., Hafer, H. R., Long, R. and Perdue, R. R. (1993) 'Rural residents' attitudes toward recreation and tourism development', *Journal of Travel Research*, 31 (4): 27–33.

Andereck, K. L. and Vogt, C. A. (2000) 'The relationship between residents' attitudes toward tourism and tourism development options', *Journal of Travel Research*, 39: 27–36.

Ap, J. and Crompton, J. (1993) 'Residents strategies for responding to tourism impacts', *Journal of Travel Research*, 32 (1): 47–50.

Borooah, V. K. (2002) *Logit and Probit: Ordered and Multinomial Models*, Thousand Oaks, CA: Sage.

Britton, S. and Clarke, W. (1987) *Ambiguous Alternatives: Tourism in Small Developing Countries*, Suva, Fiji: University of the South Pacific.

Bujosa, A. and Rosselló, J. (2007) 'Modeling environmental attitudes toward tourism'. *Tourism Management*, 28 (3): 688–695.

Buswell, R. J. (1996) 'Tourism in the Balearic Islands', in M. Barke, J. Towner and M. T. Newton (eds) *Tourism in Spain: Critical Issues*, Wallingford, UK: CAB International.

Carlsen, J. (1999) 'Tourism impacts on small islands: a longitudinal study of community attitudes to tourism on the Cocos (Keeling) Islands', *Pacific Tourism Review*, 3: 25–35.

Cheng, J. R. (1980) 'Tourism: how much is too much? Lessons for Canmore from Banff', *Canadian Geographer*, 23: 72–80.

Davis, D., Allen, J. and Cosenza, R. (1988) 'Segmenting local residents by their attitudes, interests, and opinions toward tourism', *Journal of Travel Research*, 27 (2): 2–8.

Dyer, P., Gursoy, D., Sharma, B. and Carter, J. (2007) 'Structural modeling of resident perceptions of tourism and associated development on the Sunshine Coast, Australia', *Tourism Management*, 28 (2): 409–422.

Fishbein, M., and Ajzen, I. (1975) *Belief, Attitude, Intention, and Behavior: An Introduction to Theory and Research*, Reading, MA: Addison-Wesley.

Floyd, M. F. and Johnson, C. Y. (2002) 'Coming to terms with environmental justice in outdoor recreation: a conceptual discussion with research implications', *Leisure Sciences*, 24: 59–77.

Fredline, E. and Faulkner, B. (2000) 'Host community reactions: a cluster analysis', *Annals of Tourism Research*, 27: 763–784.

Getz, D. (1994) 'Residents' attitudes toward tourism: a longitudinal study in Spey Valley, Scotland', *Tourism Management*, 15: 247–258.

Greene, W. H. (2003) *Econometric Analysis*, Upper Saddle River, NJ: Prentice-Hall.

Gursoy, D., Jurowski, C. and Uysal, M. (2002) 'Resident attitudes: a structural modeling approach', *Annals of Tourism Research*, 29: 79–105.

Johnson, J., Snepenger, D. and Akis, S. (1994) 'Residents' perceptions of tourism development', *Annals of Tourism Research*, 21: 629–642.

Jurowski, C., Uysal, M. and Williams, R. D. (1997) 'A theoretical analysis of host community resident reactions to tourism', *Journal of Travel Research*, 36 (2): 3–11.

Korça. P. (1998) 'Resident perceptions of tourism in a resort town', *Leisure Sciences*, 20: 193–212.

Krolzig, H. M. and Hendry, D. F. (2001) 'Computer automation of general-to-specific model selection procedures', *Journal of Economic Dynamics and Control*, 25: 831–866.

Lankford, S. (1994) 'Attitudes and perceptions toward tourism and rural regional development', *Journal of Travel Research*, 33 (4): 35–43.

Long, P., Perdue, R. and Allen, L. (1990) 'Rural resident tourism perceptions and attitudes by community levels of tourism', *Journal of Travel Research*, 28 (3): 3–9.

Lubotsky, D. H. and Wittenberg, M. (2001) 'Interpretation of regressions with multiple proxies', MacArthur Network on Poverty and Inequality in a Broader Perspective Working Paper. Online, available at: http://ssrn.com/abstract=284165 (accessed 22 February 2010).

Madrigal, R. (1995) 'Residents' perceptions and the role of government', *Annals of Tourism Research*, 22: 86–102.

Mateu, J. and Riera, A. (2006) 'Demografia i inmigració', in A. Riera (ed.) *Informe Econòmic i Social 2005*, Palma de Mallorca: UIB-'Sa Nostra'.

O'Connell, A. A. (2006) *Logistic Regression Models for Ordinal Response Variables*, Thousand Oaks, CA: Sage.

Perdue, R., Long, P. and Allen, L. (1990) 'Resident support for tourism development', *Annals of Tourism Research*, 17: 586–599.

Pizam, A. (1978) 'Tourism's impacts: the social costs to the destination community as perceived by its residents', *Journal of Travel Research*, 16 (4): 8–12.

Sheldon, P. and Abenoja, Y. (2001) 'Resident attitudes in a mature destination: the case of Waikiki', *Tourism Management*, 22: 435–443.

Sheldon, P. and Var, T. (1984) 'Resident attitudes to tourism in North Wales', *Tourism Management*, 15: 40–47.

Smith, M. and Krannich, R. (1998) 'Tourism dependence and resident attitudes', *Annals of Tourism Research*, 25 (4): 783–801.

Stodolska, M. (2005) 'A conditioned attitude model of individual discriminatory behavior', *Leisure Sciences*, 27: 1–20.

Teye, V., Sirakaya, E. and Sönmez, S. (2002) 'Residents' attitudes toward tourism development', *Annals of Tourism Research*, 29: 668–688.

Turner, L. and Ash, J. (1975) *The Golden Hordes: International Tourism and the Pleasure Periphery*, London: Constable.

Williams, J. and Lawson, R. (2001) 'Community issues and resident opinions of tourism', *Annals of Tourism Research*, 28: 269–290.

4 A panel data analysis of residential water demand in a Mediterranean tourist region

The case of Sardinia

Vania Statzu and Elisabetta Strazzera

4.1 Introduction

The Mediterranean basin is one of the main tourist destinations in the world, and tourism has been a fundamental factor of economic growth for coastal regions. But just like any other economic activity, the tourism industry generates a variety of external effects on the economy and the natural environment, effects that should be properly taken into account in order to attain socially efficient allocations. Unfortunately, regulatory instruments have often been weak in controlling the environmental and sustainability problems related to the tourist presence.

A clear signal of this under-regulation is the uncontrolled and irrational urbanization of coastal areas (WWF, 2004; PNUE/PAM, 2005). Many regions in Southern Europe are characterized by a tourist demand which only in part is addressed to official tourist structures, while the remaining part is satisfied by holiday homes. This form of tourism has a strong environmental impact in coastal areas and in small islands, since local infrastructure is usually built for a number of residents much smaller than the peak tourist season population. The consequence is congestion of roads and beaches, and an excess of pressure on scarce natural resources such as land and water.

It is well known that Mediterranean regions suffer from endemic water scarcity conditions, which are expected to worsen in the future owing to supply reductions related to climate change and desertification processes, and demand increases related to agricultural, industrial and residential uses. In periods of drought, the competition between alternative uses can be tight, and the water agencies may be compelled to restrict use in one sector to allow a sufficient level of consumption in another. Generally, some priority is given to the residential sector, since basic human needs are at stake. However, if the residential sector needs are inflated by the presence of tourists in the holiday homes, it is possible for undesired distributive effects to occur.

In order to design policies aimed at correcting environmental and allocative distortions, it would be useful to measure the impact on domestic water demand produced by the presence of tourists in holiday homes. Unfortunately, although the relationship between secondary homes tourism and excess demand of water in the residential sector is recognized (Kent *et al.*, 2002; Garcia and Servera, 2003; Essex *et al.*, 2004), lack of data on unofficial tourist accommodation hinders a measurement of the impact (WWF, 2004; see also Margat, 2002, for a general discussion of measurement problems in domestic consumption). The objective of the present work is to take a step in this direction, estimating the effect of the presence of tourists in unofficial structures on the demand for water in the domestic sector, along with other factors influencing the residential demand for water.

We analyse a data set on water consumption in a Mediterranean region, Sardinia, for a period of six years (2000–2005), using aggregated data on municipalities. We estimate the value of the price and income elasticity, and analyse the influence of socio-economic, demographic and geographical characteristics, as well as climate conditions, on consumption levels and trends. In order to estimate the effect of holiday-home tourism on the residential demand for water, we use an index of residential tourist pressure obtained by Sistu (2008). The results of our analysis will help to uncover the driving factors of different trends in water consumption, and will be useful to evaluate past and current policies and management practices and to suggest indications for future plans and programmes.

The chapter is structured as follows: the next section reviews previous relevant literature on the domestic and tourist demand of water; section 4.3 presents the case study, while section 4.4 illustrates the econometric methods; estimation results are discussed in section 4.5; finally, section 4.6 concludes the chapter.

4.2 Background

The impact of tourism on environment and natural resources has been analysed in many environmental studies: effects on water supply and demand, the production of waste and sewage, beach erosion and congestion, and increasing indiscriminate development along coasts to increase the supply of holiday homes and other tourist structures. In tourist locations such as the Balearic Islands or Sardinia, the population in the peak months (July and August) outnumbers the resident population (Garcia and Servera, 2003; RAS, 2007). Congestion and excessive pressure on the resources can be a serious problem in economic terms, too, especially if the tourist location is perceived as a 'luxury' good: tourists may be willing to pay high prices for high environmental quality, and the effect on the total revenues produced by an increase in the number of visitors may be negative.

One effect of the tourist pressure on natural resources is an increase in the demand for water. According to some estimates, tourists consume nearly twice as much water as residents do (EEA, 1999); hence, it can be expected that the impact on the overall demand is more than proportional to the increase in population determined by the tourist presence. In order to alleviate this pressure, innovative management policies may be required in economies where tourism is growing. Tirado *et al.* (2006) have applied a general equilibrium model to the water market in the Balearic Islands, and find that a specific combination of water efficiency measures and price instruments may reduce the amount of water allocated to the tourism sector without having a negative impact on the economy. Kent *et al.* (2002), Garcia and Servera (2003) and Fortuny *et al.* (2008) share the opinion that a change in management policies regarding water resources is required. Until recently, supply-side strategies have mainly been used: either increasing groundwater extraction, with problems of depletion of reserves and salt intrusion; or the desalination of sea water, which is an energy-intensive and costly method. Recently, the introduction of tools for promoting sustainable pro-duction processes in the tourist sector, such as EMAS, ISO 14001 or the Euro-pean Eco-label and others, has called for more attention on the side of the tourist demand of water: tourist structures are encouraged to install flow-reducers on taps and double-discharge devices on lavatories, to use water-efficient appliances and to install systems for the reuse of grey water (Fortuny *et al.*, 2008). However, these tools apply only to official structures such as hotels, resorts, campsites, and so on, and do not have any effect on the pressure of tourists who stay in second homes; specific programmes should be designed to control the water consumption of tourists who lodge in holiday houses.

In order to help policy design, it is necessary to have a better understanding of the effect that holiday-home tourism has on the demand for water. As far as we know, only one previous study, by Martínez-Espiñeira (2002), has attempted to estimate the impact on the demand for water produced by this kind of tourism. The author analysed a balanced panel of aggregated data on water consumption in 122 towns of north-west Spain during a 23-month period. They estimated a model of demand, which includes a dummy variable for municipalities with a large number of tourists with second homes in order to estimate its effect on the overall demand of water for residential uses. The estimated effects turned out not to be significant. The author argued that more information on the presence of tourists with second homes would be required to capture the effect properly.

In order to obtain a correct specification for the model, all relevant factors should be taken into account when analysing the demand of water for domestic uses: price of water, household size, income, housing characteristics, climatic vari-ables. Previous empirical studies (see Arbués *et al.*, 2003, for an extensive survey) show that water is an ordinary good (its demand is expected to decrease when price increases), but its own price elasticity can be very low. The problem of how to correctly estimate the price elasticity in the presence of complex tariff structures – as usually is the case for water utilities – is still open in the literature: when fea-sible, a discrete–continuous maximum likelihood approach is to be recommended (see Hewitt and Hanemann, 1995; Olmstead *et al.*, 2007; Strazzera, 2006). The effect of price could be influenced by the frequency of billing, since it can be expected that a high (and, especially, regular) frequency of bills induces people to be more aware of the relationship between the use of water and the amount paid (Nieswiadomy and Molina, 1991; Martínez-Espiñeira, 2002; Gaudin, 2006).

Water consumption is also expected to increase when income increases (it is a normal good). The effect of the household size is expected to be positive, since large households consume more than smaller ones; in general, the presence of scale economies in some uses of water (for cooking, cleaning the house, washing clothes and dishes) should lead to a increase less than proportional to the increase in the number of household components (but Cavanagh *et al.*, 2002, finds an increase that is more than proportional).

The influence of climate in indoor and outdoor consumption should also be accounted for. Previous work has used precipitation levels and temperature (e.g. Nauges and Thomas, 2000; Moncur, 1987; Corral *et al.*, 1998), or the evapotranspiration rate (Billings and Agthe, 1980; Billings, 1982; Agthe *et al.*, 1986; Nieswiadomy and Molina, 1988; Hewitt and Hanemann, 1995).

Some work has considered the effect of age of the population on the aggregate consumption of water, finding that older populations consume less than young ones (Nauges and Thomas, 2000). Also, the age of the house may have an impact on water consumption: new houses have new plumbing systems and are expected to help water saving (Nauges and Thomas, 2000); but Olmstead *et al.* (2007) find a non-monotonic pattern, with houses of intermediate age consuming more than either old or recent constructions.

Moncur (1987) was the first author to explicitly analyse differences in consumer behaviour during drought and non-drought periods: a water rationing dummy variable was inserted in the model to take into account restrictions in the supply. A similar approach was taken by Renwick and Green (2000), while Martínez-Espiñeira and Nauges (2004) use a more informative variable, namely the number of daily hours of supply restrictions.

The results and insights obtained from the existing literature will be used to construct our model for the demand of water for residential uses in Sardinia.

4.3 Area of study

Sardinia is an important tourist site for summer vacations in Europe, being especially renowned for transparency of the sea water surrounding it and the beauty of its beaches and coves. Official data (ISTAT, 2007a) indicate that in 2004, 10,203,401 tourists stayed in Sardinia in registered structures, prevalently in coastal locations. This is an extremely high number if compared to the official population of Sardinia, which is approximately 1,600,000. Moreover, this number does not show the real size of the tourist phenomenon. According to the survey '*Viaggi e Vacanze degli Italiani*' conducted in 2004 (ISTAT, 2007b), 34,514,000 tourists spent at least a night in Sardinia; comparing this figure to the number of tourists lodging in official structures, CRENoS (2007) finds that 79 per cent of these tourists stayed in secondary houses.

Sistu (2008) uses a different methodology to estimate the number of home-holiday tourists, based on the differential in the amount of solid waste produced in peak summer months with respect to other periods of the year. Seaside tourist towns show a large increase in the summer period, which is due to the presence of tourists staying in holiday homes. Estimates of the increase in the population due to the presence of tourists in Sardinia's provinces are shown in Table 4.1. All provinces show high impacts: Medio Campidano appears to be the least attractive province,

Table 4.1. Estimated daily presences in Sardinia in peak season at 2005

Administrative provinces of Sardinia	Official tourist presences[a]	Estimated presence in home holidays[b]	Total presence of non-residents (A)	Resident population[c] (B)	Tourist impact (A–B)/B
Cagliari	2,066,000	6,960,384	9,026,384	545,666	15.54
Medio Campidano	94,000	351,173	445,173	106,624	3.18
Carbonia Iglesias	158,000	2,905,006	3,063,006	131,766	22.25
Nuoro	749,000	2,165,232	2,914,232	163,531	16.82
Ogliastra	339,000	2,051,131	2,390,131	59,004	39.51
Oristano	301,000	2,326,928	2,627,928	168,163	14.63
Sassari	844,000	4,912,551	5,756,551	314,823	17.29
Olbia Tempio	2,737,000	9,915,874	12,652,874	153,519	81.42
Sardinia	7,288,000	31,588,280	38,876,280	1,643,096	22.66

Sources of data: a ISTAT (2008); b RAS (2007); c ISTAT (2001).

and Olbia-Tempio and Ogliastra the most. To Olbia-Tempio belongs one of the most attractive – and luxurious – Mediterranean tourist locations, the Costa Smeralda (Emerald Coast), characterized by a highly developed tourist system; while in Ogliastra, which is much less developed, the ratio of tourists to residents is driven up by the small number of residents in that area. As yet, tourism in the Medio Campidano province is still in its embryonic stage, so that the tourist population in the summer peak period is much lower than that in other provinces of Sardinia.

Figure 4.1 in the appendix to this chapter shows the impact of tourism in Sardinian towns, classified in terms of the ratio between estimated tourist presences and resident population. Since the infrastructure, such as water pipes, sewage and filtering systems, not to mention roads and railways, is in most locations built with the needs of the resident population in mind, it is obvious that such a mass of visitors concentrated in a limited period of the year will generate strong congestion problems in the use of infrastructure and public utilities. It can be expected that similar congestion problems will arise in the future in less developed areas such as Medio Campidano after planned investment in tourist development in that province has taken take place.

Like other Mediterranean regions, Sardinia is characterized by water scarcity, the supply often being unable to meet the demand for industrial, residential and agricultural uses. This is partly due to climatic reasons, but also the resource is managed inefficiently: water has been, and in the agricultural sector still is, provided at political prices by a number of public agencies and utilities with often overlapping tasks, and scant commitment to efficiency.

The consequence has been that there has not been enough money to invest in new infrastructure (or just replace old pipes), and the percentage of water losses in the residential sector was as high as 60 per cent in 2001 (RAS, 2006). However, in 2004 the regional government accomplished the reform process in the residential water sector promoted by the National Law 36/1994. One of the fundamental acts in the reform process was the institution of a unique water agency for the whole regional area, and the application of a unique tariff system designed to cover variable costs and to penalize excessive use of the resource. The tariff is now structured with smaller blocks and higher marginal prices than they used to be, especially for high levels of consumptions; furthermore, it introduces a different (higher) tariff for non-residents (see Tables 4.2 and 4.3).

4.4 Methodology

Assuming a linear functional form for the demand function, the equation to be estimated is:

$$DEPVAR_{it} = \beta\ X_{it} + \gamma\ Z_i + \alpha_i + \varepsilon_{it} \qquad (4.1)$$

where i indexes individuals and t indexes time periods, $WATCON_{it}$ is the dependent variable, X_{it} is a $1xK$ vector of time-varying regressors (cross-sectional time series variables) and Z_i is a $1xG$ vector of time-invariant

Table 4.2 Tariff system and price level, 2000–2005

		Marginal prices (euros)					
ESAF	Block size (m³)	2000	2001	2002ᵃ		2003	2004
	0–84	0.25	0.25	0.28		0.295	0.295
	85–124	0.45	0.45	0.49		0.517	0.517
	125–164	0.64	0.64	0.695		0.738	0.738
	>165	0.76	0.76	0.825		0.886	0.886
CGB	Block size (m³)	2000	2001	Block size (m³)	2002ᵇ	2003ᶜ	2004ᵈ
	0–90	0.21	0.21	0–60	0.22	0.26	0.28
	91–180	0.47	0.47	61–120	0.51	0.57	0.62
	181–300	0.53	0.53	121–200	0.54	0.63	0.69
	>300	0.71	0.71	>200	0.67	0.85	0.96
SIINOS	Block size (m³)	2000	2001	2002		2003	2004
	0–120	0.276	0.290	0.290		0.290	0.290
	121–180	0.516	0.542	0.542		0.542	0.542
	181–240	0.705	0.740	0.740		0.740	0.740
	>240	0.930	0.976	0.976		0.976	0.976
SIM	Block size (m³)	2000	2001	2002		2003	2004
	0–100	0.25	0.25	0.25		0.25	0.25
	101–150	0.42	0.42	0.42		0.42	0.42
	151–200	0.51	0.51	0.50		0.50	0.50
	>200	0.63	0.63	0.63		0.63	0.63

Notes
(a), (b), (c), (d) values reported are means of different prices applied in a same year.

regressors (cross-sectional variables). α_i is an individual specific and time-invariant error component, assumed *iid* N $(0, \sigma_\alpha^2)$, and ε_{it} is a classical mean zero disturbance, *iid* N $(0, \sigma_\varepsilon^2)$. β and γ are vectors of parameters associated with regressors, α_i is the component of variation not explained by the equation, i.e. any factor that is specific to each town and that has not been included among the independent variables will be included in ε_i and may be correlated with parts of X and Z. ε_{it} is assumed to be uncorrelated with both the explanatory variables and the effect α_i.

Different estimators can be used depending on specific assumptions regarding individual heterogeneity.

The simplest model that could be applied to the data is the pooled OLS model. It consists of an ordinary least squares (OLS) estimation of model (1). If we assume that α_i is identical for every town (so that individual heterogeneity is completely explained by regressors and the usual error term), the OLS estimates are unbiased and consistent. If heteroscedasticity is present, it is still possible to obtain a correct variance–covariance matrix using the White–Huber 'sandwich' correction in order to obtain a robust estimation.

If individual heterogeneity is present, we can insert a dummy variable for each individual observation (least-squares dummy variables), but such a model can be difficult to manage if N is quite large. In that case, it is possible to use a

Table 4.3 Tariff system and prices applied in 2005 by ABBANOA

Residential uses – local resident tariff system	
Block size (cubic metres)	Prices (euros)
0–70	0.25
71–140	0.55
141–200	0.90
201–250	1.30
Oltre 250	1.80
Fixed charge	15
Residential uses – no resident tariff system	
0–140	0.55
141–200	0.90
201–250	1.30
Oltre 250	1.80
Fixed charge	50

panel specific estimator in order to take into account the individual heterogeneity. If we assume that individual effects are fixed for each town, we can apply the 'within' transformation. It consists of an estimation of the model taking all variables as deviations from individual (town) means. The fixed effect (FE) model can be written as

$$\Delta DEPVAR_{it} = \alpha_i + \beta \ \Delta X_{it} + \gamma \ \Delta Z_i + \Delta \varepsilon_{it}$$

where $\varepsilon_{it} = iid$ N $(0, \sigma_\varepsilon^2)$ and $\Delta DEPVAR_{it} = (DEPVAR_{it} - \overline{DEPVAR_i})$, $\Delta X_{it} = (X_{it} - \overline{X_i})$, $\Delta Z_{it} = (Z_i - \overline{Z_i})$. e $\Delta \varepsilon_{it} = (\varepsilon_{it} - \varepsilon_i)$.

The individual effects are modelled by the intercept, which varies across all observations. This estimation is consistent and unbiased even if the independent variables are correlated with the individual error.

The problem with the within transformation is that it drops out all time-invariant regressors from the model. But time-invariant variables can be important to explain an economic behaviour. Socio-economic variables are generally time invariant or are not available as time series, and the fixed effect specification reduces the explanatory power of the model. In order to maintain time-invariant variables in the model, we can adopt a random-effects GLS (generalized least squares) procedure (RE). The model can be written as follows:

$$DEPVAR_{it} = \alpha + \beta X_{it} + \gamma \ Z_i + (\alpha_i + \varepsilon_{it})$$

In this specification, individual effects are random variables and individual heterogeneity is explained by a second error term, α_i *iid* N $(0, \sigma_\alpha^2)$, and ε_{it} is the idiosyncratic error *iid* N $(0, \sigma_\varepsilon^2)$. The random-effects model is consistent and more efficient than the fixed-effect one if there is no correlation between α_i and regressors.

A Breusch–Pagan test allows us to compare the validity of the pooled OLS versus the random effect estimator. The null hypothesis is that the variance of ε_i is zero. If the null is not rejected, then we can presume that the pooled OLS is unbiased and consistent; if the null is rejected, the random-effects estimator should be preferred to the pooled OLS.

A Hausman test (1978) can be used to compare fixed and random effects. The Hausman test verifies exogeneity of individual effects: rejection of the null hypothesis of no systematic differences between FE and RE coefficients implies that there is correlation between regressors and unobserved individual heterogeneity. If this is the case, RE, as well as OLS, are not consistent and should be rejected, and the fixed-effects model, or alternative models such as the instrumental variables models, should be used instead. Unfortunately, in some cases the application of the Hausman test is not conclusive: when the matrix of the squares of the differences of the variances of the coefficients is not positive definite, the test is not reliable. Alternatively, Wooldridge (2002: 290–291) proposes a test to compare fixed- and random-effects models. This test consists in estimating a random-effects model where the time-demeaning variables of time-variant variables are inserted. Then a Wald test is used to see whether the time-demeaning variables are jointly not significantly different from zero; if this is the case, the random-effects model can be accepted.

4.5 Econometric analysis

Our study of the demand of water in Sardinia uses data on 240 towns over a period of six years (2000–2005). Data concerning domestic water consumption, prices, and number of users were directly collected from the four main water utilities involved in our research: ESAF, which managed 220 of the towns in the data set; CBG, which managed 18 towns; SIM, which managed the City of Cagliari Water Services; and SIINOS, which managed the City of Sassari Water Services. All these utilities have since been merged into a single water utility, Abbanoa.

Sardinia experienced a drought from 1998 to 2003. In order to keep the level of supplies under control, some restrictions on the water service were imposed, with the supply being cut off for several hours each day. The actual level of restrictions varied in different towns, depending on the specific hydrological subsystem they belong to.

The dependent variable used in the econometric analysis is the annual average consumption (*WATCON*) per user per town. The data were collected for the period 2000–2005 and expressed in cubic metres. The model presented in this work includes the following covariates:

- annual average price variable [the ratio of the total amount billed over the total consumption in a town (*AP*)];

- annual income variable per tax payer (*INCOME*);
- demographic variables [household size (*HHSIZE*), proportion of people not part of the workforce (*NWF*)];
- housing characteristics [share of property homes (*OWNERS*), share of houses not renovated in the period 1991–2001 (*NORENOV*)];
- geographical variables [altitude of municipalities (*ALT*), population of towns (*POP5000, POPOV15000*) and the tourist impact dummy variables (*TOUR1, TOUR2, TOUR3*)];
- climate variable [summer evapotranspiration rate (*SUMEVATRA*)];
- water utilities dummies [(*SIINOS, SIM, GOVOSSAI*)];
- a variable that takes into account the number of hours of regular water distribution (*HOURS*);
- year dummies (*YEAR 2001, YEAR 2002, YEAR 2003, YEAR 2004, YEAR 2005*).

The tourist impact variable and the summer evapotranspiration rate require some explanation. The tourist dummy variables indicate different levels of impact produced by tourists lodged in holiday homes: *TOUR1* indicates towns with low impact (ratio tourists/residents less than 40 per cent), *TOUR2* an intermediate impact (ratio tourists/residents between 40 per cent and 90 per cent) and *TOUR3* high impact (ratio tourists/residents over 90 per cent). The summer evapotranspiration rate indicates the environmental demand for water due to the interaction between climate and vegetation. This variable considers the influence on indoor and outdoor consumption, since it represents the interaction between temperature and other climatic variables and allows one to account for the perceived climate in a region: areas with higher evapotranspiration in the summer months are characterized by higher perceived temperatures.

Average price, income, the summer evapotranspiration rate, the tourist impact and the water utilities variables are cross-sectional time series variables; the year dummies are time series variables; all other variables are cross-sectional time-invariant variables. Descriptive statistics can be found in Table 4.4.

We estimate the water demand model as an equation, linear in logarithms:

$$Log(WATCON_{it}) = \beta_0 + \beta_1 \log(AP_{it}) + \beta_2 \log(INCOME_{it}) + \beta_3 \log(HHSIZE_i) +$$

$$\beta_4 \log(NLF_i) + \beta_5 \log(OWNERS_i) + \beta_6 \log(NORENOV_i) + \beta_7 \log(ALT_i) +$$

$$\beta_8(POP5000_i) + \beta_9(POPOV15000_i) + \beta_{10}(TOUR2_i) + \beta_{11}(TOUR3_i) +$$

$$\beta_{12}(TOUR4) + \beta_{13} \log(SUMEVATRA_{it}) + \beta_{14} \log(HOURS_{it})$$

$$+ \beta_{15}(SIM_{it}) + \beta_{16}(SIINOS_{it}) + \beta_{17}(GOVOSSAI_{it}) + \beta_{18}(YEAR2001_{it}) +$$

$$\beta_{19}(YEAR2002_{it}) + \beta_{20}(YEAR2003_{it}) + \beta_{21}(YEAR2004_{it}) + \beta_{22}(YEAR2005_{it}) + u_{it}$$

when $u_{it} = \alpha_i + \varepsilon_{it}$.

The estimation results are reported in Table 4.5.

We start the analysis with the simplest model, the pooled OLS: its covariate specification was selected using standard Wald and F tests. Next, we test the OLS pooled model against the random effect estimator. Finally, we test the random-effects against the fixed-effects estimator.

The Breusch–Pagan test (test value: 327.96; *p*-value: 0.000) for the presence of random effects rejects the null hypothesis, which implies that the pooled OLS is inefficient and the random-effects estimator should be preferred.

In order to compare the random-effects and the fixed-effects estimators, we first used a Hausman test: however, in our application this test is not reliable since the matrix of the squares of the differences of the variances of the coefficients is not positive definite. As was explained in section 4.4, we can apply an alternative test: the Wooldridge test does not reject the random-effects model, so we select this model as our preferred specification.

Further tests for heteroscedasticity and serial correlation in data (the Breusch–Pagan test for heteroscedasticity: test value: 0.00; *p*-value: 0.979; the

Table 4.4 Statistical description of variables

	Media	*Std. dev.*	*Data*	*Measure*	*Source*
WATCON	130	49	CS–TS	mc	Water utilities
AP	1.06	0.96	CS–TS	Euros	Water utilities
INCOME	9541	2560	CS–TS	Euros	Ministry of Treasury
HHSIZE	2.74	0.23	CS	Number	ISTAT[a]
NLF	0.57	0.05	CS	Share	ISTAT
OWNERS	0.85	0.07	CS	Share	ISTAT
NORENOV	0.75	0.06	CS	Share	ISTAT
ALT	264	222	CS	Metres	ISTAT
POP5000	0.87	0.34	CS	Dummy	ISTAT
POPOV15000	0.008	0.090	CS	Dummy	ISTAT
TOUR2	0.03	0.17	CS	Dummy	ISTAT
TOUR3	0.09	0.29	CS	Dummy	ISTAT
TOUR4	0.04	0.19	CS	Dummy	ISTAT
SUMEVATRA	151.13	16.17	CS–TS	Mm	RAS
HOURS	5880	2472	CS–TS	Number	Water utilities and RAS
SIM	0.003	0.059	CS–TS	Dummy	
SIINOS	0.003	0.059	CS–TS	Dummy	
GOVOSSAI	0.06	0.24	CS–TS	Dummy	
YEAR2001	0.17	0.37	TS	Dummy	
YEAR2002	0.17	0.37	TS	Dummy	
YEAR2003	0.17	0.37	TS	Dummy	
YEAR2004	0.17	0.37	TS	Dummy	
YEAR2005	0.17	0.37	TS	Dummy	

Note
a ISTAT (Italian Institute of Statistics), National Census, 2001.

Table 4.5 Estimation results

	OLS	FIXED EFFECT	RANDOM EFFECT – GLS
INTERCEPT	0.207	2.50***	0.609
	(0.35)	(3.35)	(1.00)
AP	−0.136***	−0.139***	−0.146***
	(−6.36)	(−6.49)	(−7.50)
INCOME	0.194***	0.066	0.163***
	(5.61)	(1.61)	(3.61)
HHSIZE	1.138***		1.141***
	(13.33)		(8.34)
NLF	−0.254***		−0.281**
	(−3.15)		(−2.16)
OWNERS	−0.434***		−0.453***
	(−4.35)		(−2.81)
NORENOV	0.189**		0.154
	(2.25)		(1.14)
ALT	−0.020***		−0.022**
	(−3.53)		(−2.44)
POP5000	0.075***		0.639*
	(3.28)		(1.75)
POPOV15000	0.458***		0.449***
	(6.34)		(3.87)
TOUR2	0.093***		0.095**
	(3.85)		(2.42)
TOUR3	0.193***		0.172***
	(4.59)		(2.57)
TOUR4	0.253***		0.250***
	(6.55)		(4.01)
SUMEVATRA	0.157***	0.083	0.108**
	(2.75)	(1.41)	(1.97)
HOURS	0.032	0.052	0.045
	(0.65)	(1.24)	(1.08)
SIM	0.705***	0.086	0.505***
	(6.35)	(0.40)	(3.47)
SIINOS	−0.211*	0.154	−0.079
	(−1.84)	(0.73)	(−0.54)
GOVOSSAI	0.093**	−0.046	0.038
	(2.24)	(−0.80)	(0.88)
YEAR 2001	0.668***	0.677***	0.669***
	(28.47)	(33.50)	(33.87)
YEAR 2002	0.516***	0.551***	0.532***
	(13.90)	(16.23)	(16.58)
YEAR 2003	0.551***	0.574***	0.558***
	(19.88)	(20.72)	(22.58)
YEAR 2004	0.509***	0.531***	0.515***
	(12.90)	(13.81)	(14.73)
YEAR 2005	0.465***	0.480***	0.470***
	(10.98)	(11.18)	(12.36)
N	1440	1440	1440
R-squared	0.63	0.43	0.63

Notes
In parentheses: *t* statistics: * 10% significance level; ** 5% significance level; *** 1% significance level.

Table 4.6 Test results

Test	Test value	p-value
Breusch–Pagan test for no heteroscedasticity in pooled OLS	0.00	0.979
Wooldridge test for no autocorrelation in panel data	9.284	0.0026
Durbin–Watson test for serial correlation	1.62	Lower DW bound: about 1.89
Hausman test for no endogeneity between FE and RE	23.38	0.025*
Wooldridge test for no differences between FE and RE	7.57	0.1085

Note
* Matrix of coefficients is not positive definite.

Wooldridge test for serial correlation of order 1: test value: 9.284; *p*-value: 0.026; DW = 1.62) show the absence of heteroscedasticity and a slight presence of serial correlation. Wooldridge (2002: 274) notes that serial correlation could be a problem when strong correlation is present and T is quite large. If serial correlation is low and T is short, as in our application, it may be preferable not to correct for this problem, as this would imply a cost in terms of loss of observations.

The random-effects estimates show a significant effect of price, with an elasticity value of −0.146. This value is somewhat lower than the value (about −0.20) found in other studies that use average price and aggregated data (Höglund, 1999; Nauges and Thomas, 2000). Also, the income variable is significant and shows the correct positive sign. The elasticity value is +0.105, close to the values found in previous literature, apart from Mazzanti and Montini (2006), who find higher values (a range varying from +0.40 to +0.71).

The household size variable is significant, and its coefficient indicates that consumption increases a little more than proportionally following an increase in the household size.

The proportion of people not in the workforce is significant and with a negative sign. In the literature, similar variables (housewives, retired and unemployed people) are inserted to see whether people who spend more time at home have different levels of water consumption as compared with the rest of the population. Our result could be explained by a reduction in social life consequent on the reduction in working activity, as argued by Liao and Chang (2002) in a survey study of the consumption of hot water and electricity by older people in the United States. Another explanation could be that people who spend more time at home may control leaks or other water waste more efficiently.

Homeowners consume less than renters. This result is found quite often in the literature and is probably due to the fact that often the rent includes the water bill, so that renters do not receive the correct price signals in relation to their consumption behaviour. The efficiency of the indoor and outdoor water system (pipes, taps and toilets) should influence the total consumption amount, but the variable indicating renovation is not significant in the random-effects model.

The altitude variable has a significant negative effect on water consumption. This may be due to the characteristics of houses in different territories in Sardinia: houses in hilly towns generally do not have gardens, unlike valley and coastal towns. Unfortunately, lack of data on the presence and size of gardens in the municipalities prevents us from explicitly evaluating the influence of the presence of gardens on water demand. The dummy variables for population indicate that water consumption is not monotonic with town size, since medium-sized municipalities consume less than do either small or large towns. The climate variable is significant and with the expected sign. Where the summer evapotranspiration rate is higher, water consumption increases. High values of this variable imply that the climate is more arid (the level of precipitation is low) and the temperature is higher: this situation leads to high water consumption, probably for outdoor uses. As we said earlier, lack of data prevents us from directly measuring the influence of the presence of gardens on water consumption.

Considering the water management variables, we notice that the coefficient of the variable *hours* (i.e. hours in a day with regular service) is not significant: this implies that water-rationing measures did not have a significant influence on consumer behaviour. In fact, after a first year (2000) when the restrictions were effective in reducing consumption, users adopted defensive measures (water tanks) that offset the regulations imposed. Year dummies show that even though water-rationing measures were implemented, 2001 and 2003 are characterized by the highest average yearly consumption. Lower coefficient values are associated with 2004 and 2005, when there was a regular distribution of water; the lowest coefficient is that for 2005; we may recall that this is the year when the reform of the water supply system came into effect. The water utilities dummies indicate that SIM customers consume more than the ESAF customers, while the opposite is the case for the SIINOS customers. These differences can be explained by differences in the tariff systems (the number and size of blocks applied by SIINOS penalize higher consumption more than do SIM tariffs) and in the management of the billing procedures (SIM had not sent bills to customers for a long period, while SIINOS sent out its bills every six months).

Finally, the estimated coefficients give a measure of how tourism in holiday homes affects the level of water consumption for residential uses. The effect is quite relevant: towns characterized by a high tourism impact are expected to consume about 32 cubic metres per year per user more than non-tourist towns (see Table 4.7).

For a relatively small number of visitors (a ratio of tourists to residents of less than 40), tourism is estimated to induce a 10 per cent increase in the levels of consumption of water; when the ratio of tourists to residents is between 40 and

Table 4.7 Water consumption estimates

	Average consumption (in cubic metres) of:			
	no tourist impact	*low tourist impact*	*intermediate tourist impact*	*high tourist impact*
2000	108.83	119.68	129.25	139.74
2001	111.21	122.30	132.09	142.80
2002	110.63	121.66	131.39	142.05
2003	115.32	126.82	136.97	148.08
2004	117.24	128.92	139.24	150.54
2005	113.33	124.63	134.60	145.52

90, we expect a rise of about 19 per cent; while higher ratios of tourists to residents will increase the residential yearly water consumption by about 28 per cent per user.

4.6 Conclusions and policy indications

Tourist development produces several externalities that should be properly taken into account for a correct allocation of resources: real estate development and loss of natural ecosystems; excessive pressure on natural resources; congestion in the use of public utilities. In this chapter, we have analysed the effect that tourism has on water resources and their provision. In particular, we deal with a particular form of tourism, namely tourists staying in holiday homes, which can be thought of as affecting the water service for residential uses quite significantly, in terms both of an increase in the demand for water and in discharges into the sewage system. Previous work has recognized the need to estimate the effect of this form of tourism on the residential demand for water, but the analysis has been hindered by lack of data. In this work, we make use of results obtained by Sistu (2008) and RAS (2007) to build an index of tourism impact, which is employed as a regressor in the estimation of the water demand equation, along with other determinants of the demand function: price, income, household size, climatic variables, characteristics of the house, and other socio-economic variables. The estimation results allow us to quantify the impact of unofficial tourism on the water system.

These results can be useful for estimating future pressure on the water service in territories that are not yet developed but where tourist investments are planned. Moreover, they show that in regions where an important share of tourism is accommodated in holiday homes, the average level of residential water consumption is significantly inflated by the tourist presences. This is an element that should be taken into account when comparing regional or district consumption levels: higher average consumption levels may be due to less responsible consumption behaviour, or lower efficiency in the maintenance of water infrastructure, but also a stronger impact of unofficial tourism may play an important role.

Appendix

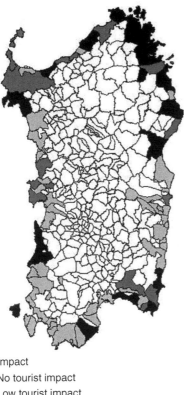

Tourist impact

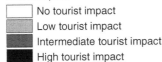

   No tourist impact
   Low tourist impact
   Intermediate tourist impact
   High tourist impact

Figure 4.1 Tourist impact map of municipalities of Sardinia (IT)
(source: our elaboration on RAS (2007) data).

References

Agthe, D. E., Billings, R. B., Dobra, J. L. and Rafiee, K. (1986) 'A simultaneous equation demand model for block rates', *Water Resources Research*, 22 (1): 1–4.

Arbués, F., García-Valiñas, M. A. and Martínez-Espiñeira, R. (2003) 'Estimation of residential water demand: a state-of-the-art review', *Journal of Socio-Economics*, 32 (1): 81–102.

Billings, R. B. (1982) 'Specification of block rate price variables in demand models', *Land Economics*, 58 (3): 386–393.

Billings, R. B. and Agthe, D. E. (1980) 'Price elasticities for water: a case of increasing block rates', *Land Economics*, 56 (1): 73–84.

Cavanagh, S. M., Hanemann, W. M. and Stavins, R. N. (2002) 'Muffled price signals: household water demand under increasing-block prices', FEEM Working Paper no.

40.2002. Online, available at: www.feem.it/userfiles/attach/Publication/NDL2002/NDL2002-040.pdf (accessed 23 February 2010).

Corral, L., Fisher, A. C. and Hatch, N. W. (1998) 'Price and non-price influences on water conservation: an econometric model of aggregate demand under nonlinear budget constraint', Working Paper no. 881, Department of Agricultural and Resource Economics and Policy, University of California at Berkeley. Online, available at: www.escholarship.org/uc/item/3gx868tg (accessed 23 February 2010).

CRENoS (2007) *Economia della Sardegna (14° Rapporto)*, Cagliari: CUEC.

EEA (1999) *State and Pressures of the Marine and Coastal Mediterranean Environment*, Copenhagen: European Environment Agency. Online, available at: www.eea.europa.eu/publications/ENVSERIES05 (accessed 23 February 2010).

Essex, S., Kent, M. and Newnham, R. (2004) 'Tourism development in Mallorca: is water supply a constraint?', *Journal of Sustainable Tourism*, 12 (1): 4–28.

Fortuny, M., Soler, R., Canovas, C. and Sanchez, A. (2008) 'Technical approach for a sustainable tourism development: case study in the Balearic Islands', *Journal of Cleaner Production*, 16 (7): 860–869.

Garcia, C. and Servera, J. (2003) 'Impacts of tourism development on water demand and beach degradation on the island of Mallorca (Spain)', *Geografiska Annaler*, 85A (3/4): 287–300.

Gaudin, S. (2006) 'Effect of price information on residential water demand', *Applied Economics*, 8 (4): 383–393.

Hausman, J. (1978) 'Specification tests in econometrics', *Econometrica*, 46 (6): 1251–1271.

Hewitt, J. A. and Hanemann, W. M. (1995) 'A discrete/continuous choice approach to residential water demand under block rate pricing', *Land Economics*, 71 (2): 173–192.

Höglund, L. (1999) 'Household demand for water in Sweden with implications of a potential tax on water use', *Water Resources Research*, 35 (12): 3853–3863.

Kent, M., Newnham, R. and Essex, S. (2002) 'Tourism and sustainable water supply in Mallorca: a geographical analysis', *Applied Geography*, 22 (4): 351–374.

ISTAT (2007a) *Capacità e movimento degli esercizi ricettivi (anno 2004)*. Online, available at: www.istat.it/dati/dataset/20070215_00/ (accessed 23 February 2010).

ISTAT (2007b) *Viaggi e vacanze in Italia e all'estero (anno 2004)*, Rome: ISTAT (Istituto nazionale di statistica). Online, available at: www.istat.it/salastampa/comunicati/non_calendario/20070219_00/ (accessed 23 February 2010).

Liao, H. C. and Chang, T. F. (2002) 'Space-heating and water-heating energy demands of the aged in the US', *Energy Economics*, 24 (3): 267–284.

Margat, J. (2002) 'Avancées de la gestion de la demande en eau en Méditerranée. Tendances contemporaines et perspectives d'évolution des demandes en eau dans les pays méditerranéens', Sophia Antipolis, France: PNUE/PAM Plan Bleu, Centre d'activités régionales. Online, available at: www.planbleu.org/publications/fiuggi_margat.pdf (accessed 23 February 2010).

Martínez-Espiñeira, R. (2002) 'Residential water demand in the Northwest of Spain', *Environmental and Resource Economics*, 21 (2): 161–187.

Martínez-Espiñeira, R. and Nauges, C. (2004) 'Is all domestic water consumption sensitive to price control?', *Applied Economics*, 36 (15): 1697–1703.

Mazzanti, M. and Montini, A. (2006) 'The determinants of residential water demand', *Applied Economics Letters*, 13 (2): 107–111.

Moncur, J. (1987) 'Urban water pricing and drought management', *Water Resources Research*, 23 (3): 393–398.

Nauges, C. and Thomas, A. (2000) 'Privately operated water utilities, municipal price negotiation, and estimation of residential water demand: the case of France', *Land Economics*, 76 (1): 68–85.

Nieswiadomy, M. L. and Molina, D. J. (1988) 'Urban water demand estimates under increasing block rates', *Growth and Change*, 19 (1): 1–12.

Nieswiadomy, M. L. and Molina, D. J. (1991) 'A note on price perception in water demand models', *Land Economics*, 67 (3): 352–359.

Olmstead, S. M., Hanemann, W. M. and Stavins, R. N. (2007) 'Water demand under alternative price structures', *Journal of Environmental Economics and Management*, 54 (2): 181–198.

PNUE/PAM (2005) 'Dossier sur le tourisme et le développement durable en Méditerranée', MAP Technical Report Series no. 159, Athens: PNUE/PAM. Online, available at: http://195.97.36.231/acrobatfiles/MTSacrobatfiles/mts159.pdf (accessed 23 February 2010).

RAS (Regione Autonoma della Sardegna) (2006) *Piano Regolatore Regionale degli Acquedotti*. Online, available at: www.regione.sardegna.it/j/v/25?s=16966&v=2&c=1323&t=1 (accessed 23 February 2010).

RAS (Regione Autonoma della Sardegna) (2007) *Piano Regionale per il Turismo Sostenibile*. Online, available at: www.regione.sardegna.it/documenti/1_13_20050223123036.pdf (accessed 23 February 2010).

Renwick, M. E. and Green, R. (2000) 'Do residential water demand side management policies measure up? An analysis of eight California water agencies', *Journal of Environmental Economics and Management*, 40 (1): 37–55.

Sistu, G. (2008) *Vagamondo. Turisti e Turismi in Sardegna*, Cagliari: CUEC.

Strazzera, E. (2006) 'Application of the ML Hausman approach to the demand of water for residential use: heterogeneity vs two-error specification', WP 06/04 CRENoS. Online, available at: http://crenos.unica.it/crenos/en/node/237 (accessed 23 February 2010).

Tirado, D., Gomez, C. M. and Lozano, J. (2006) 'Efficiency improvements and water policy in the Balearic Islands: a general equilibrium approach', *Investigaciones Economicas*, 30 (3): 441–463.

Wooldridge, J. M. (2002) *Econometric of Cross Section and Panel Data*, Cambridge, MA: MIT Press.

WWF (2004) *Freshwater and Tourism in the Mediterranean*, Rome: WWF International. Online, available at: http://assets.panda.org/downloads/medpotourismreportfinal_ofnc.pdf (accessed 23 February 2010).

Part II
Tourism and productivity

5 Pollution-averse tourists and growth

Fabio Cerina and Sauveur Giannoni

5.1 Introduction

The literature on tourism development highlights the role of environmental attractions to explain the success of a destination (Davies and Cahill, 2000; Tisdell, 2001). But developing tourism implies building tourist facilities and receiving a large number of visitors. Tourism development contributes to increasing pollution and might ultimately bring about the destruction of the attraction factor. From this point of view, a positive growth performance by economies that specialize in tourism (Brau *et al.*, 2007) might be interpreted as a phase of transition towards a long-run equilibrium characterized by the death of the destination and a zero-growth performance. The aim of this chapter is to find conditions that avoid this outcome and enable a tourist destination to experience long-term positive growth in the presence of pollution.

We build a growth model in which tourism development generates pollution while tourists are pollution-averse. We establish that long-run positive growth exists only for a particular value of tourists' pollution aversion. Furthermore, we show that intensive use of facilities is associated with a lower growth rate for destinations that specialize in green tourism.

We also see that if the destination can choose the degree of use of facilities, tourism will generate positive growth only if tourists are not too pollution-averse. In this case, the growth rate of the economy will be a negative function of tourists' aversion to pollution, so that the 'greener' the kind of tourism the destination promotes, the slower its growth rate.

This chapter mainly refers to the recent literature strand analysing the dynamic evolution of an economy that specializes in tourism based on natural resources. Among this work, we mention Lozano *et al.* (2008), who build a dynamic general equilibrium model where investment in accommodation capacity and public goods are taken into account; Giannoni and Maupertuis (2007) and Candela and Cellini (2006), who adopt the point of view of a representative tourism firm aiming to maximize its lifetime profit; Rey-Maquieira *et al.* (2005), who analyse the dynamic consequences of the conflict between agricultural and tourism sector for the use of land; Cerina (2007, 2008), who introduces several kind of abatement policies and provides respective analyses of the transitional dynamics of the economy; and finally Hernández and León (2007), who present a model of tourist life cycle highlighting the interactions between natural resources and physical capital. None of these papers, however, faces the issue of the conditions for endogenous, sustained and sustainable growth in an economy specializing in tourism based on natural resources, which is the issue we deal with here.

The rest of the chapter is organized as follow: section 5.2 describes the analytical structure of our economy, section 5.3 presents a discussion of the growth rate of such an economy, section 5.4 derives the optimal growth rate as a result of central planners' decisions, section 5.5 analyses the consequences of endogenizing the intensity in the utilization of tourism facilities, and section 5.6 concludes the chapter.

5.2 The analytical framework

5.2.1 Production of the tourism economy

We consider an economy producing only one kind of good (tourism services) which is supplied in an international tourism market in which a large number of tourism economies participate. Tourism services are only sold to non-residents. The production of tourism services implies the building of facilities and the training of human capital in order to make these facilities work. Tourism production is given by the following function

$$T_t^S(k_t) = Ak_t^\eta \tag{5.1}$$

This supply function is a neoclassical production function. k is the stock of facilities and of human capital while, for the moment, we simply take A as a scale parameter. In section 5.5 we will propose an interpretation of A in terms of intensity in the utilization of tourism facilities. In any case, an increase in A allows the economy to produce more tourism services with the same stock of capital. η is a parameter reflecting the elasticity of tourism supply with respect to capital. For simplicity, we consider that tourism supply is inelastic with respect to price.

5.2.2 Tourists' preferences

We assume that, at any time t, tourist satisfaction is affected by two factors: (1) the stock of tourism facilities supplied by private tourist operators (accommodation, restaurants, leisure facilities), k_t, and (2) the quality of the environment, which is measured at each point in time by the intensity of the pollution flow, P_t. P_t is an inverse measure of environmental quality: it increases as environmental quality decreases.

In formalizing tourists' preferences, we follow the approach used by Gómez *et al.* (2004), which relies on the hedonic price theory (Rosen, 1974). Given the above considerations, the willingness to pay (WTP) for tourism services is then given by

$$q_t = \gamma q(k_t, P_t) \tag{5.2}$$

We assume $\dfrac{\partial q_t}{\partial k_t} \geq 0$ (the higher k_t, the higher the quality of the experience for a

tourist) and $\dfrac{\partial q_t}{\partial P_t} \leq 0$ (the higher the level of pollution, the lower the quality of

the experience for a tourist). γ is a scale parameter.[1]

5.2.3 The international tourism market, revenues and residents' behaviour

Our economy supplies tourism services in an international tourism market where a large number of small tourism economies participate. It is important to highlight that although international competition fixes the price for a given quality of the services, a country could charge a higher price provided that its services are considered of a higher quality (i.e. characterized by a higher stock of environmental, cultural and social resources) than other countries'. In other words, the international market consists of a continuum of tourism markets differentiated by their quality and the (equilibrium) price paid for the tourism services. In each of them, the suppliers are price-takers but they can move along the quality ladder through changes in their environmental quality and level of facilities.

We assume that each tourist, at any time t, buys one unit of tourism services so that output at time t is measured in terms of tourist entries. The supply side of the economy is made up of a large number of identical 'household firms' which we normalize to 1. We assume that the international demand for tourism is infinite for the price level which corresponds to tourists' WTP and is nil for any other price level. So, the market clears all the time and the quantity exchanged is totally determined by the supply side.

Aggregate tourism revenues are represented by the value of the economy's output. If P_t is the level of tourism inflows at time t, this is given by

$$TR_t = \gamma_t q(k_t, P_t) T_t$$

5.2.4 Pollution

Like Smulders and Gradus (1996), we consider pollution as a flow. We will consider the following functional form:

$$P_t = P(k_t, T_t, Z_t) \tag{5.3}$$

We assume $\dfrac{\partial P}{\partial k} \geq 0$: the construction of facilities generates different kinds of pollution (destruction of biodiversity, visual pollution, waste generation, etc.) that damage the image of the destination. Analogously, we assume $\dfrac{\partial P}{\partial T}$ positive since tourist inflows (like facilities) generate pollution due to, for example, the overcrowding of tourism sites. Furthermore, when a tourist pollutes a site, this has a negative impact on the global quality of the experience for other tourists. Z denotes costless abatement and represents the capacity of each specific destination to 'resist pollution'. It can be considered as a generic variable which can be affected by several other factors such as eco-system features, country-specific characteristics, natural regeneration, different impacts of different kinds of tourism, and so on. Since Z is meant to gather all the factors that mitigate the effect of k and T on pollution, we assume $\dfrac{\partial P}{\partial Z} \leq 0$.

5.3 The rate of growth in a tourism economy

We now face the issue of the determinant of the rate of growth in an economy specialized in tourism. Assuming that residents' income is allocated between consumption of an imported good (sold at a unitary price) and investment in facilities, the dynamic budget constraint of our economy can be written as

$$\dot{k} = q_t T_t - c_t$$

The budget constraint implies that

$$\frac{\dot{k}_t}{k_t} = \frac{q_t T_t}{k_t} - \frac{c_t}{k_t} \tag{5.4}$$

Relation (5.4) is quite general and tells us that the growth rate depends positively on income per unit of capital and is negatively affected by the consumption to capital ratio. Therefore, if this economy admits a constant steady-state long-run growth rate, it must be the following:

$$g = \frac{q_{ss} T_{ss}}{k_{ss}} - \frac{c_{ss}}{k_{ss}} \tag{5.5}$$

where x_{ss} is the steady state value of the variable x. One can check that the previous condition is verified if, and only if, the income to capital ratio is constant. Hence:

$$\frac{\dot{q}_{ss}}{q_{ss}} + \frac{\dot{T}_{ss}}{T_{ss}} - \frac{\dot{k}_{ss}}{k_{ss}} = 0$$

and since $\dfrac{\dot{k}_{ss}}{k_{ss}} = g$, in the long run we have

$$g = \frac{\dot{q}_{ss}}{q_{ss}} + \frac{\dot{T}_{ss}}{T_{ss}}$$

In the steady state, the rate of growth of the tourism-specialized economy is equal to the sum of the growth rate of tourists' willingness to pay and of the growth rate of tourist inflows. Moreover, in order for g to be constant, we need both $\dfrac{\dot{q}_{ss}}{q_{ss}} = g_q$ and $\dfrac{\dot{T}_{ss}}{T_{ss}} = g_T$ to be constant in the steady state.

Log-differentiating (5.2) and (5.1), we find

$$\frac{\dot{T}}{T} = \frac{\dot{A}}{A} + \eta \frac{\dot{k}_t}{k_t}$$

$$\frac{\dot{q}_t}{q_t} = \frac{\dot{\gamma}_t}{\gamma_t} + \frac{q_k k_t}{q(k_t, P_t)} \frac{\dot{k}_t}{k_t} + \frac{q_P P_t}{q(k_t, P_t)} \frac{\dot{P}_t}{P_t}$$

So, for balanced growth, it must be true that

$$g_T = g_A + \eta g$$
$$g_q = g_\gamma + \alpha(k_{ss}, P_{ss}) g - \beta(k_{ss}, P_{ss}) g_P$$

where g_A, g_γ are the steady-state growth rate of respectively A and γ. Again, in order for a balanced growth path to exist in a tourism economy, these two values should be constant. Also,

$$\alpha(k_{ss}, P_{ss}) = \frac{q_k(k_{ss}, P_{ss})}{q(k_{ss}, P_{ss})} k_{ss}$$

and

$$\beta(k_{ss}, P_{ss}) = -\frac{q_P(k_{ss}, P_{ss})}{q(k_{ss}, P_{ss})} P_{ss}$$

which are the steady-state values of, respectively, the elasticity of tourists' WTP with respect to facilities and pollution, should be constant too. Since k_{ss} is not constant, P_{ss} may not be constant and g_P may not be zero, we need both $\alpha(\cdot)$ and $\beta(\cdot)$ to be constant for *any* value of k and P. That means that the only functional form for the WTP which can be compatible with a balanced growth path in a tourist economy is a Cobb–Douglas one. Hence, it must be

$$q(k_t, P_t) = \gamma_t k_t^\alpha P_t^{-\beta}$$

5.3.1 Growth and pollution

Substituting for the expression for T_{ss} and q_{ss} in Equation 5.5, we find that

$$g = \gamma_{ss} P_{ss}^{-\beta} A_{ss} k_{ss}^{\alpha+\eta-1} - \frac{c_{ss}}{k_{ss}} \tag{5.6}$$

From this expression, we can clearly note that the rate of growth is (negatively) affected by the level of pollution. But what are the determinants of pollution? By log-differentiating (5.3),

$$g_P = \frac{P_k k_{ss}}{P(k_{ss},T_{ss},Z_{ss})} g + \frac{P_T T_{ss}}{P(k_{ss},T_{ss},Z_{ss})} g_T + \frac{P_Z Z_{ss}}{P(k_{ss},T_{ss},Z_{ss})} g_Z$$

but since $g_T = g_A + \eta g$, we finally have

$$g_P = g\left(\frac{P_k k_{ss}}{P(k_{ss},T_{ss},Z_{ss})} + \frac{\eta P_T T_{ss}}{P(k_{ss},T_{ss},Z_{ss})} \right) + \frac{P_T T_{ss}}{P(k_{ss},T_{ss},Z_{ss})} g_A + \frac{P_Z Z_{ss}}{P(k_{ss},T_{ss},Z_{ss})} g_Z$$

g_P being constant, we again need g_Z, $\dfrac{P_k k_{ss}}{P(k_{ss},T_{ss},Z_{ss})}$, $\dfrac{\eta P_T T_{ss}}{P(k_{ss},T_{ss},Z_{ss})}$ and $\dfrac{P_Z Z_{ss}}{P(k_{ss},T_{ss},Z_{ss})}$ to be constant too. This is tantamount to saying that the only functional form for pollution that is compatible to a balanced growth path in such a tourism economy is a Cobb–Douglas one. Hence, we set $\phi = \dfrac{P_k}{P(k_{ss},T_{ss},Z_{ss})}$, $\varphi = \dfrac{\eta P_T}{P(k_{ss},T_{ss},Z_{ss})}$ and $-1 = \dfrac{P_Z}{P(k_{ss},T_{ss},Z_{ss})}$ in order to have

$$P(k_t,T_t,Z_t) = \frac{k_t^{\phi} T_t^{\varphi}}{Z_t}$$

which, by using Equation 5.1, becomes

$$P_t = \frac{k_t^{\phi+\varphi\eta} A_t^{\varphi}}{Z_t}$$

As a consequence,

$$g_P = (\phi+\varphi\eta)g + \varphi g_A - g_Z$$

It is then clear that in order to have constant pollution in the steady state, we need Z (resistance to pollution) to grow at the rate

$$g_Z = (\phi+\varphi\eta)g + \varphi g_A$$

Hence, in the absence of any abatement effort, environmental quality is doomed to decrease more and more in a tourist economy that experiences a positive and sustained growth in the stock of capital. As long as g is strictly positive, this is true even if $g_A = 0$. Hence, unless we assume some kind of exogenous growth given, for example, by ever-increasing terms of trade (g_γ positive), we cannot have any sustainable tourism (i.e. $g_T \geq 0$, $g \geq 0$, $g_P \leq 0$) without any form of abatement.

5.3.2 Restrictions on parameters

By substituting for the new expression for pollution in Equation 5.6, we find

$$g = \gamma_{ss} A_{ss}^{1-\beta\varphi} k_{ss}^{\alpha+\eta-1-\beta(\phi+\varphi\eta)} Z_{ss}^\beta - \frac{c_{ss}}{k_{ss}} \tag{5.7}$$

This is our final expression for the rate of growth of the economy and it deserves some further explanation.

First, it is clear that not only k but also γ (the pressure on the relative price of tourism), A (the capital stock 'efficiency') and Z (resistance to pollution) have an important role in determining the rate of growth of the economy.

Second, since $\frac{c_{ss}}{k_{ss}}$ is constant, $\gamma_{ss} A_{ss}^{1-\beta\varphi} k_{ss}^{\alpha+\eta-1-\beta(\phi+\varphi\eta)} Z_{ss}^P$ should be constant too. An important implication is that different assumptions concerning the dynamic behaviour of γ, A and Z would lead to different requirements that the parameters α, β, ϕ, φ and η should satisfy in order for a balanced growth path to be feasible. Since our aim is to focus on the dynamic properties of a tourist economy that experiences some kind of *endogenous* growth, we exclude any kind of exogenous growth in the model and hence we treat γ, A and Z as constant variables.[2]

When γ, A and Z are exogenously fixed, in order to have constant steady-state growth we need (net) constant returns to scale on the accumulable factor k.

Proposition 1: *A necessary condition in order to have a constant steady-state growth in the long run is to have:*[3]

$$\beta^* = \frac{\alpha+\eta-1}{(\phi+\eta\varphi)}$$

Proof: *In order for g to be constant, it should not be affected by k_{ss}. That only happens when the exponent of k_{ss} in equation (7) is null so that $\alpha - \beta(\phi+\eta\varphi) + \eta - 1 = 0$. This will be true if and only if $\beta = \frac{\alpha+\eta-1}{(\phi+\eta\varphi)}$.*

Table 5.1 shows how environmental preferences of tourists must evolve through a change in the value of one parameter in order for positive long-term growth to occur. Any increase in love for facilities α is associated with an increase in hate for pollution. Furthermore, any increase in the elasticity of pollution with respect to facilities ϕ and/or with respect to tourist flows φ induces

Table 5.1 Steady-state analysis of β*

	α	η	φ	φ
β*	+	+/−	−	−

a decrease in pollution aversion. The effect of a change in the elasticity of supply with respect to capital η is ambiguous. If $\phi + (1 - \alpha)\varphi > 0$ (resp. <0) an increase in η leads to an increase (resp. a decrease) in β*. In particular, we see that when the love for facility is low any increase in η increases β*.

If we substitute β for β*, we obtain that the growth rate is simply

$$\frac{\dot{k}}{k} = \gamma A^{1-\beta^*\varphi} Z^{\beta^*} - \frac{c}{k}$$

And this is also true in the steady state so that:

$$g = \gamma A^{1-\beta^*\varphi} Z^{\beta^*} - \frac{c_{ss}}{k_{ss}} \tag{5.8}$$

Even if γ, A and Z are constant variables in our model, it is useful to draw some comparative statics conclusions. In particular, we can easily see that an exogenous increase in γ (higher pressure on the relative price of tourism) will increase the growth rate of the economy. The same conclusion can be drawn concerning the resistance to pollution, Z: other things being equal, an increase in the capacity of the economy to resist pollution will allow faster growth. As long as we let γ and Z be 'country-specific' or associated with the particular kind of tourism good produced, they can have a role in explaining some cross-country difference in the growth rate.

As for A, we can conclude that it is not always good for growth. If $\beta > \dfrac{1}{\varphi}$, a higher level of A implies a slower growth rate. If pollution aversion and/or the impact of tourists on pollution are too high, the destination grows more slowly as capital become more efficient. This result has some interesting implications as long as we can associate a high level of β* with green tourism and a low level of β* with mass tourism. In particular, a destination producing green tourism $\left(\beta^* > \dfrac{1}{\varphi}\right)$ will experience high growth rates in the long run provided the efficiency of each unit of capital is low enough. The reverse is true for a destination producing mass tourism.

5.4 The optimal growth rate

In the previous section, we established the necessary conditions to obtain a positive and sustained growth. The problem is now to compute this growth rate as a result of residents' maximizing behaviour. Residents' aggregate utility, at time t, is positively influenced by the aggregate level of consumption at time t of a homogeneous good purchased from abroad at a unitary price c_t:

$$U_t = \int_t^\infty u(c_t)e^{-\rho t}dt = \int_t^\infty \ln c_t e^{-\rho t}dt \qquad (5.9)$$

We assume there is a benevolent central planner whose objective is to choose the consumption plan in order to maximize (5.9) respecting the dynamic budget constraint which can be expressed as

$$\dot{k} = \gamma A^{1-\beta\varphi}k_t^{\alpha+\eta-\beta(\phi+\varphi\eta)}Z^\beta - c_t \qquad (5.10)$$

In the previous section, we showed that positive constant growth exists only for a particular combination of parameter values such that $\beta=\beta^*$. As long as we look for a positive constant growth, we will use β^* instead of β. In this case, the accumulation equation simply becomes

$$\dot{k} = \gamma A^{1-\beta^*\varphi}k_t Z^{\beta^*} - c_t \qquad (5.11)$$

After we substitute for the value of P_t, the Hamiltonian looks as follows:

$$H = \ln c + \lambda\left(\gamma A^{1-\beta^*\varphi}k_t Z^{\beta^*} - c_t\right)$$

First-order and Euler conditions are the following:

$$H_c = 0 : \frac{1}{\lambda} = c$$

$$\dot{\lambda} = \lambda\left(\rho - \gamma A^{1-\beta^*\varphi}Z^{\beta^*}\right)$$

From these equations we obtain the growth rate of consumption over time:

$$\frac{\dot{c}}{c} = \gamma A^{1-\beta^*\varphi}Z^{\beta^*} - \rho$$

which, in conjunction with Equation 5.11, gives us the dynamic system describing the evolution of the economy over time.

We know that, along the balanced growth path, $\dfrac{\dot{c}}{c} = \dfrac{\dot{k}}{k} = g$, hence

$$g = \gamma A^{1-\beta^*\varphi}Z^{\beta^*} - \rho$$

Equating this equation with Equation 5.8, we find the optimal steady-state consumption to capital ratio, which is equal to

$$\frac{c_{ss}}{k_{ss}} = \rho$$

This model is similar to that of Rebelo (1991). This means that there is no transitional dynamics so that the growth rate is constant over time and that the consumption to capital ratio is equal to ρ all along the time-path. But if in the Rebelo model any growth in A increases the growth rate, it is not the case in our model, owing to tourists' aversion towards pollution.

5.5 Endogenous capital efficiency

As long as an increase in A allows for larger tourist inflows using the same amount of capital stock, it can be interpreted as an increase in the intensity with which existing facilities are used.

From this point of view, the value of A may be associated with the degree of utilization of the tourism structure – that is, the length of the tourism season.[4] In so far as residents are those who decide how long such facilities should be kept open and available to foreign tourists, the level of A might be treated as a further control variable. In choosing the optimal value of A, residents should make a trade-off between its benefits and its costs. A higher value of A leads to larger tourism inflows and then to higher income and higher growth if $\left(\beta^* < \dfrac{1}{\varphi}\right)$.

However, a higher A entails a higher direct cost (a longer tourism season means harder work, and we assume residents are work-averse) and an indirect cost that is associated with the higher pollution flow due to the increase in tourist inflows.

In this case, residents' utility might be represented by

$$U_t = \int_t^\infty u\left(c_t, A_t\right) e^{-\rho t} dt = \int_t^\infty \left(\ln c_t - A_t^{1+\omega}\right) e^{-\rho t} dt \tag{5.12}$$

where $\omega > 0$ and $1+\omega$ reflects residents' disutility to work. The benevolent planner maximizes (5.12) under the same budget constraint (5.8).

The Hamiltonian of this function is given by

$$H = \ln c - A^{1+\omega} + \lambda\left(\gamma A^{1-\beta^*\varphi} k Z^{\beta^*} - c\right)$$

The Maximum principle gives:

$$H_c = 0 \ : \ \lambda = \frac{1}{c}$$

$$H_A = 0 \ : \ \lambda = \frac{(1+\omega) A^\omega}{\gamma\left(1-\beta^*\varphi\right) A^{-\beta^*\varphi} k Z^{\beta^*}}$$

$$H_k = \rho\lambda - \dot{\lambda} \ : \ \dot{\lambda} = \lambda\left(\rho - \gamma A^{1-\beta^*\varphi} Z^{\beta^*}\right)$$

We can then obtain the optimal growth rate of consumption:

$$\frac{\dot{c}}{c} = \gamma A^{1-\beta^*\varphi} Z^{\beta^*} - \rho$$

As in the previous section, we can check that at every point in time the ratio $\dfrac{c}{k}$ is equal to ρ.

By solving the system, we find that the optimal length of the season A is constant over time and is equal to:

$$A = \left(\frac{\left(1-\beta^*\varphi\right)\gamma Z^{\beta^*}}{\left(1+\omega\right)\rho} \right)^{\frac{1}{\omega+\beta^*\varphi}}.$$

It is worth observing that a meaningful (positive) value of A requires $\beta^* < \dfrac{1}{\varphi}$. In other words, if tourists are *too* averse to pollution, residents find it optimal to keep the tourism structure closed for the whole year. An important implication is that, from Equation 5.8, the rate of growth of the economy is always a positive function of the optimal A.

It is possible to substitute A for its optimal in the growth rate in order to obtain:

$$g = \gamma^{1+\frac{1-\beta^*\varphi}{\omega+\beta^*\varphi}} Z^{\beta^*+\frac{1-\beta^*\varphi}{\omega+\beta^*\varphi}} \left(\frac{1-\beta^*\varphi}{\left(1+\omega\right)\rho} \right)^{\frac{1-\beta^*\varphi}{\omega+\beta^*\varphi}} - \rho$$

One can observe that any exogenous increase in the willingness to pay, γ, or in the capacity of the destination to resist pollution, Z, is beneficial for growth. Moreover, the higher β^*, or tourists' impact on pollution, the slower the growth rate. And, clearly enough, the larger residents' disutility to work, ω, the slower the growth rate.

5.6 Conclusions

In this chapter, we have investigated the impact of tourists' aversion to pollution on the growth rate of an economy specializing in tourism.

We built a model of optimal growth and we showed that the destination can experience endogenous growth. In fact, there exists for each destination a unique level of pollution aversion (β^*) that enables the destination to have a positive and constant growth.

Our model is akin to that of Rebelo (1991), but we found that because of pollution aversion, a higher level of productivity of capital is not always associated with a higher growth rate. More precisely, we established that for a destination specializing in green tourism (high level of β^*), there exists a negative relationship between the 'efficiency of capital' and the rate of growth. It means that an intensive use of the capital stock may be harmful to growth when green tourism is produced.

Furthermore, under the assumption that the destination can choose the length of the season, we observed that if tourists' aversion to pollution is too high, then the growth rate will tend to zero. It means that if tourists really hate pollution, one should not develop tourism unless the destination has some control over abatement policies (Z), or the exogenous price dynamic (γ) is particularly favourable.

We believe this chapter raises some interesting questions and draws some relevant policy issues for an economy facing the choice of specializing in the production of tourism services. The analysis of such problems should be deepened by a framework in which the supply side is modelled in a more detailed way.

Notes

1 An increase in γ might reflect the pressure on the relative price of tourism for any perceived quality of tourism services depending on the interplay between growth in foreign income and the luxury nature of the tourism good (Crouch, 1995; Smeral, 2003) or its small elasticity of substitution with respect to other kinds of goods (Lanza and Pigliaru, 1994, 2000).
2 Actually, in the last section we will treat A as an endogenous variable, and its constancy in the steady state will be a result of consumers' optimization.
3 This condition can obviously be expressed in terms of other parameters. The choice to express it in terms of β is suggested by the fact that β can be considered as a sort of policy tool: different values of β mean different preferences towards pollution and therefore a different kind of tourist. The country may influence its own value of β by addressing itself to different kinds of tourism.
4 In interpreting an increase in A as a longer tourism season, we are only considering one particular aspect of it, specifically the increase in the number of tourist *per unit of time* (say a year). We are then leaving aside other important aspects related to the increase in the length of the season, such as the decrease in the concentration of tourists per unit of time (which might have a positive effect on pollution and then on willingness to pay). The analytical framework we propose in this chapter is not suitable for dealing with this complex issue and thus we leave its analysis to future research.

References

Brau, R., Lanza, A. and Pigliaru, F. (2007) 'How fast are small tourism countries growing? Evidence from the data for 1980–2003', *Tourism Economics*, 13: 603–614.
Candela, G. and Cellini, R. (2006) 'Investment in tourism market: a dynamic model of differentiated oligopoly', *Environmental and Resource Economics*, 35: 41–58.
Cerina, F. (2007) 'Tourism specialization and environmental sustainability in a dynamic economy', *Tourism Economics*, 13: 553–582.
Cerina, F. (2008) 'Tourism specialization, environmental quality and pollution abatement', in R. Brau, A. Lanza and S. Usai (eds) *The Economics of Tourism and Sustainable Development II*, Cheltenham, UK: Edward Elgar, pp. 3–27.
Crouch, G. I. (1995) 'A meta-analysis of tourism demand', *Annals of Tourism Research*, 22: 103–118.
Davies, T. and Cahill S. (2000) 'Environmental implications of the tourism industry: resources for the future', Discussion Paper 00-14.
Giannoni, S. and Maupertuis, M. A. (2007) 'Is tourism specialization sustainable for a small island economy? A cyclical perspective', in A. Matias, P. Nijkamp and P. Neto (eds) *Advances in Modern Tourism Research*, Heidelberg: Springer, pp. 87–105.
Gómez, C., Lozano, J. and Rey-Maquieira, J. (2004) 'A dynamic analysis of environmental and tourism policies', in *Economía del Turismo*, Proceedings of the First 'Jornadas de Economía del Turismo', held in Palma de Mallorca, 28–29 May, pp. 435–456.

Hernández, J. and León, C. (2007) 'The interactions between natural and physical capitals in the tourist lifecycle model', *Ecological Economics*, 62: 184–193.

Lanza, A. and Pigliaru, F. (1994) 'The tourist sector in the open economy', *Rivista Internazionale di Scienze Economiche e Commerciali*, 41: 15–28.

Lanza, A. and Pigliaru, F. (2000) 'Tourism and economic growth: does country's size matter?', *Rivista Internazionale di Scienze Economiche e Commerciali*, 47: 77–85.

Lozano, J., Gómez, C. and Rey-Maquieira, J. (2008) 'The TALC hypothesis and economic growth theory', *Tourism Economics*, 14: 727–750.

Rebelo, S. (1991) 'Long-run policy analysis and long-run growth', *Journal of Political Economy*, 99: 500–521.

Rey-Maquieira, J., Lozano, J. and Gómez, G. M. (2005) 'Land, environmental externalities and tourism development', in A. Lanza, A. Markandya and F. Pigliaru (eds) *The Economics of Tourism and Sustainable Development*, Cheltenham, UK: Edward Elgar.

Rosen, S. (1974) 'Hedonic prices and implicit markets: product differentiation in pure competition', *Journal of Political Economy*, 82: 34–55.

Smeral, E. (2003) 'A structural view of tourism growth', *Tourism Economics*, 9: 77–93.

Smulders, S. and Gradus, R. (1996) 'Pollution abatement and long-term growth', *European Journal of Political Economy*, 12: 505–532.

Tisdell, C. A. (2001), *Tourism Economics, the Environment and Development*, Cheltenham, UK: Edward Elgar.

6 On the relationship between tourism and trade

María Santana Gallego,
Francisco J. Ledesma Rodríguez and
Jorge V. Pérez Rodríguez

6.1 Introduction

In recent decades, international tourism has increased greatly. Data from the World Tourism Organization indicate that tourist trips increased in number from 25 million in 1950 to 700 million in 2000. At the same time, World Trade Organization data show that exports per capita grew from US$44 in 1961 to US$1,200 in 2000. This, therefore, provides a very good reason to investigate whether there is a significant relationship between tourism and trade.

International trade theory studies the causes of international flows of goods when factors are internationally immobile. Several extensions have allowed the main new features of the international economy to be addressed. However, the issue of consumers travelling to another country and consuming goods and services there has received less attention. This lack of attention in mainstream literature in this area is an important factor motivating this analysis.

The relevance of this relationship is direct since both tourism and trade increase the market size, thus promoting growth. The influence of international trade on economic growth has been extensively studied by Marin (1992). Marin analysed whether a link between exports and productivity exists. To demonstrate this, co-integration and Granger causality techniques were applied. Using four OECD countries, his results suggest that exports Granger-cause productivity; consequently, the hypothesis of export-led growth cannot be rejected. Recent research has also found that tourism has encouraged economic development in many countries.[1] For this reason, the study of the potential complementary relationship between flows of goods and international tourism could be of major interest, since such a relationship could promote economic growth.

In this chapter, the empirical relationship between tourism and trade is explored. With this objective in mind, the link between tourism and trade is studied for the case study of the United Kingdom. In this case, a longer data set allows us to analyse whether trade and tourism are co-integrated. Again, the relationship is tested in a long-run perspective. The results suggest a long- and a short-run significant relationship between tourism flows and international trade.

The chapter is organized as follows. In section 6.2, the literature and the reasons for the reciprocal relationship are presented. In section 6.3, the so-called integrated world economy approach is used to describe two basic effects of tourism on trade: a *shifting consumption* and a *biased consumption* effect. Section 6.4 investigates the existence of a long-run and a short-run relationship between tourism and trade in a case study of the United Kingdom. Finally, in section 6.5, some conclusions are drawn.

6.2 The links

In this section, the literature about the relationship between tourism and trade is analysed. Previous work is reviewed in order to present some suggestions that could explain the causes of the relationship between trade and tourism.

First, we present several explanations of how trade can promote tourism. If we consider business travel, this type of travel may motivate other people (particularly friends and relatives of those who are involved in business) to take holiday or pleasure trips to the destinations concerned.[2] Moreover, the direction of causality in the sense that 'trade causes tourism' can be shown, as business travel is required to begin and to maintain the international trade of goods and services.

Transactions and dealings between countries create interest among consumers not only about the products but also about the source countries of the goods, and this may subsequently lead to a surge in the flow of holiday visits to these countries. Furthermore, international trade requires infrastructure and conditions, such as transport, currency exchange, knowledge of the language, etc., that also promote tourism. Finally, another reason to explain the relationship 'trade causes tourism' is that tourists may want to find in the tourist destination the same products that they consume in their own country; therefore, imports could promote tourist arrivals.

Second, to explain the opposite relationship, we suggest some reasons for why tourism causes trade. The literature points out that the influence of travel on trade might result from several causes: for instance, (1) via direct, indirect and induced impacts on production; (2) by facilitating commercial relations when information failures occur (Aradhyula and Tronstad, 2003) or (3) through foreign direct investment via business travel; and (4) growing the market size of the foreign country in the presence of increasing returns.

If we concentrate on business travel alone (visitors who travel mainly for business purposes), the idea is quite straightforward. Business visitors travel to a tourist destination to buy or sell certain products. Therefore, successful business trips directly create a flow of exports and/or imports in subsequent periods. However, visitors with other motives can influence trade as well. International visitors for pleasure or on holiday may identify business opportunities that could lead to either exports or imports in subsequent periods. Moreover, tourists may consume certain types of goods that are not produced in the tourist destination (and therefore have to be imported), leading to a surge in import requirements for that country.

An additional reason is described in more detail in the following section: tourism implies a shift in consumption from visitors' country of origin to the tourist destination. Thus, tourism and trade can present a relationship of complementarity or substitutability, depending on the good being importable or exportable. Moreover, we can recognize that the consumption pattern in tourism destinations is different, thus affecting the volume of international trade.

Up to this point, we have presented some suggestions given in the literature on the relationship between trade and tourism. However, few papers have focused on the empirical analysis of this relationship. Some empirical evidence in favour of the existence of a bilateral relationship between tourism and trade flows has been found.

Kulendran and Wilson (2000) investigate whether there is a relationship between international trade and tourism using Australian data. By applying co-integration techniques and Granger causality tests, their paper finds support for a bilateral link. In related work, Khan *et al.* (2005) analyse the empirical connection between trade and tourism using data from Singapore. They found a strong link between business visits and imports.

Chul *et al.* (1995) and Eilat and Einav (2004) estimate a model for tourist demand where international trade is considered as one of its determinants. In both papers, the results show that international trade is relevant in explaining tourist demand, and hence it is suggested that there is a relationship in the sense 'international trade causes tourism'. In a similar way, Turner and Witt (2001) analyse tourist demand and find that international trade is one of the main determinants for business trips.

In the literature, several papers study the relationship between trade and tourism for some products or specific regions. Aradhyula and Tronstad (2003) suggest that there is a role for government agencies to play in overcoming imperfect information related to trade opportunities through facilitating exploratory business ventures and tourist visits. Easton (1998) studied whether Canadian aggregate exports are complementary or substitutive to tourist arrivals. The study finds 'some evidence of substitution of Canadian exports for tourist excursions to Canada'. Finally, Fischer and Gil-Alana (2005) focus on the case of German imports of Spanish wines, finding that tourism has a positive effect on imports.

6.3 An illustration of the relationship between trade and tourism

Turning to a direct effect of tourism on international trade, we can recognize that tourism implies a shift of consumption from visitors' country of origin to the tourist destination. In this section, two direct effects of tourism on trade are illustrated. (1) The *shifting consumption* effect provides both a complementarity and a substitutability nexus between trade and tourism. If consumption switches from the home country to the foreign country, tourism increases the supply excess in exportable goods and reduces the demand excess in importable goods in the home country. Thus, tourism and trade can present a relation of complementarity or substitutability depending on whether the good is importable or exportable. (2) The *biased consumption* effect achieves a switch in the consumption pattern in tourism destinations.

To illustrate these effects, the so-called *integrated world economy* (IWE) approach is used.[3] Both the integrated world equilibrium and the trading equilibrium in a $2 \times 2 \times 2$ model are represented in Figure 6.1. The dimensions of the box diagram are the world factor endowments, labour and capital. The integrated world equilibrium is given by a vector of prices and an allocation of resources $OQ=O'Q'$ to the most capital-intensive good (manufactures) and $O'Q=OQ'$ to the most labour-intensive good (food). Then, the lower-left corner at O is the origin for representing factor endowments of the home country, and the upper-right corner at O' is the origin for representing available quantities of factors of the foreign country. Suppose that point E measures the distribution of factor endowments in the international economy. In this way, the home country is capital-rich and the foreign country is labour-rich. Factor price equalization takes place in the parallelogram $OQO'Q'$.

If YY' represents the budget restraint with slope w/r, i.e. the relative price of labour, the intersection point C of YY' with the diagonal of the box divides the diagonal into two parts, $OC/O'C$ being the relative GDP of the home country. Provided that preferences are assumed to be identical and homothetic, both parts of the diagonal represent the factor content of consumption in both countries. The factor content of net trade is given by vector EC. The pattern of trade in terms of goods is easily obtained by drawing the vectors parallel to OQ and QO' through E (and C). The exports of manufactures (net if it is a differentiated good in a monopolistic competition model) of the home country are measured by vector $Q_m C_m^0$, and its imports of food are measured by $Q_f C_f^0$. The pattern of trade

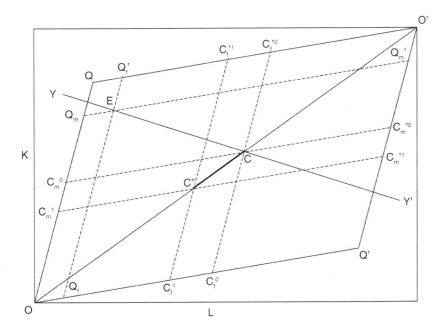

Figure 6.1 The shifting-consumption effect of tourism on trade.

is explained by the factor proportions theory – that is, the home country is relatively capital-rich and exports manufactures that are capital-intensive.

Now, assuming one-way tourism from the home country to the foreign country and maintaining the assumption of identical preferences, we can examine tourism by measuring the consumption of visitors from the home country to the foreign country through the vector, say C'C. So, people of the home country consume a factorial content OC' in their own country and C'C as visitors in the foreign country. Obviously the total consumption of both goods in the home country is reduced and it is increased in the foreign country. $OC_m'^1$ and $OC_f'^1$ represent consumption of manufactures and food in the foreign country, both by residents and non-residents. The result is that the registered trade in the home country is characterized by smaller imports of food $Q_fC_f^1$ and greater exports of manufactures $Q_mC_m^1$. Now the factor content of trade is given by EC'.[4]

The pattern of trade can be explained by the factor proportions theory, but the volume of imports and of exports are modified by tourism flows. For the country of origin of tourists, tourism is revealed as complementary for exports and substitutive for imports. For the foreign country, the direction of the relationship is the opposite.

The *biased consumption* effect is presented in Figure 6.2. In order to focus on this effect, this figure is constructed assuming balanced flows of tourists (i.e. C''C=CC'). Let C'A=BC'' be the factor content of consumption by home-country people in the foreign country, and C''A=C'B represent the consumption by foreign-country people in the home country.[5] The sum of both vectors equals C''C', assuring clearing of markets.

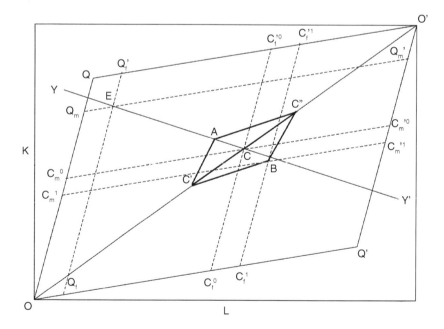

Figure 6.2 The biased-consumption effect of tourism on trade.

Point A represents the division of world consumption between residents in the home country and residents in the foreign country, while point B shows the distribution according to a territorial criterion (i.e. between consumption within the home country and consumption within the foreign country). This last division must be taken into account in order to determine the exports and imports of each country.

As can be observed in Figure 6.2, both exports and imports are increased by the *biased consumption effect*. Since tourists are biased towards goods exported from their country of origin, tourism and trade are complementary. It can easily be checked that if the bias is the contrary one, tourism and trade are substitutive. Therefore, if tourists modify their pattern of purchases in the destination, the pattern of trade is affected. This influence on trade can reinforce or reduce the *shifting consumption* effect. Under unbalanced tourism and asymmetrical behaviour of consumers, the net result depends on the relative importance and the sign of each effect (the *shifted consumption effect* and the *biased consumption effect*).

To summarize, trade and tourism can be connected by several links. More direct links can be illustrated by the IWE, considering that tourism means a shift in consumption from the origin to the destination of tourists.

6.4 Empirical analysis

In this section, the case study of the United Kindom is used to carry out the Granger causality test augmented with the error correction mechanism (ECM) in order to analyse the relationship between trade and tourism. The ECM implies a co-integration relationship between the variables. Hence, the long-run equilibrium relationship and the short-run causality can be tested in this section. Moreover, we present the impulse–response functions, which help to support the findings of the Granger causality tests.

The United Kingdom is an important travel destination, as well as being a major source of tourists. So, the main reasons for choosing the United Kingdom are (1) the availability of data for a long-run analysis, and (2) the fact that the United Kingdom is a very open economy with an important tourist sector. Tourism makes a major contribution to the UK economy. According to the Office for National Statistics, the travel and tourism industry was expected to contribute directly 3.4 per cent to GDP in 2008. At the same time, the share of this sector in the total employment was expected to be 8.6 per cent.

With regard to tourist data, we use monthly *tourist arrivals* (A_t), *tourist departures* (D_t) and *total tourism* (TT_t), as the sum of arrivals and departures, from January 1980 to February 2007. These data are obtained from the International Passenger Survey (IPS). Regarding the trade data, we consider *exports* (E_t), *imports* (I_t) and *total trade* (T_t). Trade data are obtained from the Direction of Trade Statistics of the International Monetary Fund (IMF). All data are seasonally adjusted applying X12ARIMA, and all variables are logarithms. Table 6.1 presents the descriptive statistics for all the variables.

Figure 6.3 plots the original series of *total tourism* in the United Kingdom. A look at the figure suggests the variable presents an increasing trend. The same

Table 6.1 Descriptive statistics

Variable	Obs	Mean	Std Dev.	Min	Max
Exports	326	9.4838	0.2405	8.9676	10.1952
Imports	326	9.6352	0.2845	9.1078	10.3274
Total trade	326	10.2566	0.2618	9.7328	10.9604
Arrivals	326	14.2934	0.3125	13.6841	14.8886
Departures	326	14.9294	0.4276	14.1068	15.6239
Total tourism	326	15.3572	0.3847	14.6451	15.9947

features can be observed in the series of *total trade*, presented in Figure 6.4. This pattern could indicate that both variables are I(1).

The first step of the analysis is the study of the statistical properties of each variable individually. For this purpose, we first implement some classic methods to investigate whether the series are stationary I(0) or non-stationary I(1). In particular, we carry out the augmented Dickey–Fuller (ADF) test to formally test the non-stationarity of trade and tourism flows.

As can be observed in Table 6.2, the null hypothesis of a unit root cannot be rejected at the 1 per cent significance level for all variables. This result implies that all series are integrated of the same order, and hence we can analyse the co-integration between variables.

As was mentioned above, the main objective of this chapter is to analyse the causal link between trade and tourism and its long-run relationship. The classical model to study the causality is the vector autoregression model (VAR). The VAR can be written as:

$$Eq.1: \Delta y_{1t} = \sum_{i=1}^{p} \alpha_{1i} \Delta y_{1t-i} + \sum_{i=1}^{p} \beta_{1i} \Delta y_{2t-i} + u_{1t}$$

$$Eq.2: \Delta y_{2t} = \sum_{i=1}^{p} \alpha_{2i} \Delta y_{1t-i} + \sum_{i=1}^{p} \beta_{2i} \Delta y_{2t-i} + u_{2t} \tag{6.1}$$

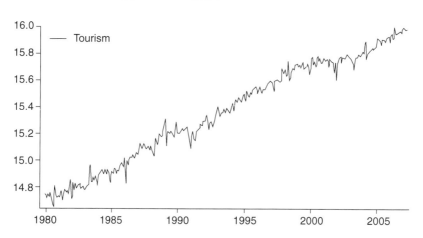

Figure 6.3 Total tourism, United Kingdom.

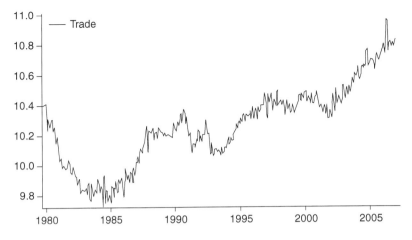

Figure 6.4 Total trade, United Kingdom.

where y_{1t} and y_{2t} are the endogenous variables, both integrated of order 1, p is the lag length and u_{1t} are u_{1t} are the residuals.[6] Following Granger (1988), if y_{1t} and y_{2t} are both I(1) and are co-integrated, then they can be represented by an error correction mechanism (ECM). As a consequence, either Δy_{1t}, Δy_{2t} or both could be caused by ECM_{t-1}, being $ECM_t = y_{1t} - \alpha - \beta y_{2t}$, which is a function of y_{1t} and y_{2t-1}. Thus, the omission of ECM_{t-1} from the VAR would imply misspecification and the OLS method being biased.

For that reason, the VAR should be redefined as a dynamic multi-equational model augmented with the error correction mechanism (VECM). The equation system (6.1) is rewritten as a new system of equations such as

$$Eq.1: \Delta y_{1t} = \sum_{i=1}^{p} \alpha_{1i} \Delta y_{1t-i} + \sum_{i=1}^{p} \beta_{1i} \Delta y_{2t-i} + \gamma_1 ECM_{t-1} + u_{1t}$$

$$Eq.2: \Delta y_{2t} = \sum_{i=1}^{p} \alpha_{2i} \Delta y_{1t-i} + \sum_{i=1}^{p} \beta_{2i} \Delta y_{2t-i} + \gamma_2 ECM_{t-1} + u_{2t} \qquad (6.2)$$

Table 6.2 Augmented Dickey–Fuller test

Variable	Constant	Trend
Exports	0.84	0.01
Imports	0.95	0.15
Trade	0.91	0.03
Arrivals	0.90	0.14
Departures	0.74	0.43
Total	0.90	0.52

Note
MacKinnon approximate *p*-value.

By doing this, we can analyse not only the co-integration between variables but also the Granger causality between them, which implies short-run causality and give us the direction of the relationship.

System (6.2) allows us to test two different hypothesises. The first is related to co-integration where the null hypothesis is H_0: $\gamma_1 = 0$ or H_0: $\gamma_2 = 0$ in equations (6.1) and (6.2) respectively. We use a chi-square statistic as $\chi(p)$, where p is the number of coefficients estimated in each equation, in this case $p = 1$. The rejection of the null hypothesis indicates that both variables are co-integrated. Sims *et al.* (1990) interpret this hypothesis as long-run neutrality, while Corradi *et al.* (1990) consider the rejection of the null hypothesis as the existence of a long-run equilibrium relationship.

The second hypothesis that can be tested is the presence of short-run causality. So, in the first equation of system (6.2) the null hypothesis is H_0: $\beta_{11} = \ldots = \beta_{1p} = 0$, while in the second equation the null hypothesis is H_0: $\alpha_{21} = \ldots = \alpha_{2p} = 0$. In this case, the statistic is distributed as $\chi(p)$, with p being the lag length of the VECM. The rejection of the null hypothesis implies the existence of a short-run causality in the sense of Granger (1981).

Tables 6.3–6.5 present the results of the estimation of the VECM for various relationships. These tables contain the estimations of VAR parameters, the ECM parameter, the long-run parameter, the χ^2-test statistics and R^2. We also apply the Lagrange multiplier test, and find that there is not a residual autocorrelation.

As can be observed, the ECM is significant in all cases in at least one way. These results imply that tourism and trade are co-integrated, and hence a long-run relationship exists between them in at least one direction. Furthermore, coefficient β obtained from $ECM_t = y_{1t} - \alpha - \beta y_{2t}$, is significant and positive in all cases. As a consequence, tourism and trade seem to be complementary.

Regarding the short-run causal nexus, the tables show the results associated with Granger tests. These results support a short-run link between trade and tourism. However, the most consistent direction in this relationship is from trade to tourism. It can be observed how for almost all the cases (eight out of nine) there is a short-run causal relationship in the sense 'trade causes tourism'. For the opposite relationship, the effects of tourist departures on exports, imports and total trade are near to significance.

Thus, the short-run causal relationship is the sense trade causes tourism. Earlier in the chapter, we suggested some channels through which this relationship might go. For instance, business travel is required in order to begin and to maintain the international trade of goods and services, and transactions and dealings between countries create interest among consumers about the source countries of the goods, interest that may subsequently lead to a surge in the flow of holiday visits to these countries. Moreover, international trade also requires some infrastructure and conditions that promote tourism. The evidence in favour of a relationship between tourist departures and trade can be explained from the effects studied by the IWE and by successful business trips that can create flows of trade.

Table 6.3 Co-integration and causality between exports and tourism

	Eq.1: E_t	Eq.2: A_t	Eq.1: E_t		Eq.2: D_t	Eq.1: E_t	Eq.2: TT_t
Constant	0.0012	0.0064	0.0015		0.0010	0.0002	0.0087
	(0.41)	(2.07)	(0.47)		(3.99)	(0.07)	(4.10)
E_{t-1}	−0.1008	0.1230	−0.6514	E_{t-1}	0.0770	−0.6546	0.0986
	(−4.38)	(2.19)	(−11.78)		(1.70)	(−11.86)	(2.58)
E_{t-2}	−0.6569	0.1434	−0.3863	E_{t-2}	0.0310	−0.3870	0.0697
	(−12.06)	(2.28)	(−6.30)		(0.62)	(−6.32)	(1.64)
E_{t-3}	−0.3970	0.1013	0.1235	E_{t-3}	−0.0499	0.1156	−0.0032
	(−6.49)	(1.84)	(2.30)		(−1.14)	(2.16)	(−0.08)
D_{t-1}	−0.0349	−0.6134	0.1326	TT_{t-1}	−0.7378	0.1026	−0.6842
	(−0.61)	(−10.45)	(1.92)		(−13.06)	(1.25)	(−12.04)
D_{t-2}	0.0382	−0.3339	0.1712	TT_{t-2}	−0.4443	0.1996	−0.4244
	(0.61)	(−5.17)	(2.13)		(−6.77)	(2.15)	(−6.60)
D_{t-3}	−0.0216	−0.1079	0.0354	TT_{t-3}	−0.1981	0.0300	−0.1794
	(−0.39)	(−1.91)	(0.52)		(−3.53)	(0.37)	(−3.18)
ECM	−0.1008	0.0195	−0.0773		0.0112	−0.0870	0.0023
X(1)	19.18	0.82	13.67		0.43	15.31	0.02
β	0.8758	—	0.6464		—	0.7040	—
	(9.10)	—	(7.05)		—	(7.77)	—
R^2	0.5016	0.3042	0.5021		0.4015	0.504	0.3649
X(p)	2.4	6.24	5.98		7.8	5.61	9.23
	[0.4937]	[0.1004]	[0.1125]		[0.0504]	[0.1321]	[0.0264]

Note
Student's t is given in parentheses and p values in square brackets.

Table 6.4 Co-integration and causality between imports and tourism

	Eq.1: I_t	Eq.2: A_t		Eq.1: I_t	Eq.2: D_t		Eq.1: I_t	Eq.2: TT_t
Constant	0.0031	0.0056		0.0021	0.0099		0.0014	0.0086
	(1.31)	(1.82)		(0.90)	(3.92)		(0.58)	(4.00)
I_{t-1}	−0.5306	0.1988	I_{t-1}	−0.5031	0.0768	I_{t-1}	−0.5158	0.1181
	(−9.80)	(2.83)		(−9.24)	(1.32)		(−9.50)	(2.45)
I_{t-2}	−0.2038	0.2220	I_{t-2}	−0.1995	0.0971	I_{t-2}	−0.2054	0.1362
	(−3.39)	(2.85)		(−3.37)	(1.54)		(−3.45)	(2.57)
I_{t-3}	0.1536	0.1203	I_{t-3}	0.1424	0.0064	I_{t-3}	0.1376	0.0327
	(2.86)	(1.73)		(2.69)	(0.11)		(2.58)	(0.69)
A_{t-1}	−0.0357	−0.6055	D_{t-1}	0.1058	−0.7458	TT_{t-1}	0.0732	−0.6894
	(−0.80)	(−10.43)		(1.97)	(−13.06)		(1.15)	(−12.13)
A_{t-2}	−0.0044	−0.3266	D_{t-2}	0.0229	−0.4433	TT_{t-2}	0.0238	−0.4245
	(−0.09)	(−5.12)		(0.37)	(−6.69)		(0.33)	(−6.62)
A_{t-3}	−0.0188	−0.1010	D_{t-3}	−0.0393	−0.1778	TT_{t-3}	−0.0576	−0.1618
	(−0.44)	(−1.82)		(−0.74)	(−3.13)		(−0.92)	(−2.90)
ECM	−0.0564	0.0315		−0.0588	0.0126		−0.0624	0.0101
X(1)	14.99	2.80		16.55	0.67		17.11	0.57
β	1.1417	—		0.8251	—		0.9075	—
	(8.91)	—		(8.71)	—		(9.11)	—
R^2	0.3396	0.3167		0.3614	0.3912		0.3537	0.3641
X(p)	1.02	10.71		6.04	3.38		3.25	8.94
	[0.797]	[0.0134]		[0.1098]	[0.3367]		[0.3548]	[0.0301]

Note
Student's t is given in parentheses and p values in square brackets.

Table 6.5 Co-integration and causality between total trade and tourism

	Eq.1: T_t	Eq.2: A_t		Eq.1: T_t	Eq.2: D_t		Eq.1: T_t	Eq.2: TT_t
Constant	0.0027	0.0057		0.0020	0.0099		0.0012	0.0085
	(1.13)	(1.88)		(0.84)	(3.92)		(0.48)	(4.02)
T_{t-1}	−0.6164	0.1968	T_{t-1}	−0.5962	0.1098	T_{t-1}	−0.6048	0.1442
	(−11.58)	(2.89)		(−11.06)	(1.96)		(−11.25)	(3.08)
T_{t-2}	−0.2845	0.2342	T_{t-2}	−0.2754	0.0779	T_{t-2}	−0.2797	0.1338
	(−4.67)	(3.01)		(−4.56)	(1.24)		(−4.61)	(2.53)
T_{t-3}	0.1883	0.1634	T_{t-3}	0.1894	−0.0270	T_{t-3}	0.1784	0.0310
	(3.56)	(2.41)		(3.59)	(−0.49)		(3.37)	(0.67)
A_{t-1}	−0.0395	−0.6053	D_{t-1}	0.1243	−0.7380	TT_{t-1}	0.0822	−0.6818
	(−0.87)	(−10.41)		(2.27)	(−12.98)		(1.26)	(−1.20)
A_{t-2}	0.0092	−0.3281	D_{t-2}	0.0983	−0.4482	TT_{t-2}	0.0955	−0.4249
	(0.18)	(−5.13)		(1.55)	(−6.80)		(1.30)	(−6.63)
A_{t-3}	−0.0223	−0.1030	D_{t-3}	0.0066	−0.1929	TT_{t-3}	−0.0197	−0.1736
	(−0.51)	(−1.85)		(0.12)	(−3.42)		(−0.31)	(−3.10)
ECM	−0.0706	0.0333		−0.0619	0.0127		−0.0689	0.0095
X(1)	11.25	2.45		6.45	0.61		11.56	0.43
β	1.0250	—		0.7536	—		0.8223	—
	(9.66)	—		(8.23)	—		(8.95)	—
R^2	0.4618	0.3167		0.472	0.3979		0.4683	0.3694
X(p)	2.4	6.24		5.98	7.8		5.61	9.23
	[0.4937]	[0.1004]		[0.1125]	[0.0504]		[0.1321]	[0.0264]

Note
Student's t is given in parentheses and p values in square brackets.

Finally, to complement the results obtained from the Granger causality test, the impulse–response functions are estimated. Impulse–response functions are computed to give an indication of the system's dynamic behaviour. Also, an impulse–response function shows how a variable in the VECM system responds to a single 1 per cent exogenous change in another variable of interest.

Figures 6.5 and 6.6 illustrate the estimated impulse–response function for eight months. Figure 6.5 represents the response of total tourism to a 1 per cent exogenous shock in total trade while Figure 6.6 represents the opposite relationship. It can be observed how in both cases an exogenous shock has an effect on the other variable and also that this effect appears to die down very quickly. Specifically, the shock in trade has a greater influence on total tourism during the next few months than it does over longer-term horizons. The same happens for the case of a shock in total tourism.

Generally, the results of the impulse response functions for the variables in this study are consistent with the results obtained from the Granger causality test that suggest evidence of a nexus between trade and tourism.

6.5 Conclusions

In this chapter, empirical evidence for a relationship between tourism and trade is provided. Several ways through which the link can go are described. For instance, tourism implies shifting the consumption from the country of origin of visitors to the tourist destination. Moreover, tourists modify the consumption pattern with respect to one of their countries. This could directly change the volume of trade. Other links between tourism and trade are explored.

The empirical analysis used two approaches. We analysed both the co-integration or long-run equilibrium relationship and the short-run causality

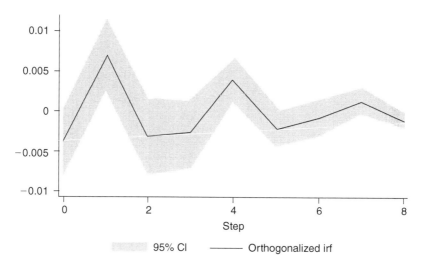

Figure 6.5 Impulse(trade)–response(total tourism).

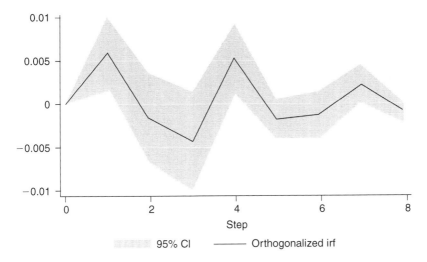

Figure 6.6 Impulse(total tourism)–response(trade).

applying Granger causality tests. The results suggest a long-term nexus between tourism and trade. Though evidence of a two-way relationship is found, when the short-run nexus is tested it is mainly in the direction 'trade causes tourism'.

In all cases, a complementary link between tourism and trade is obtained. Since growth theory provides that trade (and tourism as a kind of trade) promotes growth via increased market size, this effect can be encouraged by a virtuous complementary relationship between international flows of tourists and international trade.

Acknowledgements

We thank Professor Adam Blake and Sylvain Petit for their useful comments and suggestions regarding a previous version of the chapter. We also thank participants at the First Meeting of the International Tourism Economics Association in Palma de Mallorca. We also thank the Spanish Ministry of Education and Science for financial support (SEJ09094/ECON), and María Santana Gallego acknowledges, in particular, the support of CajaCanarias and the University of La Laguna. Finally, we want to thank the World Tourism Organization for kindly providing tourism data.

Notes

1 See, for instance, Balaguer and Cantavella (2002) for the case of Spain and Oh (2005) for the Korean economy.
2 Ledesma *et al.* (2001, 2005) consider the hypothesis that repeated purchases in tourism markets could be considered as a consequence of asymmetrical information problems.

The willingness to return increased with the number of previous visits, the degree of satisfaction declared by visitors, and when the sources of information about the destination were from relatives, friends and previous visits.

3 See Dixit and Norman (1980), Helpman and Krugman (1985) and Krugman (1995) for a description of this approach used in the international trade theory.

4 If tourism occurs in both directions, these relationships are diminished. In the limiting case of balanced tourism, trade data would reveal independence between tourism and trade.

5 Note that both vectors have to fall into the diversification cone, since manufacture and food are consumed in the tourist destinations.

6 In order to define the VAR, it is necessary to determine the optimum lag to assure that residuals are white noise. A reduced number of lags could impede the adequate capturing of the dynamics of the series. An excessive number of lags could lead to a loss of degrees of freedom in the estimation. The number of lags considered is three, according to the Akaike information criterion and the final prediction error. Furthermore, a number of three lags ensures the absence of autocorrelation since the hypothesis of absence of autocorrelation cannot be rejected at 5 per cent when the Breusch–Godfrey test is computed.

References

Aradhyula, S. and Tronstad, R. (2003) 'Does tourism promote cross-border trade?', *American Journal of Agricultural Economics*, 85 (3): 569–579.

Balaguer, J. and Cantavella, M. (2002) 'Tourism as a long-run economic growth factor: the Spanish case', *Applied Economics*, 34: 877–884.

Chul, H., Muzaffer, U. and Weaver, P. A. (1995) 'Product bundles and market segments based on travel motivations: a canonical correlation approach', *International Journal of Hospitality Management*, 14 (2): 123–137.

Corradi, V., Galeotti, M. and Rovelli, R. (1990) 'A cointegration analysis of the relationship between bank reserves, deposits and loans: the case of Italy, 1965–1987', *Journal of Banking and Finance*, 14: 199–214.

Dixit, A. and Norman, V. (1980) *Theory of International Trade*, Cambridge: Cambridge University Press.

Easton, S. T. (1998) 'Is tourism just another commodity? Links between commodity trade and tourism', *Journal of Economic Integration*, 13: 522–543.

Eilat, Y. and Einav, L. (2004) 'Determinants of international tourism: a three-dimensional panel data analysis', *Applied Economics*, 36: 1315–1327.

Fischer, C. and Gil-Alana, L. A. (2005) 'The nature of the relationship between international tourism and international trade: the case of German imports of Spanish wine', Working Paper 15/05, Navarra: School of Economics and Business Administration, University of Navarra.

Granger, C. W. J. (1981) 'Some properties of time series data and their use in econometric model specification', *Journal of Econometrics*, 16: 121–130.

Granger, C. W. J. (1988) 'Some recent developments in a concept of causality', *Journal of Econometrics*, 39: 199–211.

Helpman, E. and Krugman, P. R. (1985) *Market Structure and Foreign Trade: Increasing Returns, Imperfect Competition and the International Economy*, Cambridge, MA: MIT Press.

Khan, H., Toh, R. S. and Chua, L. (2005) 'Tourism and trade: cointegration and Granger causality tests', *Journal of Travel Research*, 44: 171–176.

Krugman, P. R. (1995) 'Increasing returns, imperfect competition and the positive theory of international trade', in G. Grossman and K. Rogoff (eds) *Handbook of International Economics*, vol. 2, Amsterdam: North-Holland, pp. 1245–1260.

Kulendran, N. and Wilson, K. (2000) 'Is there a relationship between international trade and international travel?', *Applied Economics*, 32: 1001–1009.

Ledesma, F. J., Navarro, M. and Pérez, J. V. (2001) 'Panel data and tourism demand: a case study of Tenerife', *Tourism Economics*, 7 (1): 75–88.

Ledesma, F. J., Navarro, M. and Pérez, J. V. (2005) 'Return to tourist destinations: is it reputation, after all?', *Applied Economics*, 37: 2055–2065.

Marin, D. (1992) 'Is the export-led growth hypothesis valid for industrialized countries?', *Review of Economics and Statistics*, 74: 678–688.

Oh, C.-O. (2005) 'The contribution of tourism development to economic growth in the Korean economy', *Tourism Management*, 26: 39–44.

Sims, C., Stock, H. and Watson, M. (1990) 'Inference in linear time series models with some unit root', *Econometrica*, 58: 113–145.

Turner, L. W. and Witt, S. F. (2001) 'Factors influencing demand for international tourism: tourism demand analysis using structural equation modelling, revisited', *Tourism Economics*, 7 (1): 21–38.

7 Evaluating labour productivity of diversifying rural tourism
Evidence from Japan

Yasuo Ohe

7.1 Introduction

Activities in rural tourism have been diversifying and some of these activities have grown into a firm market. There has been little investigation conceptually and empirically from an economic perspective on the relationship between endogenous utilization of rural resources, including agriculture and actual rural tourism activities. However, there have been intensive analyses of farm and rural tourism from various disciplines (Bryden *et al.*, 1993, for the British, French and German cases; Maude and van Rest, 1985, Hoyland, 1982, Evans and Ilbery, 1989, 1992a, b, for the British; Pevetz, 1992, and Pichler, 1991, for the Austrian; Oppermann, 1997, for the German; Vanslembrouck *et al.*, 2005, for the Flemish; Ohe and Ciani, 1998, for the Italian; and Ohe, 2008a, 2010, for the Japanese case), as well as anecdotal reports (Nakamichi, 2003).

Rural tourism's endogenous utilization of rural resources increases in importance in this context. Sustainable development of rural tourism depends on how the rural side will be able to respond appropriately to emerging new social demands for recreational and educational functions of agriculture and the rural environment. Exploration of these functions will lead to the establishment of new roles for agriculture and the countryside and eventually to diversification of rural tourism activities.

Thus, bearing in mind the characteristic of rural tourism as a labour-intensive service activity that differs from the production of traditional farm products, it is necessary to examine the factor input relationship of human resources and utilization of rural resources and to clarify conditions for the viable development of new markets for these services. For this purpose, we should evaluate each activity involved in rural tourism, not rural tourism in general. Hall *et al.* (2004) deal with rural tourism from the aspect of sustainable business, and Hall and Richards (2000) approach it from community development aspects. Fleischer and Tchetchik (2002) take the approach of the production function and Vanslembrouck *et al.* (2005) and Ohe (2007, 2008b) deal with the relationship between multifunctional aspects of farming and rural tourism. Robinson *et al.* (2000) and Pender and Sharpley (2005) study management issues. None of these studies, however, has fully addressed the necessity mentioned above.

This chapter, thus, first conceptually characterizes rural tourism activity in comparison with past farm products resulting from rural resource use and gives a basic framework with which to conduct an empirical evaluation of the state of market formation of rural tourism activity in Japan. Second, we examine the relationship between utilization of rural resources and rural tourism. Third, we estimate the marginal labour productivity of rural tourism activities and examine the formation of the market for rural tourism in connection with the utilization of rural resources. Finally, we consider policy implications for the development of rural tourism.

7.2 Conceptual considerations

Recently, there has been a trend towards rising demand for rural tourism, rural amenities and the educational function of the rural heritage and environment, which are generalized as components of multifunctionality of agriculture (for multifunctionality, see OECD, 2001, 2003; Brower, 2004; van Huylenbroeck and Durand, 2003). The rural indigenous environment and heritage are reflected in this new demand. In this context, there is commonality with the traditional products in terms of products made from rural resources. Nevertheless, this is not the demand for traditional farm products per se, but a different demand emerging as a new market resulting from social development.

The following points explain how new market goods and services differ from past products. First, these new social demands for recreational and educational purposes have characteristics of service goods in addition to farm-processed products. Second, these new services have the positive externality typically observed as multifunctionality due to the initial stage of the market formation and partly to their characteristic of being public goods such as maintenance of cultural heritage, biodiversity and cultural diversity, and educational effects with regard to these aspects and the rural environment. The woodland and grassland adjacent to agricultural settlements, called 'Satoyama' in Japanese, and the terrace paddy are the most typical traditional rural resources that are now attracting increasing attention for this purpose in Japan (Takeuchi *et al.*, 2003). Therefore, we need to position services related to these resources as a new market.

In Figure 7.1, *D* symbolizes the demand line for a rural tourism service and *MC* the marginal cost line measuring the quantity of farm products by farm and rural resources horizontally and the value vertically. To simplify the discussion here, other things being equal, only labour input is considered because these products require intensive labour input. Figure 6.1 has two kinds of marginal cost lines, owing to the existence of positive externality: *MC* represents the farmer's private marginal cost line and *SC* represents the social marginal cost line.

In taking into account the newness of markets, I shall consider two cases: one is at the initial stage of market formation (initial stage), and in the other case the markets are already formed (evolutionary stage). First, suppose an activity having a market at the initial stage and the market equilibrium is attained at point e_g (activity level *ok*). The price e_g is low and slightly higher than the break-even

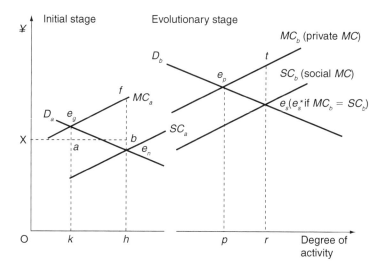

Figure 7.1 Diversified markets for rural tourism and market equilibrium.

level xo (= ak), and the market size is small. If this activity has positive external-ity to society, then the social optimal point is achieved at e_n. The price at e_n, however, is lower than the break-even price ak. This point, therefore, is not a private optimal point for farmers. A typical example of this case is when farmers provide these services free of charge or only recover the costs of materials. The cause of this phenomenon is considered to result from asymmetric information in that people do not know these services provided by farmers well and thus in general do not recognize these services as an object of payment, but think of them as a kind of free externality. Another reason is that farmers themselves often think of these services as a kind of volunteer activity, and the traditional rural mentality tends to avoid talking about the issue of money. In this respect, it is considered to be a market in which the rational factor input relationship to be reflected upon has not yet been established. In this context, the activity is not viable and therefore not a sustainable activity. In that case, it is rational for farmers not to be involved on a full-time basis, but on a part-time basis at most.

The evolutionary case is that a market has been formed. Point e_p is a private optimal point if externality does not exist. If externality exists, then the social optimal point is e_s. When farmers are not compensated by society for the exter-nality they produce, e_s is not an optimal point for farmers, but e_p is. Unless farmers are paid for te_s – that is, the vertical difference between MC_b and SC_b – the unit of externality they produce, e_s, is not optimal for farmers. Thus, in terms of the factor input relationship, farmers' rational choice is to stay at e_p. However, this is not socially an optimal point, although the gap between MC_b and SC_b narrows more than that between MC_a and SC_a ($fe_n > te_s$) because some of the externality has already been internalized in the development of the market.

To attain socially optimal resource allocation, a subsidy such as the direct payment programme will be effective for the moment, as implemented in EU countries and Japan. In this respect, it is true that the direct payment programme gives an incentive to farmers to maintain the activity level at *or* and to internalize the externality, to some extent, into the farm business. Nevertheless, because direct payment is a product of the political process and there is difficulty in accurately measuring externality, this programme does not always guarantee the achievement of internalization. Unless the new activity becomes economically viable, externality is not internalized essentially. In short, this is a limitation of the multifunctionality perspective. Put differently, the multifunctionality perspective can underpin direct payment, but cannot always sustain the success of rural tourism activity. This is why it is necessary for farm policy to promote rural tourism by way of internalization of the externality into the farm business.

If farmers try to internalize the externality by their managerial efforts, the MC_b line will shift to the SC_b line. Eventually, when MC_b overlaps SC_b, both social optimal and private optimal resource allocations are attained all at once (e_s*). What is important here is that this process inevitably activates a way of utilizing rural resources effectively and uniquely. It is safe to say that this is an endogenous innovation in utilization of rural resources. It is an empirical issue to evaluate how these managerial efforts are reflected upon in the outcome of rural tourism activities.

As has been mentioned, the positive connection between rural resources and rural tourism is not established without necessary conditions being met. It is not enough to evaluate the formation of a market by evaluating simply the relationship between rural resources and activities of rural tourism. Therefore, I shed light on the supply side of rural tourism by paying attention to the following two points under the assumption that the demand conditions are constant.

The first point to look at is the factor input relationship, to judge whether a market is formed and viable. This is because rural tourism is not a service for which the market is already established. Thus, if we observe the state of a factor input relationship in the market, we then can recognize whether the market is formed and viable. I focus on labour as an input factor because endowment of rural resources and rural culture embodies labour, and rural tourism involves labour-intensive services. Also, although capital, too, is an important input, data are not available.

However, we cannot recognize the managerial effort of internalization, narrowing the gap between *SC* and *MC*, from the estimation results of production elasticity because production elasticity only shows that private optimal behaviour is taken. Thus, we need to consider the second point.

In the second point, we estimate supply shift effects to evaluate the relationship between endogenous utilization of rural resources and rural tourism. There are two kinds of causes of supply shift: internal factors that farmers can control, and external factors that farmers cannot control, such as external technological innovation. What we mainly focus on are internal factors such as labour conditions for agricultural production, richness of traditional food culture and activities for utilization of rural resources, etc. For instance, the value of the terrace paddy, despite its having been considered a low-productivity area and often being abandoned, has now been rediscovered and maintained in an innovative way in cooperation with urban dwellers who want to enjoy farming and the rural heritage. Newly developed products processed on the farm, rural cuisine and a farming experience menu are also included in this category. If we detect any shift effect from these factors, we can say that these factors represent managerial efforts by farmers and local residents to narrow the gap between *MC* and *SC*.

All of these aspects are empirical questions to be tested.

7.3 Analytical model

Keeping in mind the above aspects, I set up a simple analytical model that has two parameters of labour input: W_f and W_t. These parameters basically give information on full-time and part-time labour and the factor input relationship from the level of significance, hence whether a market for each activity is formed or not and the local employment effect. Another parameter is to determine the supply shift effect: X.

$$Y = F(X, W_f, W_t) \tag{7.1}$$

where Y=sales of rural tourism activity, X=endogenous innovation of rural resource use, W_f=full-time labour input and W_t=part-time labour input.

We interpret the formation of a market from the two parameters of labour input as summarized in Table 7.1. If neither multicollinearity nor heteroscedasticity exists, the parameters of labour are classified into four types, sequentially indicating the degree of market formation.

In case 1, neither of the two labour parameters is statistically significant, which indicates that the factor input relationship does not exist. This means that the activity is not viable, which corresponds to point e_n in Figure 7.1. In case 2 and case 3, only one of the two parameters is significant, meaning that the market is partially formed and viable. In case 2, only the parameter of part-time labour is significant, so it can be said that this market is at the part-time stage.

Table 7.1 Relationship between the viability of a market and statistical significance

Case	Parameter of full-time labour	Parameter of part-time labour	Viability of market
1	NS	NS	None
2	NS	S	Partially viable
3	S	NS	Partially viable
4	S	S	Yes

Note
S, statistical significance; NS, not significant

Case 3 is the stage at which we observe a factor input relationship only in full-time labour, while the market size is not large enough to hire part-time labour. These two cases are considered being partially established and/or small size markets, which correspond to point e_g.

In contrast, case 4 has two significant parameters, which indicates that a factor input relationship is formed and viable for both types of labour and consequently indicates that the local employment effect is the highest among the four cases. Case 4 corresponds to point e_p in Figure 7.1.

In addition to the two parameters with significance, if we observe a significant parameter of the supply shift effect endogenously caused by innovative utilization of rural resources, then externality is internalized resulting in the shift of MC_b to SC_b and the optimal internalization is attained at e_s^*.

7.4 Data

In terms of data on rural tourism, since there are no regular official data and limited data availability in general, data pooling and linkage with several sources of data are effective and necessary. I combined data as follows.

I obtained the main data on rural tourism activity from a survey on the Organization for Urban–Rural Interchange Revitalization in 2003, 'Data on Survey Results on Socio-economic Activity of Public Green Tourism Facilities', reported by the Committee for Understanding the Structure and Function of the Green Tourism Market published in 2004. This survey focused on public facilities, and the published data are aggregated at the prefectural level, which is a limitation of these data. This does not mean that private activities are omitted in this survey, because an activity itself is operated by local residents, including farmers, in public facilities. Surveyed were the amount of sales for each activity, wages paid to full-time and part-time labour, and the number of employees as of 2002. Regarding factor input, no data other than those on labour are available. Although the data constraints are significant, there are no other nationwide data on rural tourism.

Specifically, the activities surveyed were accommodation, direct selling, restaurant operation, recreation (sports, hot springs, aromatherapy, etc.), appreciation or viewing (visiting rural heritage sites, museums, walking in the countryside, etc.), and three experience services (farming, food processing, craft work). Experience services and appreciation or viewing have an educational function and others have a recreational function. I evaluated these eight activities. Regarding market size, direct selling accounts for nearly half of the total sales from the eight activities and is the largest activity, followed by accommodation (23 per cent) and restaurant operation (16 per cent). These three major activities account for nearly 90 per cent of total sales. The remainder are minor activities, with 8 per cent of sales from recreation, less than 5 per cent from three experience services and 1 per cent from appreciation/viewing.

Data on agricultural conditions were obtained from the Pocket Statistics of Agriculture, Forestry and Fisheries, MAFFJ, in 2004. Data on local food culture come from 'Results of Survey on Activities Regarding Succession of Food Culture Including Traditional Food and Utilization of Local Farm Products', MAFFJ, in 2002. Unemployment rates in the prefectures were from the Labour Survey by the Ministry of Internal Affairs and Communications (MIAC) in 2002. Average income per capita in each prefecture was obtained from 'Economic Statistics in the Prefectures' by the Cabinet Office in 2002.

7.5 Correlation coefficients between rural tourism and utilization of rural resources

I examined the relationship between the eight activities and utilization of rural resources. As indicators of the utilization of rural resources, I take into consideration agricultural conditions, local food culture, facilities and conditions of the local economy.

Conditions of agriculture and the local economy are not directly connected with the *MC* to *SC* shift in Figure 7.1, but the local food culture is, because local food culture typically represents the richness of rural heritage and cultural diversity of the country, and thus it has multifunctional traits and externality. Table 7.2 shows partial correlation coefficients between rural tourism and utilization of rural resources. Only significant coefficients are listed. Variables of activities took the logarithm form to make it possible to compare the results with those of the model estimation in the next section. Most of the coefficients are around 0.3, which is not high. We mainly look at variables with higher than 5 per cent significance.

Three major activities have conditions of agriculture and factors related to local food culture to a certain extent. There is a correlation between women's roles in agricultural conditions and direct selling and restaurant operation, because of the significant role of women in rural tourism.

Accommodation has a positive correlation with village agreement for direct payment and the portion of farm households in the village. These facts indicate that the cohesiveness of the rural community is important for accommodation activity because accommodation activity is often practised as a community business in rural Japan.

With respect to food culture, as a software aspect, research on how to utilize local farm products has a correlation with the three major activities. Another interesting software aspect that has a connection with restaurant activity is the portion of municipalities where people have a daily habit of eating traditional food. This proves the connection between the local food culture and restaurant activity.

As a hardware aspect, having a traditional Japanese-style facility is related to sales by direct selling. Thus, the local food culture has, to a certain extent, a relationship with rural tourism from both software and hardware aspects.

Among conditions of the local economy, average income per capita has a negative correlation with accommodation activity. The reason is considered to be that remote areas tend to have lower average incomes and give more importance to accommodation activity than central areas do.

To summarize, I was able to confirm a positive relationship between farm women and rural tourism and between traditional food culture and restaurant activity. These factors could lead to endogenous innovation. Thus, when one controls the factor input relationship of labour, how these endogenous factors work needs to be examined, as shown in the next section.

7.6 Estimation model of marginal labour productivity

The estimation model in activity i ($i = 1, \ldots, 8$) is as follows:

$$Y = e^{c + aX} W_f^{\alpha} W_t^{\beta} \tag{7.2}$$

Taking the double logarithm of Equation 7.2, then

$$\ln Y = c + aX + \alpha \ln W_f + \beta \ln W_t + v \tag{7.3}$$

where Y = annual sales of activity (10,000 yen), X_i = variable i representing the degree of utilization of rural resources, W_f = wage payment of full-time labour (10,000 yen), W_t = wage payment of part-time labour (10,000 yen), c = constant, a_i = shift effect by endogenous utilization of rural resources, α = production elasticity of full-time labour, β = production elasticity of part-time labour and v = stochastic error.

We look at the eight activities. The explained variable is annual sales for each activity. The two explanatory variables of labour input are W_f, wage payment of full-time labour, and W_t, wage payment of part-time labour. Parameters α and β represent the production elasticity of full-time labour and part-time labour, respectively. One must take care to measure the shift effect of revenue instead of the supply shift because it is hard to measure the actual supply shift accurately. If the supply curve, is elastic, however, one can assume a similar shift effect. I take this assumption since rural tourism goods are considered to be more elastic than ordinary farm products.

Another explanatory variable, X, demonstrates the status of utilization of rural resources, and data are obtained from one of the variables in the above correlation analysis because these variables are correlated with each other.

The full sample size was 47 prefectures and the estimation method was ordinary least squares (OLS) except when heteroscedasticity was observed. When it was observed, then the bootstrap method was used.

7.7 Estimation results

7.7.1 Evaluation of factor input relationship

Table 7.3 shows the results of the estimation. To judge from the smallness of vif, there was no multicollinearity problem. Since heteroscedasticity was observed in appreciation/viewing activity, bootstrap estimation was performed. Only

Table 7.2 Partial correlation coefficients between rural tourism activities and variables of rural resources

Variables	Accommodation	Direct selling	Restaurant operation	Recreation	Food processing experience	Craft experience	Farming experience	Appreciation/ viewing
% share of agricultural sales	0.2824*	0.3455**	0.3654**					
Rice share in agricultural sales						0.2751*		
% women in farm population		0.3882***	0.4950***	−0.2872*				−0.2859*
% women in farm workforce			0.3349**			0.3206**	0.2943**	
No. of village agreements for direct payment	0.3853***							
% farm households in village	0.4443***		0.2431*			0.2567*		
No. of local farm products utilized	0.2941**	0.3773***	0.2707*	0.2850*				
No. of financial support and PR activity for local farm products		0.3179**	0.2624*					

	(1)	(2)	(3)	(4)	(5)
No. of studies on utilization of local farm products	0.3318**	0.2976**	0.3326**		
No. of facility buildings for processing and selling		0.3735***	0.3566**	0.3569**	
No. of activities utilizing local farm products		0.3219**	0.3202**	0.3057*	
% municipalities where residents have daily habit of eating local traditional food		0.2737*	0.3392**		0.2763*
Traditional Japanese-style facility		0.3111**			
Unemployment rate			−0.2487*		
Average income per capita	−0.3891***				

Source
Survey Results on Socio-economic Activity of Public Green Tourism Facilities, by the Organization for Urban-Rural Interchange Revitalization in 2004. Variables of agricultural conditions, local farm products, traditional local food are from MAFFJ; unemployment rate is from MIAC; and average income per capita from Cabinet Office in 2002.

Notes
***, **, * correspond to $p < 0.01$, $p < 0.05$, $p < 0.1$, respectively.
Variables of activity took the logarithm form.

Table 7.3 Estimation results of marginal labour productivity of rural tourism

Variables	ln (Sales)							
	Accommodation	Direct selling	Restaurant operation	Recreation	Food processing experience	Farming experience	Craft experience	Appreciation/ viewing
ln (Wage payment of full-time labour)	0.4644*** (5.95)	0.6267*** (5.95)	0.3552*** (4.36)	0.4367*** (3.85)	0.3638+ (1.47)	0.4493* (1.86)	0.5959*** (3.55)	1.2810** (2.22)
ln (Wage payment of part-time labour)	0.3079*** (3.44)	0.1815*** (2.75)	0.3770*** (3.49)	0.3131** (2.26)	0.3214* (1.82)	0.3784+ (1.68)	0.1674+ (1.32)	0.1487 (0.26)
No. of activities utilizing local farm products (yes = 1, no = 0)	— —	— —	— —	0.0048* (1.75)	— —	—	—	—
Unemployment rate	— —	— —	−0.1618** (−2.19)	— —	— —	—	—	—
Japanese traditional style facility (yes = 1, no = 0)	— —	1.7389** (2.10)	— —	— —	— —	—	—	—
Constant	3.8967*** (8.08)	4.2575*** (5.99)	5.1656*** (5.85)	3.4610*** (3.33)	3.4848** (2.74)	2.3770+ (1.52)	2.3814* (1.99)	−3.0878 (−0.69)
ajstR²	0.8412	0.7348	0.6909	0.5650	0.3829	0.2699	0.3353	0.3536
Vif	2.68	1.45	1.44	1.26	1.97	1.43	1.05	
Breusch–Pagan test	n.s.	n.s.	n.s.	n.s.	n.s.	n.s.	n.s.	
Wald chi²								7.17**
Method of estimation	ols	ols	ols	ols	ols	ols	ols	bootstrap
Sample size	41	43	42	32	27	33	31	22

Source: Same as Table 7.2.

Notes:
Figures in parentheses are t static, or z-value when bootstrap estimation is applied.
***, **, *, + (as reference) correspond to p < 0.01, p < 0.05, p < 0.1 and p < 0.2, respectively.

parameters of rural resources with statistical significance are listed. First, let us look at the overall results and the production elasticity of labour. The results of the three major activities (providing accommodation, direct selling and restaurant operation) and recreation showed relatively large goodness of fit, and the two parameters of labour were both positive and statistically significant – the supposed results of a factor input relationship and corresponding to case 4. Activity-wise, direct selling and accommodation have the larger full-time parameters while restaurant activity has the larger part-time parameter. In service activities such as restaurant operation, sales will be determined by how to cope with fluctuations in daily or weekly demand. For this purpose, waiting staff will play an important role. This is why restaurant activity has the higher part-time parameter.

To summarize, among the three major activities, direct selling has the highest production elasticity of full-time labour while restaurant activity has the highest production elasticity of part-time labour. In any case, these three major activities as well as recreation have a firm factor input relationship, hence these facts prove that the markets for these activities have been established and that they have a larger employment effect than the other activities. These four activities commonly have a recreational characteristic.

We cannot, however, observe any apparent shift effect caused by software aspects with regard to utilization of rural resources with up to 5 per cent significance. Only recreation activity has a positive shift effect caused by the number of activities utilizing local farm products in local food (with 10 per cent significance). There is no shift effect in accommodation, while there is a negative shift effect between the jobless rate and restaurant activity. This result suggests that the restaurant business depends on local purchasing power, which is provided by income. Direct selling has a shift effect by the hardware aspect, indicating that a traditional Japanese-style facility is effective in raising sales at direct selling stations. Strictly speaking, however, this is not exactly revitalized or innovative utilization of rural resources.

Thus, while I observed a positive correlation between sales and rural resources, I could not observe a noteworthy relationship between them with a high degree of significance. A likely explanation is that even if a region has rich and diverse local resources as well as food culture, the effects of an endogenously innovative way of rural resource use will not be sufficient to create a shift effect that generates internalization of externality even if such a cultural background has already been reflected in labour itself to some extent.

The results of other activities show lower goodness of fit and only one of the two labour parameters has significance; only full-time labour parameters have significance in craft and appreciation/viewing, and these parameters indicate relatively higher production elasticity. This single parameter with significance means that the market is not large enough for employment of both full-time and part-time labour even if it is not small enough to be managed only by part-time labour. Craft exactly fits this example, owing to its requirement of specialized techniques. The full-time parameter in appreciation/viewing is greater than unity, which suggests economy of scale in this activity. In the case of ordinary tangible goods, labour is the operating input that has no economy of scale. On the contrary, in the case of appreciation/viewing, providing an explanation of the exhibition can be elastic in terms of acceptance of numbers of visitors so that economy of scale can work easily.

Food processing and farming experiences have neither full-time nor part-time parameters with significance up to the 5 per cent level, but only a 10 per cent level of significance in the part-time parameter of food processing. This means that the factor input relationship and the markets for these services have not been established yet, or at most are partially established in food processing on a part-time basis. These two experience services are considered as being provided not as economically viable services, but rather as collateral-free services.

In short, the educational function corresponds to case 2 or case 3, which indicates a factor input relationship and that markets are partially but not yet fully established.

7.7.2 Estimated labour productivity

Calculated marginal labour productivity from the estimation results is shown in Table 7.4. For instance, in the case of full-time labour we can obtain marginal labour productivity from the formula

$$\alpha = \ln Y / \ln W_f = (W_f / Y) \cdot (dY / dW_f)$$
$$= (\text{employment coefficient}) \cdot (\text{marginal labour productivity}) \tag{7.4}$$

Production elasticity was obtained by the estimated parameters and the employment coefficient by the average of (full-time or part-time wage payment in each activity/sales in each activity). Marginal labour productivity is greater than unity if dY (marginal revenue) > dW_f (marginal cost) due to the value term evaluation here. If the estimated parameter did not reach the 10 per cent significance level, then we consider that marginal labour productivity is zero.

The difference between the two types of activities, i.e. recreational and educational, is obvious. The three major activities show nearly unity or greater than unity, and direct selling has the highest marginal productivity for both types of labour input. Roughly speaking, labour productivity in every activity of the recreational function is nearly equal to unity or is greater than unity. This means that marginal revenue nearly equals or surpasses marginal cost and that marginal labour productivity in direct selling is the greatest among the eight activities examined.

In contrast, activities with an educational function show less than unity in marginal productivity, except for food processing. This means that the marginal revenue of these activities is lower than the marginal cost, and therefore we can say that these activities are not conducted as rational economic behaviour.

Table 7.4 Estimated labour productivity of rural tourism activity

Activity	Full-time labour			Part-time labour		
	Marginal labour productivity	Production elasticity	Employment coefficient	Marginal labour productivity	Production elasticity	Employment coefficient
Accommodation	1.441	0.464	0.322	2.197	0.308	0.140
Direct selling	9.734	0.627	0.064	5.706	0.182	0.032
Restaurant operation	0.989	0.355	0.359	3.159	0.377	0.119
Recreation	1.771	0.437	0.247	0.759	0.313	0.412
Food processing	0	0	0.773	0.979	0.321	0.328
Craft making	0.448	0.596	1.330	0	0	0.313
Farming experiences	0.264	0.450	1.704	0	0	0.296
Appreciation/viewing	0.147	1.281	8.699	0	0	10.836

Notes
Marginal labour productivity = production elasticity/employment coefficient. Production coefficient is obtained by the estimated parameters with up to 10% significance and employment coefficient by (wage payment/sales). If MR (marginal revenue) > MC (marginal cost) then labour productivity > 1.

7.8 Discussion

Now we summarize characteristics of each activity from the estimation results in Table 7.5. Direct selling, restaurants and the provision of accommodation have relatively larger market and factor input relationships, and therefore are at least at a private equilibrium point e_p. These major activities have a local employment effect. It is considered that there is still, however, a gap between the private marginal cost and the social marginal cost; thus, we cannot say that the social equilibrium point has been attained.

In contrast, recreation has a small market size and is considered as being at a private equilibrium point e_g. Appreciation/viewing and the three experience services have only a partial factor input relationship, and from the estimated marginal productivities even private equilibrium has not been attained and only externality is provided without receiving its full cost. Thus, it is considered to remain at point e_n, the social optimal but not the private optimal point. The market in this state is not viable and thus is not a sustainable situation over the long term.

In short, we can sum up the findings as follows. The first point is that while certain markets have already been established and are viable for those activities with a recreational function, the markets for activities with an educational function remain to be fully established and viable. The second is that endogenous innovation in utilizing rural resources remains to be detected.

The most probable reasons that I was not able to confirm this endogenous innovation are the indigenous nature of the utilization of rural resources and the severe constraints on human resources. As a result, let us consider the following four specific factors. First, since this innovation is in the form of software, it is often hard to grasp the effect widely, unlike that with widespread hardware innovation in farming technology. Second, this effect is partly embodied in labour and realized as income for farmers. Third, it has an aspect of demand creation. Fourth, there is difficulty in creating endogenous innovations.

Consequently, it seems that there is still a gap between private cost and social cost, meaning that externality is not yet internalized. We can say that rural tourism activity in general is undersupplied at an optimal social level. Put differently, the richness of rural resources that originally exist is not as yet reflected in an economic outcome that ensures rural viability.

Finally, measures that enable farmers to cover opportunity costs should be undertaken for activities that have a mounting demand. This point is crucial for improvement of service quality, proper social recognition of roles of these services and eventually the sustainable development of the market for these services. It is effective to have policy measures that aim at reducing the information gap between supply and demand sides and an institutional design for market formation. In the long run, an integrated programme that induces endogenous innovation for sustainable utilization of rural resources should be given greater emphasis.

Table 7.5 Relationship between the existence of a market and statistical significance

Case	Function	Activity	Parameter of full-time labour	Parameter of part-time labour	Viability of market	Local employment effect	Internalization of externalities	Utilization of rural resources
2	Educational	Food processing	NS	S	Partially viable	Partially yes	Undetectable	Not high enough
3	Educational	Craft, appreciation/ viewing, farming experience	S	NS	Partially viable	Partially yes	Undetectable	Not high enough
4	Recreational	Accommodation, direct selling, restaurant operation	S	S	Yes	Yes	Undetectable	Not high enough

Note
S, statistical significance; NS, not significant.

7.9 Conclusions

Although rural tourism has reached the stage of diversification, there has been little investigation on the viability of these markets for rural tourism. This chapter conducted an empirical evaluation of market viability of rural tourism activities in Japan. These are the main points revealed.

Rural tourism is different from the products that used to be produced at these points in that it is made up of service-oriented goods with positive externality and includes activities with different market sizes. Direct selling, restaurant operation and accommodation are three major activities that account for a large share of sales in rural tourism.

From an empirical evaluation of market formation of each activity and endogenous innovation of rural resource use, the activities of the recreational function have full-time and part-time marginal labour productivity with significance while the activities of the educational function have only partial marginal labour productivity with significance. The markets for these services have not been fully established, or the services have not yet become viable activities.

I could not confirm the supply shift effect of endogenous innovative rural resource use. Overall, it was evaluated that rural tourism in Japan has not reached the level of complete internalization of externalities that farmers generate and is undersupplied at a socially optimal level.

Therefore, since rural experience services that have an educational function are attracting growing social attention, measures that increase the viability of newly formed markets should be undertaken. These measures should be developed more intensely as a part of rural tourism policy to ease the information gap on rural tourism between the rural supply and urban demand sides and to create institutional conditions for capacity building by farmers to promote endogenous innovation in the utilization of rural resources.

References

Brower, F. (ed.) (2004) *Sustaining Agriculture and the Rural Environment: Governance, Policy and Multifunctionality*, Cheltenham, UK: Edward Elgar.

Bryden, J., Keane, M., Hahne, U. and Thibal, S. (1993) *Farm and Rural Tourism in France, Germany and Ireland*, Oxford: Arkleton Trust.

Evans, N. J. and Ilbery, B. W. (1989) 'A conceptual framework for investigating farm-based accommodation and tourism in Britain', *Journal of Rural Studies*, 5 (3): 257–266.

Evans, N. J. and Ilbery, B. W. (1992a) 'The distribution of farm-based accommodation in England and Wales', *Journal of Royal Agricultural Society of England*, 153: 67–80.

Evans, N. J. and Ilbery, B. W. (1992b) 'Farm-based accommodation and the restructuring of agriculture: evidence from three English counties', *Journal of Rural Studies*, 8 (1): 85–96.

Fleischer, A. and Tchetchik, A. (2002) 'Is agriculture an important component of rural tourism?', in C. Haven, D. Botterill and S. Webb (eds) Conference Proceedings, *Tourism Research 2002: An International Interdisciplinary Conference in Wales*, Cardiff: UWIC Press, p. 150.

Hall, D. and Richards, G. (eds) (2000) *Tourism and Sustainable Community Development*, London: Routledge.

Hall, D., Kirkpatrick, I. and Mitchell, M. (eds) (2004) *Rural Tourism and Sustainable Business*, Clevedon, UK: Channel View Publications.

Hoyland, I. (1982) 'The development of farm tourism in the UK and Europe: some management and economic aspects', *Farm Management*, 4 (10): 383–289.

Maude, A. J. S. and van Rest, D. J. (1985) 'The social and economic effects of farm tourism in the United Kingdom', *Agricultural Administration*, 20: 85–99.

Nakamichi, H. (2003) 'Rural tourism in Japan: towards endogenous development of rural areas', in S. Yoshizawa (ed.) *Japanese Less Favored Areas and Regional Revitalization*, Tokyo: Tsukuba-Shobo, pp. 139–152.

OECD (2001) *Multifunctionality: Towards an Analytical Framework*, Paris: Organisation for Economic Co-operation and Development.

OECD (2003) *Multifunctionality: The Policy Implications*, Paris: Organisation for Economic Co-operation and Development.

Ohe, Y. (2007) 'Multifunctionality and rural tourism: a perspective on farm diversification', *Journal of International Farm Management*, 4: 1–23.

Ohe, Y. (2008a) 'Characteristics and issues of rural tourism in Japan', in C. A. Brebbia and F. D. Pineda (eds) *Sustainable Tourism III*, Southampton: WIT Press, pp. 305–316.

Ohe, Y. (2008b) 'Impact of rural tourism operated by retiree farmers on multifunctionality: evidence from Japan', *Asia Pacific Journal of Tourism Research*, 13 (4): 343–356.

Ohe, Y. (2010) 'Evaluating integrated on-farm tourism activity after rural road inauguration: case of pick-your-own fruit farming in Gunma, Japan', *Tourism Economics*, 16 (3): in press.

Ohe, Y. and Ciani, A. (1998) 'The activity and characteristics of agri-tourism farms: a study of Umbria, Italy', *Bulletin of the Chugoku National Agricultural Experiment Station*, 19: 1–18.

Oppermann, M. (1997) 'Rural tourism in Germany: farm and rural tourism operators', in S. J. Page and D. Getz (eds) *The Business of Rural Tourism: International Perspectives*, London: International Thomson Business Press, pp. 108–119.

Robinson, M., Sharpley, R., Evans, N., Long, P. and Swarbrooke, J. (eds) (2000) *Developments in Urban and Rural Tourism*, Sunderland, UK: Business Education Publishers.

Pender, L. and Sharpley, R. (eds) (2005) *The Management of Tourism*, London: Sage.

Pevetz, W. (1992) 'Erscheinungsformen, Voraussetzungen und Chancen des Agrotourismus', *Monatsberichte über die Österreichische Landwirtschaft*, 39 (1): 60–67.

Pichler, G. (1991) *Farm Holidays in Austria*, Vienna: Austrian Federal Ministry of Agriculture and Forestry.

Takeuchi, K., Brown, R. D., Washitani, I., Tsunekawa, A. and Yokohari, M. (eds) (2003) *Satoyama: The Traditional Rural Landscape of Japan*, Tokyo: Springer.

van Huylenbroeck, G. and Durand, G. (eds) (2003) *Multifunctional Agriculture: A New Paradigm for European Agriculture and Rural Development*, Aldershot, UK: Ashgate.

Vanslembrouck, I., van Huylenbroeck, G. and van Meensel, J. (2005) 'Impact of agriculture on rural tourism: a hedonic pricing approach', *Journal of Agricultural Economics*, 56: 1–17.

Part III

Sustainable tourism

Environment and cultural heritage conservation

8 Clustering tourism destinations by means of composite indices of sustainability[1]

Juan Ignacio Pulido Fernández and
Marcelino Sánchez Rivero

8.1 Introduction

Twenty years has passed since the United Nations World Commission on Environment and Development (UNWCED), the so-called Brundtland Commission, drafted its document on sustainable development. Since then, sustainability has become a recurrent theme in the policies of most governments and international organizations, and of a growing number of firms and other social groups. One result has been the great number of projects, tools and management models in the field of sustainable development.

The process is far from reaching the stage at which changes can be implemented in the current leading model of development. Consequently, the main causes of unsustainability still remain (Bass, 2007), even though some of its symptoms have been dealt with. Neither has the real need for firm action on these problems been accepted by government institutions or the business world, or even at the individual level.

As the World Tourism Organization (UNWTO) recognizes, progress towards sustainability in tourism has been slow (Yunis, 2003: 19), in addition to the sector's late beginning in applying monitoring models. One also observes that as yet no model for the design of indicator systems has been created in tourism. Instead, indicators have been introduced on the basis of the already existing models designed for sustainable development in general (above all, the PSR[2] and DPSIR[3] models).

There is general agreement in the literature that one of the main obstacles to attaining sustainable tourism is the difficulty in measuring the sustainability level that has been achieved by any given tourism destination. This has hindered decision-making in the corresponding management processes and made it difficult to recognize and meet the specific needs of these territories.

Although there have been notable advances in the design of indicators in the past decade (Bell and Morse, 1999; Miller, 2001; Bartelmus, 2003; Stoeckl *et al.*, 2004; Ko, 2001, 2005; Parris and Kates, 2003; Pintér *et al.*, 2005; White *et al.*, 2006), the results are still only partial. There is still no agreement on a universal list of indicators enabling the comparison of sustainability levels in different tourism destinations. This is due in part to the multivariate character of sustainability, together with the difficulty in aggregating the great amounts of information required.

With respect to tourism, in recent years there has indeed been significant progress in the definition of indicators for the sustainable management of firms and tourism destinations (Marsh, 1993; Nelson, 1993; Payne, 1993; Manning, 1999; Twining-Ward, 1999; James, 2000; Miller, 2001; Sirakaya *et al.*, 2001; Twining-Ward and Butler, 2002; Vera and Ivars, 2003; Dwyer and Kim, 2003; Liu, 2003; Bloyer *et al.*, 2004; White *et al.*, 2006; Blackstock *et al.*, 2006). Their application to real cases, however, is still slow and only partial, being restricted to specific cases, with almost no expression of generalities.

This chapter presents and compares a new methodological approach to the creation of a composite index of tourism sustainability that we have named the ST INDEX (acronym of Sustainable Tourism Index). Its aim is to resolve the lack of aggregate information in tourism sustainability, and to be of aid in evaluating management at tourism destinations and in comparing the sustainability measures taken by those destinations.

The proposed composite index is calculated from a broad system of indicators that contribute information about four dimensions of sustainability: economic, social, environmental and institutional. The resulting single indicator that synthesizes all this information will facilitate analysis of the situation in tourism destinations and decisions made by their stakeholders.

The final value of the index will depend on the quality of the system of indicators used. But because the same system of indicators is used in calculating the ST INDEX for different tourism destinations, it can be used to compare the behaviour of these destinations in terms of tourism sustainability.

To validate the ST INDEX method, it was compared with other existing methods, using the same system of indicators.

In the second section, the most recent proposals of composite index design are analysed: the Tourism-Competitiveness Monitor and the Environmental Sustainability Index. They have gained a certain degree of international acceptance and they serve as references for the design of the tourism-sustainability composite index that we propose (ST INDEX). Their structures are introduced in section 8.3.

We propose that the use of weights in the design of a sustainable-tourism composite index demonstrates differences among tourism destinations, helping the creation of a tourism-sustainability ranking. This proposal is verified in sections 8.4 and, even more so, 8.5, where results obtained through the different methodologies are analysed and the synthetic correlations among methodologies compared. The Spanish System of Environmental Tourism Indicators (SSETI) was used, and produced sustainability figures for Spain's autonomous regions and enabled these figures to be subsequently compared.

Finally, section 8.6 incorporates an additional contribution on the possibilities of segmentation of tourism destinations by means of cluster analysis using the results of the ST INDEX. The 17 Spanish autonomous regions are classified into four exclusive but complementary segments.

8.2 Methodologies for building composite indices of tourism sustainability

The two most recent proposals for constructing composite indices in tourism or sustainable development research are the Tourism Competitiveness Monitor of the World Travel and Tourism Council (WTTC) and the Environmental Sustainability Index of the World Economic Forum (WEF). Both have gained worldwide acceptance.

The Tourism Competitiveness Monitor was originally designed to measure the level of tourism competitiveness in nearly 200 countries throughout the world. It was put into practice in 2001 with 65 tourism-competitiveness indicators classified under eight main dimensions: price competitiveness, human tourism, infrastructure, environment, technology, tourism openness, social development and human resources.

Defining a global tourism-competitiveness index is essentially begun by standardizing all the indicators, used following the methodological approach proposed by the United Nations Development Programme (UNDP). Thus, for indicator j in country i, if x_{ij} designates the value, its normalized value is given by the expression:

$$y_{ij} = \frac{x_{ij} - \min(x_{ij})}{\max(x_{ij}) - \min(x_{ij})} \qquad (8.1)$$

The indicators thus range in value from 0 to 1. The value 1 corresponds to countries with the maximum indicator value, and 0 to countries with the minimum value.

If the relationship between the indicator and the competitiveness measure is inverse (the smaller the indicator's value, the greater the tourism competitiveness), the normalization procedure uses expression (8.1) but with the numerator changed to $\max(x_{ij}) - x_{ij}$.

With the normalized indicators, the WTTC method defines an aggregate index for the eight dimensions of the aforementioned competitiveness. This index is a simple sum of the normalized values of each dimension's indicators:

$$S_i^{(k)} = \sum_{j=1}^{m} y_{ij}^{(k)} \qquad (8.2)$$

where the superindex k ($k = 1, 2, \ldots, 8$) denotes the eight dimensions, and m the number of indicators needed to measure every dimension.

Finally, in order to facilitate the interpretation and comparison between countries, the aggregate index of each dimension of tourism competitiveness is defined as follows:

$$C_i^{(k)} = \frac{S_i^{(k)} - \min\left(S_i^{(k)}\right)}{\max\left(S_i^{(k)}\right) - \min\left(S_i^{(k)}\right)} \qquad (8.3)$$

This methodological approach does not synthesize all the information into a single competitiveness index. Instead, it considers eight separate aggregate indices, each corresponding to one competitive dimension. Two disadvantages need to be borne in mind:

1   The $S_i^{(k)}$ index does not use all the available indicators. Many countries are excluded from the overall calculation, owing to the lack of statistical information on some indicators.
2   Each $S_i^{(k)}$ index is obtained as a simple sum of the normalized indicators. Hence, the indicators are not weighted in the calculation of the aggregate indices.

In an attempt to secure a weighted composite tourism-competitiveness index, Gooroochurn and Sugiyarto (2005) define the following aggregate index for each dimension:

$$I_i^{(k)} = \frac{\sum_{j=1}^{m} y_{ij}}{m} \qquad (8.4)$$

They then use this to calculate a weighted composite index:

$$z_i = \sum_{k=1}^{8} \omega_k \, I_i^{(k)} \qquad (8.5)$$

where the weights ω_k are calculated from the estimated coefficients of a factorial analysis model:

$$\omega_k = \frac{\left|\hat{\beta}_k\right|}{\sum_{k=1}^{8} \left|\hat{\beta}_k\right|} \qquad (8.6)$$

The proposal thus weights the eight tourism-competitiveness dimensions at the end of the methodological development. The weights of the indicators in constructing each aggregate index $I_i^{(k)}$ remain unknown, however, since these are obtained as simple unweighted averages of those indicators.

The other initiative that has achieved relative acceptance worldwide, ESI, a proposal of the WEF, was designed by the Yale Center for Environmental Law and Policy of Yale University and by the Center for International Earth Science Information Network of Columbia University. It is obtained from 76 variables grouped into 21 environmental sustainability indicators, and calculated for 146 countries. It analyses five broad categories (environmental systems, environmental stress reduction, reduction of human vulnerability to environmental stresses, social and institutional efficiency to respond to environmental challenges, and global management). ESI should be interpreted in terms of probability since it 'quantifies the likelihood that a country will be able to pre-serve valuable environmental resources effectively over the period of several decades', and 'it evaluates a country's potential to avoid major environmental deterioration' (WEF, 2005: 23).

In the ESI approach, all variables are normalized in order to facilitate the comparison among countries and allow variable aggregation in the indicators. Some variables are then transformed before assignation and aggregation. This is done by first calculating their skewness as a check of normality. Variables with a skewness greater than 2 are then transformed using the base-10 logarithm or potential transformations.

The final step in this pre-processing of the variables is their winsorization in order to eliminate the effect of outliers. In particular, for each variable, values exceeding the 97.5 percentile are lowered to the 97.5 percentile value, and values beneath the 2.5 percentile are raised to the 2.5 percentile value.

Once the winsorized normalized values ($\tilde{z}_{ij}$) of the 76 variables have been obtained, the values of the 21 intermediate indicators are calculated as the equally weighted average of the $\tilde{z}_{ij}$:

$$I_{ir} = \sum_{j=1}^{p} w_j \, \tilde{z}_{ij} \quad \text{for } r = 1, 2, \ldots, 21 \tag{8.7}$$

where the weights w_j are the same for the p variables constituting the r-th inter-mediate indicator ($w_1 = w_2 = \ldots = w_p = 1/p$).

Finally, the ESI is obtained as the also equally weighted average of the 21 indicators:

$$\text{ESI}_i = \sum_{r=1}^{21} \omega_r \, I_{ir} \tag{8.8}$$

where the weight, ω_r, of each intermediate indicator is the same for all 21 ($\omega_1 = \omega_2 = \ldots = w_{21} = 1/21$).

The indices calculated using expression (8.8) are transformed into percentiles of the normal distribution in order to facilitate comparison among countries.

One observes, therefore, that ESI employs identical weights at the levels of both the variables and the indicators. This is because of the global (worldwide) character of ESI, notwithstanding the justification for the use of different weights in the case of an analysis of a single nation (or even a smaller territorial area):

> Our argument for equal indicator weights is based on the premise that no objective mechanism exists to determine the relative importance of the different aspects of environmental sustainability. At the country level, the indicators would almost certainly be weighted differently, but we cannot determine a globally applicable differential set of weights that would allow a fair comparison between countries.
>
> (WEF, 2005: 66)

8.3 A proposal for a tourism sustainability composite index: ST INDEX

As an alternative to these two methods, we propose a methodological framework based on the use of weights with the basic information of sustainability. The justification of the proposal is that to consider all indicators as equally important in forming a measure of sustainability is not a very realistic way of proceeding. We denote the proposed weighted composite index the ST INDEX (an acronym of Sustainable Tourism Index).

The ST INDEX method uses a factor analysis model to establish each partial indicator weight in the construction of the aggregate index. Prior to the estimation of the factor loadings, the range of all the tourism-sustainability indicators is normalized following the procedure of the UNDP calculation (which overall adopts the WTTC method).

After this first stage of normalization, the indicator values are standardized (to have means of zero and standard deviations of unity). This transformation, prior to model estimation, is usual in statistical packages that implement factorial analysis models.

Depending on the proportion of total variance explained, a single factor or more than one factor will be considered. After the values of the aggregate index of the k-th sustainability dimension as a linear weighted combination of initial indicators have been computed, a transformation function is used to facilitate interpretation of the obtained values. Finally, the ST INDEX is computed as a weighted sum of aggregate indices using a confirmatory factor analysis model.

Given the underlying character of each of the sustainability dimensions, the factor variables considered in the ST index represent the underlying measure of those dimensions. Thus, after the computation of the factor loadings the aggregate index of the k-th sustainability dimension for the case where a single factor explains a high proportion of the original indicator variances is calculated as:

$$I_k = \alpha_{11} Y_1 + \alpha_{21} Y_2 + \cdots + \alpha_{n_k 1} Y_{n_k} \qquad (8.9)$$

where n_k is the number of indicators used to measure this k-th dimension, Y_j (for $j = 1, 2, \ldots, n_k$) is the normalized value of indicator X_j, and α_{j1} is the correlation (or factor loading) between the normalized indicator Y_j and the single factor. From expression (8.9), it follows that the stronger the relation between an indicator and the underlying dimension quantifiable by the indicator (the k-th dimension of sustainability), the greater its weight in the calculation of index I_k.

At other times, it is necessary to consider more than a single factor to explain a high proportion of the Y_j variances. The optimal factorial solution is then usually the rotated one, where two or more extracted factors are transformed (by an orthogonal rotation) to make every indicator strongly correlated to just one of the rotated factors. Thus, if $m \geq 2$ rotated factors are considered, and with β_{jr} (for $j = 1, 2, \ldots, n_k$; $r = 1, 2, \ldots, m$) designating the correlation between the normalized indicator Y_j and the rotated factor G_r one obtains the following intermediate factors:

$$\theta_1 = \beta_{11}Y_1 + \beta_{21}Y_2 + \cdots + \beta_{n_k 1}Y_{n_k}$$

$$\theta_2 = \beta_{12}Y_1 + \beta_{22}Y_2 + \cdots + \beta_{n_k 2}Y_{n_k} \cdots \tag{8.10}$$

$$\theta_m = \beta_{1m}Y_1 + \beta_{2m}Y_2 + \cdots + \beta_{n_k m}Y_{n_k}$$

Since the eigenvalues are in decreasing order, θ_1 explains a greater percentage of the Y_j variances than θ_2; θ_2 explains a greater percentage of the variances than θ_3; and so on. This means that the composite index corresponding to the k-th tourism-sustainability dimension is obtained as a weighted sum (with decreasing weights) of the intermediate indicators of expression (8.10) thus:

$$I_k = \omega_1\theta_1 + \omega_2\theta_2 + \omega_3\theta_3 + \cdots + \omega_m\theta_m \tag{8.11}$$

where $\omega_1 \geq \omega_2 \geq \ldots \geq \omega_m$ are given by

$$\omega_i = \frac{\lambda_i^*}{\sum_{i=1}^{m}\lambda_i^*}; \text{ for } i = 1, 2, \ldots, m \tag{8.12}$$

and $\lambda_i^*(i = 1, 2, \ldots, m)$ is the eigenvalue associated with the factor G_i.

The resulting index I_k is not usually easy to interpret whether there is a single factor (expression (8.9)) or multiple factors (expression (8.10)). In order to facilitate the interpretation, the authors propose transforming I_k into a 0 to ϕ range, using Casalmiglia's transformation function (1990):

$$S_k = f(I_k) = \begin{cases} 1 + \dfrac{\phi-1}{2}\exp(I_k) & \text{si } I_k < 0 \\ \phi - \dfrac{\phi-1}{2}\exp(-I_k) & \text{si } I_k \geq 0 \end{cases} \tag{8.13}$$

Now it can be argued that the closer the transformed value of S_k is to ϕ for a given tourism destination, the greater that destination's (economic, social, environmental or institutional) sustainability. And, of course, the more closely S_k approaches 0, the lower the sustainability.

Finally, to obtain a single composite tourism-sustainability index, we consider Goroochurn and Sugiyarto's method (2005) to be the most appropriate. Thus, the ST INDEX is a weighted sum of the partial composite indices S_{EC}, S_{SO}, S_{EN}, and S_{IN} (representing the sustainability dimensions: economic, social, environmental and institutional). The weights are obtained from the estimated coefficients of a confirmatory factor analysis model as follows:

$$ST_i = \omega_1 S_{ECi} + \omega_2 S_{SOi} + \omega_3 S_{ENi} + \omega_4 S_{INi} \tag{8.14}$$

where $\omega_k = \dfrac{\left|\hat{\beta}_k\right|}{\sum\limits_{k=1}^{4}\left|\hat{\beta}_k\right|}$, if $k = 1,2,3,4$, and $\sum\limits_{k=1}^{4}\omega_4 = 1$.

8.4 A measurement to verify the validity of tourism sustainability synthetic indices: the composite correlation

The essence of the proposal is how to estimate the different weights for the indicators used in constructing the composite tourism sustainability index, and to show how their use helps considerably in establishing significant differences among various tourism destinations, allowing them to be ranked in terms of tourism sustainability.

The analysis is based upon the calculation of the Euclidean distances between the tourism destinations. These distances can then be used to check whether the final rankings obtained with the three methodological approaches described above are congruent with the differences that can be detected by comparing the original values of the variables corresponding to different tourism destinations.

Consider w countries (or regions, tourism destinations, etc.). Then the Euclidean distance between each pair of countries can be computed, taking as a basis the variables used to measure each dimension of tourism sustainability. Thus, if n_k tourism-sustainability indicators are taken into account for the k-th dimension, the square of the Euclidean distance is:

$$m_{rs} = \sum_{j=1}^{n_k}\left(x_{rj} - x_{sj}\right)^2 \text{ for } r,s = 1,2,\ldots,w \qquad (8.15)$$

These values form the elements of the w-th order square symmetric matrix $\mathbf{M}_k$.

Similarly, between every pair of countries the square Euclidean distance is computed using the values of the final composite indices. If I_{kw} represents the value of the final composite tourism-sustainability index reached by country w in the k-th sustainability dimension, this (squared) Euclidean distance is:

$$s_{rs} = \left(I_{kr} - I_{ks}\right)^2 \quad \text{for } r,s = 1, 2, \ldots, w \qquad (8.16)$$

Again, these distances s_{rs} form the elements of a w-th order symmetric, square matrix, $\mathbf{S}_k$.

For the composite index to be consistent and statistically reliable, there must be a strong correlation between the elements of the matrices $\mathbf{M}_k$ and $\mathbf{S}_k$. Even though both matrices have a total of w^2 values, their symmetry and the null values of the diagonals mean that the number of elements of each matrix to take as a basis for the calculation of the **composite correlation** is $g = w(w - 1)/2$. Thus, the composite correlation is obtained as follows:

$$r_{\text{M;S}} = \frac{\sum_{u=1}^{g}\left(m_u - \bar{m}\right)\left(s_u - \bar{s}\right)}{\sqrt{\sum_{u=1}^{g}\left(m_u - \bar{m}\right)^2 \sum_{u=1}^{g}\left(s_u - \bar{s}\right)^2}} \tag{8.17}$$

The greater the value of $r_{\text{M;S}}$, the more efficient is the aggregation of the partial indicators to obtain the single composite index.

8.5 Comparative analysis of results: the advantages of weighting the indicators

To compare the three methods (WTTC, ESI and ST INDEX) and calculate the composite correlation, we used the Spanish System of Environmental Tourism Indicators (SSETI). This system consists of 27 indicators targeted at evaluating the most environmentally relevant features in Spain's tourism sector, and at identifying the main stress factors and specific responses in this field. With this choice, each indicator is classified according to the element of the European Environmental Agency's DPSIR (Driving forces–Pressures–State–Impact–Responses) model (1999) that it represents.

Some comments are in order:

1   The ST INDEX method is based on obtaining a composite sustainable-tourism index as the weighted sum of the composite indices S_{EC}, S_{SO}, S_{EN} and S_{IN} (representing the economic, social, environmental and institutional dimensions of sustainability). Nevertheless, the SSETI, which is the only available homogeneous system for Spain's autonomous regions with which to validate our proposed composite index, does not classify its indicators according to the aforementioned four dimensions, but according to the elements of the DPSIR model. (No particular tourism-sustainability indicator system has as yet been officially designated in Spain.) The indicators really should be classified according to the dimensions of sustainability, so that the system could be used to make temporal and spatial comparisons of each of these dimensions. The design of the ST INDEX satisfies these methodological requirements, with the caveat that, given the information that is available, the weighted composite indices used in calculating the ST INDEX refer to the Driving forces–Pressures–State–Impact[4]–Responses categories.

The practical difference between these two classifications is that using the elements of the DPSIR model is better suited to the estimation of partial weighted indicators of independent calculation and interpretation rather than to the calculation of a final composite index. On the other hand, classifying the indicators under the four sustainability dimensions would lead to greater interdependence in calculation and interpretation, and thus be better suited to the estimation of the final composite index.

2   No environmental indicators referring to beaches and coasts are used in the analysis since there are inland autonomous regions in Spain. A comparative analysis including these characteristics would therefore not be feasible.

3   Some other SSETI indicators exclusively refer to certain tourism locations, without any presentation of aggregate data for the autonomous regions. Since the autonomous region is the basic unit that we employ in the present study, these indicators are also excluded from the analysis.

The 14 SSETI indicators finally used in the analysis are listed in Table 8.1.

The following subsections present the results of applying the WTTC, ESI and ST INDEX methods to these 14 indicators.

8.5.1 The WTTC method

Table 8.2 lists the values (on a scale of 0 to 100) of the aggregate indices for the drivers, pressures, state, and responses categories for Spain's 17 autonomous

Table 8.1 Tourism environmental indicators used in constructing the composite tourism-sustainability indices

Indicator	Description
Driving forces indicators	
DR1	Total annual tourism expenditure (millions of euros)
DR2	Percentage of employees in the hotel restaurant sector
DR3	Percentage of equivalent tourism population
DR4	Number of bed places in tourism accommodation per 100 inhabitants
Pressures indicators	
PR1	Potential pressure on natural areas (tourism density in SCIs[a])
PR2	Tourism density in urban areas
PR3	Interventions carried out by Seprona on tourism and sports activities in natural areas
PR4	Urban waste production attributable to tourism
PR5	Consumption of urban drinking water attributable to tourism
PR6	Electric energy consumption attributable to tourism
State indicators	
ST1	Natural rate of the environment
ST2	Continental bathing water quality (percentage of compliance continental bathing areas)
Responses indicators	
RE1	Hotel establishments certified under environmental management regulation systems related to their upper level
RE2	Separate collection of packaging produced by tourism

Source: Spanish Ministry of the Environment (2003). All indicators are from 2000 since no later data have been recorded.

Note
a SCIs: Sites of Community Interest.

regions resulting from applying the WTTC method, together with the region's rank in each category.

It can be seen that the Balearic Islands rank first in three out of the four categories analysed of elements of the DPSIR model. According to the WTTC method estimate, therefore, the Balearic Islands are the Spanish destination subjected to the greatest driving forces and pressures from tourism. They are also, however, the leading region in the category of responses to confront the negative effects of tourism on the environment. In this overall ranking, they precede the Canary Islands (which have a weak response to the negative effects of tourism), Catalonia and Madrid. These are the Spanish regions in which effects of tourism are most marked and the responses of their institutions are most resolute.

Extremadura is the Spanish region with the lowest levels in aggregate indices (especially in drivers and responses). The responses are null, perhaps because of the low pressure tourism exerts on its territory. The cases of Castilla-La Mancha, Aragon and La Rioja can be mentioned as having similar low levels.

From an overall analysis of the resulting indices, two observations can be made:

1   Because of the method of calculating the aggregate index, there is bound to be one destination with the highest possible value (100) and another with the lowest possible (0).
2   The method also led to a major jump in the values of the three or four top-ranked destinations and the rest (especially notable in the driver and response

Table 8.2 Aggregate indices of drivers, pressures, state and responses estimated according to the WTTC method

Autonomous regions	Driving forces		Pressures		State		Responses	
	Value	Order	Value	Order	Value	Order	Value	Order
Andalusia	22.9	4	73.2	5	56.7	9	15.1	6
Aragon	8.8	11	28.3	10	0.0	17	3.8	7
Asturias	10.4	9	35.9	8	68.8	5	3.2	10
Balearic Islands	100.0	1	100.0	1	79.9	3	100.0	1
Canary Islands	93.4	2	76.4	4	100.0	1	2.4	13
Cantabria	12.5	7	7.7	15	72.3	4	0.7	16
Castilla and León	11.2	8	22.6	11	53.3	10	3.7	8
Castilla-La Mancha	0.3	16	18.5	13	42.3	14	1.4	14
Catalonia	34.7	3	91.1	2	66.9	6	73.4	2
Valencia	19.2	6	47.1	6	60.5	7	32.2	4
Estremadura	0.0	17	16.0	14	42.5	13	0.0	17
Galicia	4.3	15	21.3	12	46.3	12	2.6	12
Madrid	19.3	5	83.5	3	40.5	15	70.5	3
Murcia	5.0	14	30.2	9	51.0	11	3.6	9
Navarre	6.3	13	4.9	16	59.9	8	2.8	11
Basque Country	6.9	12	36.4	7	35.7	16	20.1	5
La Rioja	10.2	10	0.0	17	91.1	2	1.2	15

Source: Designed by the authors based on SSETI figures.

indices) – that is, the assignation of values of the aggregate indices to the regions analysed was highly uneven. In certain cases, therefore, it would be impossible to establish a meaningful comparison between autonomous regions.

8.5.2 The ESI method

Table 8.3 lists the results for the same aggregate indices but now calculated using the ESI method proposed by the World Economic Forum. The top-ranking regions again include the Canary Islands and the Balearic Islands. Indeed, the differences between these two regions are slight except for the 'responses' index, which reflects how the regions are coping with the environmental problems deriving from tourism. Catalonia is placed third in the overall ranking, while there are three regions vying for fourth place: Madrid, Valencia and Andalusia.

Again, the use of this different method of estimation did not change Extremadura's overall position at the bottom of the ranking. Castilla-La Mancha, La Rioja and Aragon come above Extremadura in this classification, just as thjey did with the WTTC method.

Finally, one notes that the indices in Table 8.3 are generally far more evenly distributed than in the WTTC case, with the differences between regions being less marked and no region having either the maximum (100) or minimum (0) levels of the possible range. Consequently, these indices would seem to be better suited to comparing different tourism destinations.

Table 8.3 Aggregate indices of drivers, pressures, state and responses estimated according to the ESI method

Autonomous regions	Driving forces		Pressures		State		Responses	
	Value	Order	Value	Order	Value	Order	Value	Order
Andalusia	52.9	5	71.6	5	49.6	9	43.9	6
Aragon	39.4	11	40.2	10	6.2	17	32.9	7
Asturias	42.3	10	45.3	8	63.6	5	32.4	10
Balearic Islands	98.0	2	86.0	1	74.9	3	96.3	2
Canary Islands	98.3	1	81.2	4	89.5	1	31.7	13
Cantabria	46.5	7	23.5	15	67.4	4	30.1	16
Castilla and León	43.9	8	31.8	12	46.0	10	32.9	8
Castilla-La Mancha	14.9	17	26.2	13	33.5	15	30.8	14
Catalonia	73.6	3	85.5	2	61.5	6	96.4	1
Valencia	53.6	4	60.4	6	54.3	7	61.0	4
Estremadura	16.8	16	24.4	14	33.7	14	29.8	17
Galicia	24.8	15	34.5	11	38.0	13	31.9	12
Madrid	47.2	6	85.0	3	39.3	12	85.1	3
Murcia	29.3	13	43.5	9	43.3	11	32.8	9
Navarre	32.6	12	20.7	16	53.4	8	32.1	11
Basque Country	27.6	14	54.8	7	26.8	16	48.9	5
La Rioja	43.0	9	17.7	17	84.0	2	30.6	15

Source: Designed by the authors based on SSETI figures.

8.5.3 The ST INDEX method

The formulas used to calculate the aggregate indices of drivers, pressures, state, and responses with the ST INDEX method are presented in Table 8.4. The weights in these formulae are the correlations between each indicator and the factor (or factors) representing the corresponding DPSIR element. These correlations are determined from the rotated (or non-rotated, as the case may be) factor matrix.

Bearing in mind the preceding calculation, the use of Casalmiglia's transformation function (1990) with $\phi = 100$ progressivity level results in the aggregate indices shown in Table 8.5.

These results basically show great similarity to those obtained with the two previous methods. The Balearic Islands and the Canary Islands are again ranked top or near the top in all the DPSIR categories except for the 'responses' category, for which the Balearic Islands are ranked top while the Canary Islands are only thirteenth. Overall, Catalonia is in the third place, ahead of Madrid, Andalusia and Valencia. Extremadura is ranked bottom in three out of the four categories. This region, together with Castilla-La Mancha and Aragon, has, overall, the lowest values of the aggregate indices.

Hence, there appear to be no significant differences in the results of using the three different methods to obtain composite tourism-sustainability indices. The question arises, however, as to whether the resulting composite indices are coherent with the 14 SSETI indicators from which they were constructed. In other words, are the aggregate indices obtained from the statistical information of Table 8.1 equally synthesized?

To reply to this question implies verifying whether or not the distances between tourism destinations in the original raw indicators are maintained in the

Table 8.4 Weighted aggregate indices for the DPSIR model using the ST INDEX method

	F	%	FR
Driving forces: $S_{DR} = 0.884\ DR1 + 0.915\ DR2 + 0.968\ DR3 + 0.911\ DR4$	1	84.63	N
Pressures: $S_{PR} = 0.724\ G_1 + 0.276\ G_2$ $G_1 = -0.024\ PR1 + 0.373\ PR2 - 0.463\ PR3 + 0.889\ PR4 + 0.955\ PR5 + 0.927\ PR6$ $G_2 = 0.949\ PR1 + 0.804\ PR2 + 0.234\ PR3 + 0.381\ PR4 + 0.174\ PR5 + 0.269\ PR6$	2	79.44	Y
State: $S_{ST} = 0.755\ ST1 + 0.755\ ST2$	1	57.01	N
Responses: $S_{RE} = 0.816\ RE1 + 0.816\ RE2$	1	66.65	N

Source: Table designed by the authors.

Notes
F: number of resulted factors; %: explained variance percentage; FR: factorial rotation.

Table 8.5 Aggregate indices of drivers, pressures, state and responses estimated according to the ST INDEX method

Autonomous regions	Driving forces		Pressures		State		Responses	
	Value	Order	Value	Order	Value	Order	Value	Order
Andalusia	45.5	4	93.3	6	49.7	9	40.4	6
Aragon	12.8	11	7.4	11	5.0	17	25.6	7
Asturias	15.5	10	8.1	10	70.7	5	25.1	10
Balearic Islands	100.0	1	97.3	4	82.0	3	98.8	1
Canary Islands	100.0	2	99.0	3	92.5	1	24.3	13
Cantabria	20.1	7	4.9	15	74.9	4	22.6	16
Castilla and León	16.7	8	35.2	8	43.5	10	25.6	8
Castilla-La Mancha	5.1	16	4.7	16	27.0	14	23.4	14
Catalonia	85.6	3	99.5	1	68.2	6	95.2	2
Valencia	35.2	6	93.6	5	57.9	7	69.3	4
Estremadura	5.0	17	4.2	17	27.3	13	22.1	17
Galicia	7.5	15	9.1	9	32.3	12	24.5	12
Madrid	38.1	5	99.3	2	24.5	15	93.7	3
Murcia	8.4	14	5.9	14	39.4	11	25.4	9
Navarre	9.9	13	6.8	13	56.5	8	24.7	11
Basque Country	10.3	12	79.3	7	20.5	16	49.4	5
La Rioja	15.6	9	6.9	12	89.0	2	23.2	15

Source: Table designed by the authors based on SSETI figures.

final composite index. To this end, we calculated composite correlations for the drivers, pressures, state and responses indices calculated following the WTTC, ESI and ST INDEX methods. The results are listed in Table 8.6.

It can be seen that the strongest correlations correspond to the drivers index, with all three methods giving values above 0.8. One also notes the low values of the state index (from 0.25 in ESI to 0.33 in ST INDEX). Indeed, there were only two SSETI indicators in this category, and they are clearly insufficient as measures of the state of the environment in Spain's regions as tourism destinations. Hence, there needs to be an improvement in the design of the SSETI indicators, in particular in the state indicators.

The primary objective of the present study was to compare the three aggregate index methods on the basis of these composite correlations. In this sense, there are two essential deductions that can be made from the results presented in Table 8.6:

1   The ESI composite correlations are stronger than those of the WTTC method, with the exception of the state index. Thus, the statistical transformations proposed by the World Economic Forum (logarithmic or potential transformation of asymmetric indicators, and winsorization of all indicators) prior to assignment and aggregation, would seem to be better suited to obtaining a final robust index than the WTTC relativization of indicators into a range of 0 to 1.

Table 8.6 Composite correlations ($r_{M;S}$) of the DPSIR model elements in the WTTC, ESI and ST INDEX methods

	Driving forces	Pressures	State	Responses
WTTC methodology	0.8173	0.6399	0.3141	0.5075
ESI methodology	0.8485	0.7102	0.2495	0.6472
ST INDEX methodology	0.9294	0.7144	0.3361	0.7347

Source: Table designed by authors.

2   Although the ESI correlations are, in general terms, quite acceptable (apart from the state category, they are all above 0.64), they are weaker than the ST INDEX correlations. The pressure index can be considered equally consistent when either the ESI method or the ST INDEX method is applied since the two correlations are quite similar in value. For the other three categories of the DPSIR model analysed, however, the ST INDEX composite correlations are stronger than the ESI correlations. Thus, while it is convenient to perform statistical transformations prior to indicator aggregation, the use of different weights in that aggregation is even more effective in obtaining composite indices that are as robust and consistent as possible.

8.6 Possibilities of segmentation of the Spanish autonomous regions by means of cluster analysis

In order to complete this analysis, the 17 Spanish autonomous regions are classified into four exclusive but complementary segments. To make this classification, the cluster analysis technique has been used to identify similarities in the attitude of the Spanish regions towards tourism sustainability. It has been used a cluster-agglomerative hierarchic process based upon the criterion of the increased sum of squares (the Ward method). The Euclidean squared distance is employed, thus, to measure differences among regions. Results are shown in Table 8.7 and the following comments are derived from it:

a   The regions in segment A, Catalonia and the Balearic Islands (together with the Canary Islands, which belong to another segment), are the territories with the highest driving force in tourism (average value of the index equal to 92.81). The A-segment regions are subject to strong pressure from tourism. At the same time, however, they are offering a determined response to environmental impacts from tourism (the average value of the composed index is equal to 96.99), notably differing in this respect from the rest of the autonomous regions. In sum, these regions are leading the challenge for sustainability in the Spanish tourism sector.

b   Three other Spanish regions (Andalusia, the Canary Islands and Madrid) show tourism pressure levels very similar to the A-segment regions but do not reveal so determined a response with regard to tourism sustainability (the average value of the response composite index of the B-segment regions is equal to 52.80). Nevertheless, the state of environmental preservation in these regions is fairly acceptable as it is marked by the average of the joint index of state for these regions (87.12), which is, significantly, the highest of the four indices analysed.

c   Valencia and the Basque Country are classified in the third segment (C). The current situation of the environment in these two regions is the most worrisome for all the Spanish autonomous regions since the average value of their state indices is the lowest of the four segments. Anyway, tourism pressure in these two regions is in some way less than in segments A and B. The same is also noted for the driving force.

d   The largest segment is D since it is composed of ten regions (Aragon, Asturias, Cantabria, Castilla-Leon, Castilla-La Mancha, Extremadura, Galicia, Murcia, Navarre and La Rioja). For the most part, they are non-coastal regions or, traditionally, with less tourism than those classified in the three previous segments. That is the reason why the driving force of tourism in these regions is minimal and one might even say that tourism pressure on the environment is hardly relevant. For this reason, it is easy to understand why the response to environmental problems derived from tourism has been scanty so far (the average value of the response composite index is equal to 24.21). Finally, it should be said that the state of the environment is very similar to the level in the A-segment regions and slightly better than in the C-segment regions.

In conclusion, this empirical analysis shows in Figures 8.1–8.4 the profiles of the regions belonging to the four segments analysed. They are considered as attending to the composite index value. It is calculated for four out of the five elements of the DPSIR[5] model. These graphs help to show similarities and differences regarding tourism sustainability in the Spanish regions.

Table 8.7 Segmentation of Spanish autonomous regions according to tourism sustainability

	Segment A	Segment B	SegmentC	Segment D
	Balearic Islands Catalonia	Andalusia Canary Islands Madrid	Valencia Basque Country	Aragon Asturias Cantabria Castilla-León Castilla-La Mancha Extremadura Galicia Murcia Navarre La Rioja
Driving force	92.81	61.19	22.74	11.66
Pressures	98.39	97.21	86.43	9.32
State	38.94	87.12	28.74	38.82
Responses	96.99	52.80	59.37	24.21

Source: Table elaborated by the authors.

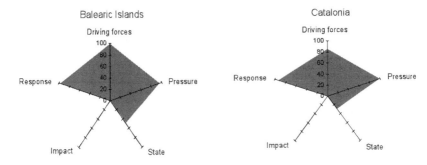

Figure 8.1 Profiles of A-segment regions.

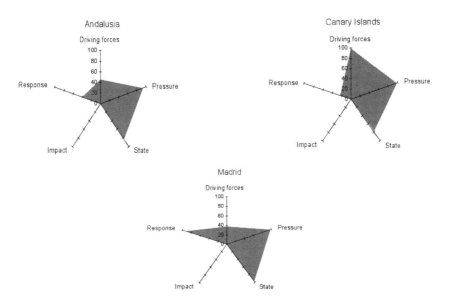

Figure 8.2 Profiles of B-segment regions.

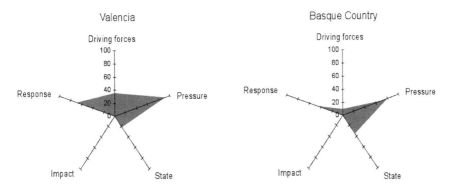

Figure 8.3 Profiles of C-segment regions.

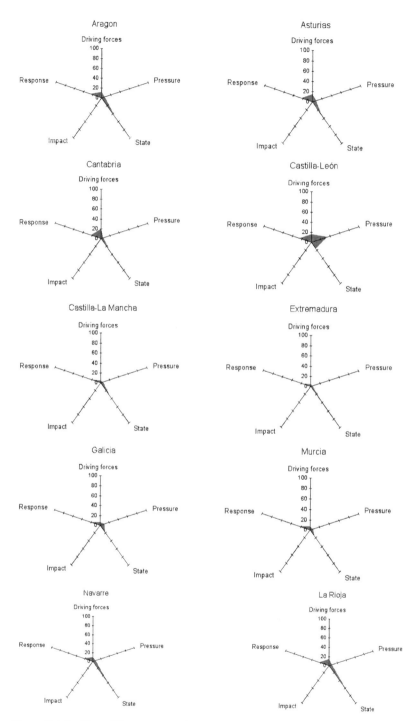

Figure 8.4 Profiles of D-segment regions.

8.7 Conclusions

We have been actively investigating this subject over recent months, and contributing to the debate on it in forums and publications. This research is the first presentation of specific data derived from an empirical analysis. The results have demonstrated the fruitfulness of the proposed index since its results showed a greater degree of consistency and robustness than the alternative methods tested.

The study has confirmed the importance that was indicated in the Introduction of weighting the different indicators that comprise a composite index of sustainable tourism. The use of different weights ensures that the composite sustainable-tourism index fulfils its main purpose of ranking tourism sustainability so that the progress of tourism destinations towards sustainability can be determined and compared. Such a tourism-sustainability ranking will encourage destinations to make their own choices concerning sustainability, to set policies and establish support programmes with well-defined targets and monitoring procedures. Also, the decision-makers involved will have more information with which to evaluate the performance of these programmes.

The method accepts the four-dimensional character of sustainability (economic, social, environmental and institutional). It uses standard factor analysis to establish all of the partial indicator weights in the construction of the aggregate index. Therefore, it is ensured that those indicators which are more correlated with each dimension have greater weights in the calculation of the aggregate index.

In addition, we proposed a measure of the validity of the aggregate indices given by the three aforementioned methods. This measure quantifies the correlation between the original raw indicators used and the calculated aggregate indices, and helps to clarify how adequately those indices have been constructed. This composite correlation was found to be stronger with the ST INDEX method than with the ESI method, and stronger with the latter than with the WTTC method. In particular, the newly proposed index proved to be the most consistent.

Nevertheless, there are still unresolved questions that the authors are currently investigating. First, the method takes for granted the availability of data for all the indicators and tourism destinations analysed. On many occasions, however, this is not the case, so that a procedure is needed to deal with missing data. Otherwise, both the indicator and the destination affected by any missing information would have to be excluded from the analysis.

Second, it would be desirable to apply the method to different tourism destinations, even destinations in different countries. At present, this is impossible, however, since there exists no common database of indicators for all of them.

Third, the ST INDEX is a static composite index because it provides a snapshot of tourism sustainability referred to a single time period (usually a year). It would be interesting to design tools to enable comparison between different time periods. Attention would have to be focused on whether the weights for different years are different or the same – that is, whether they are stable in time or, on the contrary, are volatile.

And fourth, there is the always troublesome issue of the sources of the information that the composite index depends on. Although the national statistics agencies of developed countries provide a great amount of information, it is not usually available in a systematic and homogeneous form for all the tourism destinations that one wishes to analyse. This makes it necessary to define previously a homogeneous system of indicators responding to the four dimensions (economic, social, environmental and institutional) of sustainability. Then, prior to calculating the ST INDEX, one can determine the four corresponding partial indices of sustainability (S_{EC}, S_{SO}, S_{EN} and S_{IN}, respectively), and thereby have information on the progress of each of the destinations analysed in these four components.

In sum, the present study has demonstrated the validity of the proposed method, and that its results have greater consistency than those that were obtained using two other methods that have worldwide acceptance. In future work, our aim is to address the challenges that were noted in discussing the results in order to obtain a consistent ranking of tourism sustainability for every tourism destination that is to be analysed.

Notes

1 This work was presented for the first time in the First Conference of the International Association for Tourism Economics (CIATE), held in 2007. The second version, modified and checked, has been accepted for publication in *Tourism Economics*. This third version incorporates an additional contribution on the possibilities of segmentation of tourism destinations by means of the cluster analysis using the results of the ST INDEX.

2 The PSR (Pressures–State–Responses) model conceptualizes the reality that human activities exert pressures on the environment, changing the quality and quantity of natural resources. These changes alter the state, or condition, of the environment. The human responses to these changes include any organized behaviour that aims to reduce, prevent or mitigate undesirable changes. This is the model developed by the Organisation for Economic Co-operation and Development (OECD) – the Pressures–State–Responses Framework (PSR Framework) – in the late 1980s.

3 The DPSIR (Driving forces–Pressures–State–Impact–Responses) model is used by the European Environment Agency and was developed from the PSR framework.

4 SSETI provides no indicators with which to measure the 'Impact' element in the DPSIR model. Consequently, the empirical analysis is limited to the other four elements of the model.

5 The unavailability of statistics referring to impact indicators impedes the calculation of its composite index and, hence, comparisons among the regions.

References

Bartelmus, P. (2003) 'Dematerialization and capital maintenance: two sides of the sustainability coin', *Ecological Economics*, 46: 61–81.

Bass, S. (2007) *A New Era in Sustainable Development: An IIED Briefing*, London: International Institute for Environment and Development (IIED).

Bell, S. and Morse, S. (1999) *Sustainability Indicators: Measuring the Immeasurable*, London: Earthscan.

Blackstock, K. L., McCrum, G., Scott, A. and White, V. (2006) *A Framework for Developing Indicators of Sustainable Tourism*, Aberdeen: Macaulay Institute.

Bloyer, J., Gustke, L. and Leung, Y. (2004) 'Indicators for sustainable tourism development: crossing the divide from definition to actions', in F. Pineda, C. Brebbia and M. Múgica (eds) *Sustainable Tourism*, Southampton: WIT Press, pp. 109–115.

Casalmiglia, X. (1990) 'La financiación de las Comunidades Autónomas y el principio de solidaridad', *Economía Pública*, 6: 3–43.

Dwyer, L. and Kim, C. (2003) 'Destination competitiveness: determinants and indicators', *Current Issues in Tourism*, 6 (5): 369–414.

European Environment Agency (1999) *Environmental Indicators: Typology and Overview*, Technical Report no. 25, Copenhagen: European Environment Agency.

Gooroochurn, N. and Sugiyarto, G. (2005) 'Competitiveness indicators in the travel and tourism industry', *Tourism Economics*, 11 (1): 25–43.

James, D. (2000) 'Local sustainable tourism indicator', in *Fifth International Forum on Tourism Statistics*, Conference Proceedings, Glasgow: Glasgow Caledonian University.

Ko, J. T. G. (2001) 'Assessing progress of tourism sustainability', *Annals of Tourism Research*, 28 (3): 817–820.

Ko, T. G. (2005) 'Development of a tourism sustainability assessment procedure: a conceptual approach', *Tourism Management*, 26 (3): 431–445.

Liu, Z. (2003) 'Sustainable tourism development: a critique', *Journal of Sustainable Tourism*, 11 (6): 459–475.

Manning, T. (1999) 'Indicators of tourism sustainability', *Tourism Management*, 20 (1): 179–181.

Marsh, J. (1993) 'An index of tourism sustainability', in J. Nelson, R. Butler and G. Wall (eds) *Tourism and Sustainable Development: Monitoring, Planning, Managing*, Waterloo, Ontario: Department of Geography, University of Waterloo, pp. 257–258.

Miller, G. (2001) 'The development of indicators for sustainable tourism: results of a Delphi survey of tourism researchers', *Tourism Management*, 22 (4): 351–362.

Nelson, J. G. (1993) 'Are tourism growth and sustainability objectives compatible? Civil, assessment, informed choice', in J. Nelson, R. Butler and G. Wall (eds) *Tourism and Sustainable Development: Monitoring, Planning, Managing*, Waterloo, Ontario: Department of Geography, University of Waterloo, pp. 259–268.

Parris, T. M. and Kates, R. W. (2003) 'Characterizing and measuring sustainable development', *Annual Review of Environment and Resources*, 28: 559–586.

Payne, R. J. (1993) 'Sustainable tourism: suggested indicators and monitoring techniques', in J. Nelson, R. Butler and G. Wall (eds) *Tourism and Sustainable Development: Monitoring, Planning, Managing*, Waterloo, Ontario: Department of Geography, University of Waterloo, pp. 249–254.

Pintér, L., Hardi, P. and Bartelmus, P. (2005) 'Indicators of sustainable development: proposals for a way forward', Discussion Paper Prepared under a Consulting Agreement on behalf of the UN Division for Sustainable Development, mimeo.

Sirakaya, E., Jamal, T. B. and Choy, H. S. (2001) 'Developing indicators for destination sustainability', in D. B. Weaver (ed.) *The Encyclopedia of Ecotourism*, Wallingford, UK: CAB International, pp. 411–432.

Spanish Ministry of Environment (2003) *Spanish System of Environmental Tourism Indicators*, Madrid.

Stoeckl, N., Walker, D., Mayocchi, C. and Roberts, B. (2004) *Douglas Shire Sustainable Futures: Strategic Planning for Implementation Project Report*, Canberra: CSIRO Sustainable Ecosystems.

Twining-Ward, L. (1999) 'Opinion piece: towards sustainable tourism development: observations from a distance', *Tourism Management*, 20: 187–188.

Twining-Ward, L. and Butler, R. (2002) 'Implementing sustainable tourism development on a small island: development and use of sustainable tourism development indicators in Samoa', *Journal of Sustainable Tourism*, 10 (5): 363–387.

Vera, J. F. and Ivars, J. A. (2003) 'Measuring sustainability in a mass tourist destination: pressures, perceptions and policy responses in Torrevieja, Spain', *Journal of Sustainable Tourism*, 11 (2–3): 181–203.

White, V., McCrum, G., Blackstock, K. L. and Scott, A. (2006) *Indicators and Sustainable Tourism: Literature Review*, Aberdeen: Macaulay Institute.

Yunis, E. (2003) 'El marco internacional de la gestión sostenible del turismo: la visión de la Organización Mundial del Turismo', *A DISTANCIA. Monográfico "Turismo y sostenibilidad"*, 21 (1): 16–21.

Web pages

International Institute for Sustainable Development (2005) *Compendium of Sustainability Indicators*. Online, available at www.iisd.org/measure/compendium/searchinitiatives.aspx (accessed 3 March 2010).

World Economic Forum (2005) *2005 Environmental Sustainability Index*. Online, available at: http://sedac.ciesin.columbia.edu/es/esi/ESI2005.pdf (accessed 3 March 2010).

9 Equilibrium dynamics and local indeterminacy in a model of sustainable tourism

Giovanni Bella

9.1 Introduction

Tourism economics is considered a branch of standard economic theory devoted to the study of the overall class of economic events accruing from the activity of those agents called tourists. The main interest, either theoretical or empirical, concerning tourism economics lies in the useful insights it could generate in terms of policy interventions, insights that might be of help in relation to other micro- and macroeconomic actions in an overall strategy for economic development. Tourism economics is a rather new discipline, but there is explosively growing interest in it. Unfortunately, formalized theoretical bases and well-defined assumptions are still lacking in this field, making it difficult to carry out a deep investigation and exhaustive analysis of such economic facts and implications so that they can be fully documented and accurately explained.

Like every human activity, tourism is based on a relationship with the surrounding environment, influencing it and being influenced by it in a complex way (see, for example, Budowski, 1976: 27). On the other hand, as an industrial activity, tourism will have some negative effects on the environment, for tourist firms might overuse the natural resources at their disposal, making inevitable the rise of a new 'tourism curse' (e.g. Sachs and Warner, 2001: 827). Sustainable tourism is definitely a new concept in economics, as the recurrent exploitation of natural resources still constitutes the principal source of income of tourist destinations overall.

Paraphrasing the highly cited Brundtland Report's definition of sustainable development, we may therefore outline a sustainable pathway for tourism, basically saying that each human or economic activity (from the point of view both of the tourism industry and of the hosting population) must be able to meet the needs of the present generation of tourists without compromising the capabilities of future ones to satisfy their own needs (e.g. Casagrandi and Rinaldi, 2002: 13; Swarbrooke, 1999).

However, once environmental resources are taken into account, some interesting questions then suddenly arise: 'does tourism matter for economic growth?' and therefore, 'to what extent can tourism affect economic dynamics in such a way as to lead towards a long-run stable equilibrium?', or lastly, 'may eventually an indeterminacy problem or, alternatively, stable equilibria arise when tourism, given priority when it comes to an environmental resource, is allowed to enter the maximization problem?'.

As I have mentioned, tourism's contribution to economic development has been well documented in the literature. Nonetheless, though particular attention has been paid to the empirical exploration of the economic effects produced by tourism flows in the growth performance of different countries, there has been surprisingly little interest in studying the determinants of the same relationship from a theoretical point of view instead (e.g. Giannoni and Maupertuis, 2005; Candela and Cellini, 2006: 41).

On the one hand, for example, a recent empirical study shows that small 'tourism economies' do manifest higher levels of economic growth compared to the average for OECD countries (e.g. Brau *et al.*, 2007; McElroy, 2006: 61). This is also confirmed by numerous other papers, even though there has not yet been a clear investigation of the interdependencies between tourism and the environment (see, for reference, Lanza and Pigliaru, 1994: 15; 2000: 77; Smeral, 2003: 77). On the other hand, Cerina (2006) has made a ground-breaking study involving deep investigation of the steady-state properties of an economy whose tourism sector is specifically based on use of a natural resource.

In the light of this still new theoretical literature, the present chapter studies the potential impact of mass tourism on the evolution of the surrounding environment in a long-lasting sustainable perspective. Indeed, its intention is to give an insight into how overuse of natural resources can be avoided without negatively affecting economic growth (see also Lozano *et al.*, 2005).

To this end, I develop an optimal control problem where the representative agent faces a tourism-oriented economic scenario. In this framework, tourism is based on the use of existing environmental resources, but this leads to an inevitable trade-off as both positive effects (in terms of new output) and negative impacts (in terms of environmental degradation) are generated. The problem is then finally to choose the optimal number of tourists to be hosted in this economy, as well as the long-run levels of both consumption and natural resource extraction that maximize the aggregate social welfare.

As will become clear, this chapter makes use of the seminal Uzawa–Lucas model (ULM), for it has become one of the most preferred frameworks from which predictions on the growth process of two-sector economies are commonly derived in the economic literature (see, for example, Boldrin and Rustichini, 1994: 323; Ladrón-de-Guevara *et al.*, 1997: 115; Mattana, 2004; Nishimura and Shigoka, 2006: 199). Indeed, its formal structure, accompanied by a simple mathematical characterization, offers a particularly appreciated synthesis between complexity of the topics involved and analytical tractability. I basically decide to move a step forward by substituting here human for natural capital, coupled with flows of visiting tourists, as one of the possible engines for economic growth and sustainable development.

To complete the analysis, I study the transitional dynamics of the model, and provide the whole necessary and sufficient conditions for the existence of a feasible steady-state equilibrium associated with positive long-run growth (e.g. Restepo-Ochoa and Vázquez, 2004: 285; Gómez, 2005). Moreover, in order to justify the hereafter assumed increase in produced output, jointly with higher levels of resource exploitation due to massive tourism arrivals in economies endowed with larger amounts of natural resources, I consider the presence of an externality factor enhancing the final sector of the economy. This choice of powerful consequences is rich: on the one hand, in fact, the natural result of the traditional growth theory, namely the stability/instability outcome in the saddle-point sense, is not automatically achieved, and indeterminacy results when the externality from natural capital are sufficiently high. Indeed, more complicated dynamic phenomena (such as multiple equilibria) are more likely to emerge instead. I am able to prove these results analytically and to give some insights into the economic intuition behind them.

The rest of the chapter is organized as follows. In section 9.2, I derive the formal structure of the model, with particular attention to the set of preferences, the level of technology, and the link between tourism and the environment. Section 9.3 concentrates on the solution of the optimization problem and investigates deeply the stability properties of the associated steady-state solutions. A final section concludes, and a subsequent appendix provides all the necessary proofs.

9.2 Formal structure of the model

The model is structured as follows. First, we assume the set of preferences to be defined by a standard CES utility function in the form

$$U = \frac{c^{1-\sigma} - 1}{1 - \sigma} \tag{9.1}$$

where c is the level of consumption, and σ is the inverse of the intertemporal elasticity of substitution.

Moreover, mass tourism arrivals are allowed to enter our economy and 'feed' upon an open-access natural site whose property rights are absent or unenforced, with no individual bearing the full cost of its degradation. The result is an obvious free-riding problem, accompanied by overexploitation of the available natural resources, commonly referred to in the literature as the 'tragedy of the commons' (see Hardin, 1968: 1243).

The maximizing representative agent acting this scenario, therefore, needs to modify the two constraints on both physical and natural capital to be used in his or her long-lasting policy actions in order to account for the specific effects due to the presence of a tourism sector. To this end, we devote the rest of this section to characterizing the aforementioned constraints, particularly focusing on:

- the evolution of the available natural resources, and their link to tourism inflows;
- the level of technology.

9.2.1 Tourism and the environment

In a broad sense, sustainable tourism is an industry devoted to minimizing its impact on the environment and on local culture, connected with new income and employment opportunities for the development and preservation of a site. However, tourism may have different impacts, either positive or negative, on the ecological system of a country (see, for example, Hughes, 2002: 457). As a result, it may be difficult, if not impossible, to formulate policies that allow tourism to be maintained over a long period without severely affecting the environment (e.g. Papatheodoru, 2003: 407; Hillary *et al.*, 2001: 853).[1]

In this view, deriving a theoretical approach to tourism sustainability is not an easy task. To this end, we need to properly identify the link between tourism flows, T, and the stock of the available natural resources, E, for we assume here that high levels of E may stimulate an increase in tourist visits, even though negatively impinging on future recreation for the environment as a whole.[2]

To begin with, we start our analysis by giving an explicit algebraic interpretation of the stated tourism flows. Formally, let us define tourism as a slight modification of the Schaefer harvest function:

$$T = vE \qquad (9.2)$$

where $v \in [0, 1]$ is the number (i.e. percentage) of new-coming tourists visiting (i.e. harvesting) the selected natural site, E.[3]

On the other hand, without any loss of generality, evolutionary dynamics of the environmental good, E, is assumed here to be also influenced by tourism, T, and explicitly given by

$$\dot{E} = f(E,T) = \delta E(1-T) \qquad \delta \in [0,1] \qquad (9.3)$$

where $f_T < 0$, for any increase in the number of tourists diminishes the self-reproduction capacity of the ecosystem, or rather nature's capacity to recover from tourists' resource exploitation (e.g. Smulders 1995, p. 163).

To make a whole representation of the entire dynamics described so far, we substitute (9.2) into (9.3) and let $f(\cdot)$ behave as a 3D characterization of the common Verhulst logistic function (see Verhulst, 1838: 113):

$$\dot{E} = \delta E(1-vE) \equiv f(E,v) \qquad (9.4)$$

where δ can be interpreted as the usual parameter for the internal growth rate of a natural resource, while v can be finally interpreted as a choice variable representing a measure for the carrying capacity of the place being considered.[4]

As a matter of fact, determining the correct tourist carrying capacity can be quite complicated. It might be worth fixing the appropriate lower bound of natural resource exploitation, below which the system incurs the risk of an inevitable qualitative deterioration (see also Bretschger and Smulders, 2007: 1). We can thus proxy the carrying capacity by the size of arrivals – that is, the density of tourists – that a specific destination may host per unit of land, as synthesized by $1/v$, which is commonly referred to in the literature as a 'welcoming capacity' (e.g. Costa and Manente, 2000).[5]

A representation of the environmental constraint described in (9.4) is provided in Figure 9.1.

9.2.2 Technology

Final output, y, is produced by employing both physical capital, k, and tourism flows, T, according to a Cobb–Douglas production function in the form

$$y = Ak^{\alpha}(T)^{1-\alpha}E_a^{\gamma} \tag{9.5}$$

where A is a simple parameter of scale, E_a represents any external effect due to the presence of a 'common pool' natural capital that no one will take account of when deciding how to allocate it in time, and $\gamma \in (-1, 1)$ is an externality parameter. Basically, we are assuming that, in addition to the individual effects coming from the use of natural capital on the individual's own productivity – what we may call the 'internal environmental effect' – room is left for some external effects too, denoted by E_a^{γ}. Specifically, we call this effect external because, even though everyone benefits from it (if it is positive), no individual will take it into account when making his or her optimal decision.[6] This last assumption will, of course, become critical in the derivation of the model, and the generation of multiple equilibria with the rise of some complex indeterminacy problems.

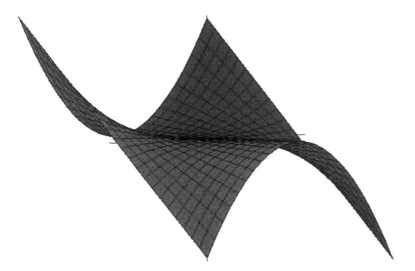

Figure 9.1 The 3D environmental constraint.

To make the analysis simpler, we may substitute (9.2) into (9.5), and finally derive the following production function, which resembles the classic ULM specification:

$$y = Ak^{\alpha}(vE)^{1-\alpha} E_a^{\gamma} \qquad (9.6)$$

where final output, y, is expressed in terms of new visitors, v, as well as physical (k) and natural capital (E) only.

The more direct specification given in Equation 9.6 allows us, for example, to differentiate the total contribution of natural capital to production of output, y, in the two classical components that are commonly referred to in the literature as the use value, E, and the non-use value, E_a. Consequently, a deepest analysis of the external parameter, γ, may signal the impact of the non-use value on the characterization of the stability properties of our economy, as will be investigated in the rest of the chapter.[7]

9.3 The optimization problem

Formally, the representative agent maximizes the present discounted utility

$$\max_{c} \int_{0}^{\infty} \frac{c^{1-\sigma}-1}{1-\sigma} e^{-\rho t} dt$$

subject to the following constraints on both physical and natural capital:

$$\dot{k} = Ak^{\alpha}(vE)^{1-\alpha} E_a^{\gamma} - c$$
$$\dot{E} = \delta E(1-vE)$$

given the initial conditions on each state variable:

$$k(0) = k_0 > 0 \text{ and } E(0) = E_0 > 0$$

The current value Hamiltonian then looks like

$$H_C = \frac{c^{1-\sigma}-1}{1-\sigma} + \lambda \left[Ak^{\alpha}(vE)^{1-\alpha} E_a^{\gamma} - c \right] + \mu \left[\delta E(1-vE) \right]$$

where λ and μ represent the shadow prices of physical and natural capital, respectively.

The first-order condition for a maximum requires that the discounted Hamiltonian be maximized with respect to its control variables (in our case, c and v):

$$\frac{\partial H_C}{\partial c} = c^{-\sigma} - \lambda = 0$$

$$\frac{\partial H_C}{\partial v} = \lambda(1-\alpha)Ak^{\alpha}v^{-\alpha}E^{1-\alpha+\gamma} - \mu\delta E^2 = 0$$

accompanied by the law of motion of each costate variable:

$$\frac{\dot{\lambda}}{\lambda} = \rho - \alpha A k^{\alpha-1} v^{1-\alpha} E^{1-\alpha+\gamma}$$

$$\frac{\dot{\mu}}{\mu} = \rho - \delta(1 - vE)$$

and the transversality condition:

$$\lim_{t\to\infty} e^{-\rho t}[\lambda_t k_t + \mu_t E_t] = 0$$

that jointly constitute the canonical system.[8]

Proposition 1 *The maximum principle associated with the decentralized optimization problem implies the following four-dimensional system of first-order differential equations:*

$$\xi_k = \frac{\dot{k}}{k} = A k^{\alpha-1} v^{1-\alpha} E^{1-\alpha+\gamma} - \frac{c}{k} \qquad (S1)$$

$$\xi_E = \frac{\dot{E}}{E} = \delta(1 - vE)$$

$$\xi_c = \frac{\dot{c}}{c} = -\frac{\rho}{\sigma} + \frac{\alpha}{\sigma} A k^{\alpha-1} v^{1-\alpha} E^{1-\alpha+\gamma}$$

$$\xi_v = \frac{\dot{v}}{v} = (\gamma - \alpha)\frac{\delta}{\alpha}(1 - vE) - \frac{c}{k}$$

Proof: see the appendix.

Lemma 1 *The system S1 implies also the following reduced version:*

$$\dot{x} = -\frac{\rho}{\sigma}x + \left(\frac{\alpha - \sigma}{\sigma}\right)mx + x^2 \qquad (S2)$$

$$\dot{q} = \frac{\gamma\delta}{\alpha}(1 - q)q - xq$$

$$\dot{m} = (\alpha - 1)m^2 + \frac{\gamma\delta}{\alpha}(1 - q)m$$

by means of the convenient variable substitutions: $x = c/k$, $q = vE$, and $m = y/k$.

Lemma 2 *The steady state is a triplet (x*, q*, m*) which solves the reduced system S2:*

$$m^* = \frac{\rho}{\alpha(1-\sigma)}$$

$$x^* = \frac{\rho(1-\alpha)}{\alpha(1-\sigma)}$$

$$q^* = 1 - \frac{\rho(1-\alpha)}{\gamma\delta(1-\sigma)}$$

given 0 < σ < 1.

Moving a step backwards, it is worth noting that q^* simply represents the optimal percentage of tourists allowed to enter the natural site ($T^*=q^*$), re-expressed in terms of parameters only, and whose magnitude depends on the sign of the externality parameter, γ ($\partial T^*/\partial\gamma > 0$), as clearly depicted in Figure 9.2.

Remark 1 *A negative externality on natural capital (γ < 0) drives a positive q* off the unit threshold (q* > 1). Unbounded mass-tourism flows are thus booming in our economy.*

Remark 2 *On the contrary, a positive externality – or rather* $\gamma > \dfrac{\rho(1-\alpha)}{\delta(1-\sigma)}$ –

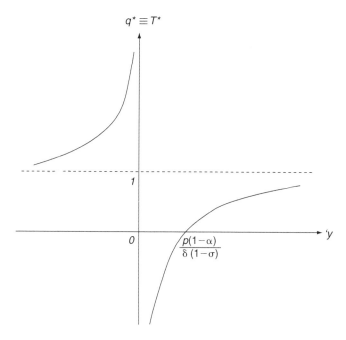

Figure 9.2 Evolution of $q^* = q^*(\gamma)$.

always leaves a positive q* within the unit threshold (q* < 1). Consequently, tourism arrivals are bounded above.

Remark 3 *Lastly, externality values lying in the interval $0 < \gamma < \dfrac{\rho(1-\alpha)}{\delta(1-\sigma)}$ imply a negative flow of tourist arrivals (T* < 0).*

The externality γ therefore plays a crucial role in the characterization of an optimal solution to our maximization problem, and does definitely matter in the process of a growth-leading tourism. It can be highly interesting to carefully analyse the path to be followed by our economy to achieve a long-run 'sustainable' stability. The next subsection is devoted to this end.

9.3.1 Stability properties of the steady state

Which path will this economy follow while converging to the steady state? Is our system stable or unstable? And if it is stable, do solutions describe uniqueness or multiplicity of equilibria, or might we face indeterminacy problems? To answer these questions, we ought to investigate the local stability properties of the solution found in the previous section and describe the reasons why an indeterminate equilibrium could possibly arise. Our scope is then to determine more precisely what kind of external effect is operating in the possible generation of multiple equilibria. To this end, we analyse the Jacobian matrix (*J**) of the reduced system *S2*, and check for the sign of the associated eigenvalues.

Proposition 2 *Let assume the following restrictions on parameters: δ > 0, 0 < α < 1, 0 < σ < 1; then there is always a continuum of equilibria if, and only if, $\gamma > \dfrac{\rho(1-\alpha)}{\delta(1-\sigma)}$; that is, J* has one positive eigenvalue and two eigenvalues with negative real parts.*

Proof: Provided that *trJ** > 0, *BJ** < 0, and *DetJ** > 0, we can thus check for local stability of the system around the steady state by means of the neat Routh-Hurwitz theorem.[9]

Proposition 3 *On the other hand, if γ < 0 then the equilibrium is locally unique, thus J* has one negative eigenvalue and two eigenvalues with positive real parts.*

Proof: Repeating the same argument, we derive the sequence *trJ** > 0, *BJ**=?, and *DetJ** < 0, which implies now having two changes of sign, and a subsequent unique equilibrium. In this case, mass tourism is overshooting, the visited place is becoming too crowded, while the quality of the environment is dramatically decreasing.

Proposition 4 *On the contrary, if $0 < \gamma < \dfrac{\rho(1-\alpha)}{\delta(1-\sigma)}$ then the equilibrium is locally unique, thus J* has one negative eigenvalue and two eigenvalues with positive real parts.*

Proof: In this case, the sequence $trJ^* > 0$, $BJ^*=?$, and $DetJ^* < 0$ resembles the previous outcome, although here the flow of tourists becomes negative ($q^* = T^* < 0$), with a decreasing percentage of newcoming visitors entering our natural site, whose regenerative capacities are consequently preserved.

We can finally synthesize the results of our analysis by means of Table 9.1, where the size of the externality parameter, γ, the flow of tourists, T, and the evolution of the environment, E, are jointly represented:

Basically, the presence of multiple equilibria has been used in the literature to explain the diversity of growth rates and income differences across different countries (e.g. Xie, 1994: 97; Benhabib and Perli, 1994: 113). It is so worth noting in this chapter that the existence of a positive externality accruing to the final output is not a necessary condition for determinacy of the equilibria.[10] Instead, depending on the magnitude of the externality parameter, either multiple or unique equilibria may consequently arise.

More specifically, we have found that, given the presence of a positive externality, the only way to allow for an increasing percentage of tourist arrivals within the carrying capacity of the environment needs a specific constraint on the externality parameter either, $\gamma > \dfrac{\rho(1-\alpha)}{\delta(1-\sigma)}$. In this case, in fact, the inward flow of tourists is upper-bounded, and no indiscriminate entries are allowed. Moreover, a positive evolution of the environment is achieved, leaving intact its regenerative capacities for the generations coming afterwards. Indeed, a positive sustainable growth rate of long-run consumption, as well as a positive inward flow of tourists with no overexploitation of the natural resources at disposal, do hopefully occur.

Nevertheless, this positive outcome is accompanied by some unexpected consequences, for indeterminacy problems and multiple equilibria do unfortunately arise.

To conclude, as is commonly assumed in the related literature, the implications of indeterminacy problems in this chapter can be synthesized as follows: two identically endowed economies with identical initial conditions may consume, and invest in the production of, natural and physical capital at completely different rates. Only in the long run will those economies converge to the same growth rate, but not to the same level of output and natural and physical capital. It is therefore possible to consider other cultural, historical or non-

Table 9.1 Results of the equilibrium analysis

$\gamma < 0$	$T^* = \nu E > 1$ (unique equilibrium)	$E_t = E_0 e^{-\varphi t}$
$0 < \gamma < \dfrac{\rho(1-\alpha)}{\delta(1-\sigma)}$	$T^* = \nu E < 0$ (unique equilibrium)	$E_t = E_0 e^{\varphi t}$
$\gamma > \dfrac{\rho(1-\alpha)}{\delta(1-\sigma)}$	$T^* = \nu E < 1$ (multiple equilibrium)	$E_t = E_0 e^{\varphi t}$

economic factors as the means for equilibria to differ on the transition path to be followed. Indeed, we refer here to local indeterminacy, and the coexistence of multiple balanced growth paths, as the device by which to theoretically reinterpret the possibility for different regions, identically endowed in terms of existing natural resources, to exhibit uneven economic development when a tourism sector is allowed to use the visited place in, hopefully, a sustainable way.

The positive implication of this chapter can be the following: given the different allocation of natural resources across countries, and assuming that multiple equilibria may exist, it is no wonder that a clear convergence among the world's economies is not observed. In the management of their natural resources, we may notice instead that, meanwhile, some countries have lagged permanently behind as a result of short-sighted policies, while others have experienced higher growth rates as a result of adopting more sustainable behaviour. It might be that a historically stagnant region continues to be so, while other regions, perhaps historically more active, may continue to flourish, even though they are the same in all other respects. History matters, then, and the management of the natural resources, perhaps directed through tourism policies, may thus act as a selection device among these different equilibria.

Further, it can be worth noting that a positive relationship does exist between the externality parameter, γ, and the inverse of the intertemporal elasticity of substitution, σ – that is, $\partial\gamma/\partial\sigma > 0$.[11] But we commonly know that the higher is σ, the less willing are supposed households to accept a deviation from a uniform pattern of consumption over time (see Barro and Sala-i-Martin, 2004). Therefore, as considered before, if we let γ represent the impact of non-use value on output production, we can finally state that a rise in σ must necessarily be accompanied by an increase in the bequest value of the natural resource we are dealing with, if we want an optimal solution that can be maintained over time – or, in other words, that the value assigned to the natural capital will rise as the need for a constant consumption increases, if we want all generations behave in a sustainable way.

9.4 Concluding remarks

The literature on tourism unfortunately lacks a sophisticated theoretical foundation, even though new work has been recently issued in this field to bridge the gap. To shed some light in this field, I have presented a model to answer the question of whether countries with similar tourist industries may exhibit very different growth experiences, arguing that a crucial aspect for the occurrence of both indeterminacy and cyclical adjustment towards the steady state might be the presence of an externality associated with natural capital in the production of final output.

Many works in macroeconomics have focused on models with multiple, or indeterminate, equilibria (see, among others, Benhabib and Perli, 1994: 113; Boldrin and Rustichini, 1994: 323; Matsuyama, 1991: 587; Boldrin *et al.*, 2001: 97), though never in the field of tourism economics, to the best of my knowledge. In such macroeconomic models, the resulting possibility of a continuum of equilibria, or indeterminacy of equilibria, arises because of market imperfections that may come from increasing returns to scale in production, often driven by external effects. It is therefore the nature of such non-competitive markets that allows for a multiplicity of equilibria.

I follow the same approach in this chapter and provide a model to better determine the properties of such external effects in generating multiple equilibria, whenever the presence of a tourism sector is assumed to influence the fundamentals of our economy. Conclusions to the analysis confirm that such externality matters in the transition towards a long-run sustainable equilibrium, but only after a certain thresholdhas been passed, thus leaving space for other, more complicated dynamic phenomena.

Appendix

Given the following current value Hamiltonian:

$$H_C = \frac{c^{1-\sigma}-1}{1-\sigma} + \lambda\left[Ak^\alpha(vE)^{1-\alpha}E_a^\gamma - c\right] + \mu\left[\delta E(1-vE)\right]$$

where λ and μ represent the shadow prices of physical and natural capital, respectively, the first-order condition for a maximum requires that the discounted Hamiltonian be maximized with respect to its control variables – that is:

$$\frac{\partial H_C}{\partial c} = c^{-\sigma} - \lambda = 0 \tag{9.A1}$$

$$\frac{\partial H_C}{\partial v} = \lambda(1-\alpha)Ak^\alpha v^{-\alpha}E^{1-\alpha+\gamma} - \mu\delta E^2 = 0 \tag{9.A2}$$

accompanied by the law of motion of each costate variable

$$\frac{\dot{\lambda}}{\lambda} = \rho - \alpha Ak^{\alpha-1}v^{1-\alpha}E^{1-\alpha+\gamma} \tag{9.A3}$$

$$\frac{\dot{\mu}}{\mu} = \rho - \delta(1-vE) \tag{9.A4}$$

Moreover, since either Arrow's or Mangasarian's second-order conditions both drive to a complex calculation, we take advantage of a more general sufficient condition, following Asada et al. (1998), according to which the optimal control problem is maximized whenever the Hamiltonian function is jointly concave in the control variables, as we can easily verify in our problem, for the minors of the Hessian matrix associated to H_C

$$\mathbf{H} = \begin{bmatrix} \frac{\partial^2 H_C}{\partial c^2} & \frac{\partial^2 H_C}{\partial c \partial v} \\ \frac{\partial^2 H_C}{\partial v \partial c} & \frac{\partial^2 H_C}{\partial v^2} \end{bmatrix}$$

do exhibit the following sequence $\mathbf{H}_1 < 0$, and $\mathbf{H}_2 > 0$, given $\dfrac{\partial^2 H_c}{\partial c^2} = -\sigma c^{-\sigma-1}$, $\dfrac{\partial^2 H_c}{\partial v^2} = -\lambda\alpha(1-\alpha)Ak^\alpha v^{-\alpha}E^{1-\alpha+\gamma}$, and $\dfrac{\partial^2 H_c}{\partial c\partial v} = \dfrac{\partial^2 H_c}{\partial v\partial c} = 0$.

To add more, given the constraints on both physical and natural capital:

$$\dot{k} = Ak^\alpha(vE)^{1-\alpha}E_a^\gamma - c$$

$$\dot{E} = \delta E(1-vE)$$

and rearranging equations (9.A1)–(9.A4) in terms of growth rates, with a little bit of mathematical manipulation we can derive the four-dimensional system of first-order differential equations, *S1*:

$$\xi_k = \frac{\dot{k}}{k} = Ak^{\alpha-1}v^{1-\alpha}E^{1-\alpha+\gamma} - \frac{c}{k}$$

$$\xi_E = \frac{\dot{E}}{E} = \delta(1-vE)$$

$$\xi_c = \frac{\dot{c}}{c} = -\frac{\rho}{\sigma} + \frac{\alpha}{\sigma}Ak^{\alpha-1}v^{1-\alpha}E^{1-\alpha+\gamma}$$

$$\xi_v = \frac{\dot{v}}{v} = (\gamma-\alpha)\frac{\delta}{\alpha}(1-vE) - \frac{c}{k}$$

or rather the more tractable reduced system, *S2*:

$$\dot{x} = -\frac{\rho}{\sigma}x + \left(\frac{\alpha-\sigma}{\sigma}\right)mx + x^2$$

$$\dot{q} = \frac{\gamma\delta}{\alpha}(1-q)q - xq$$

$$\dot{m} = (\alpha-1)m^2 + \frac{\gamma\delta}{\alpha}(1-q)m$$

by means of the convenient variable substitution: $x=c/k$, $q=vE$, and $m=y/k$, with the associated optimal steady-state values:

$$m^* = \frac{\rho}{\alpha(1-\sigma)}$$

$$x^* = \frac{\rho(1-\alpha)}{\alpha(1-\sigma)}$$

$$q^* = 1 - \frac{\rho(1-\alpha)}{\gamma\delta(1-\sigma)}$$

whose positiveness requires $0 < \sigma < 1$.

The Jacobian matrix of the reduced system *S2* is then

$$J = \begin{bmatrix} J_{11} & J_{12} & J_{13} \\ J_{21} & J_{22} & J_{23} \\ J_{31} & J_{32} & J_{33} \end{bmatrix}$$

where:

$$J_{11} = x; \; J_{12} = 0; \; J_{13} = \left(\tfrac{\alpha-\sigma}{\sigma}\right)x;$$

$$J_{21} = -q; \; J_{22} = -\tfrac{\gamma\delta}{\alpha}q; \; J_{23} = 0;$$

$$J_{31} = 0; \; J_{32} = -\tfrac{\gamma\delta}{\alpha}m; \; J_{33} = (\alpha-1)m.$$

Hence, the Jacobian evaluated at the steady state finally becomes

$$J_{(x^*,q^*,m^*)} = \begin{bmatrix} \frac{\rho(1-\alpha)}{\alpha(1-\sigma)} & 0 & \frac{\rho(1-\alpha)(\alpha-\sigma)}{\alpha\sigma(1-\sigma)} \\ 1 - \frac{\rho(1-\alpha)}{\gamma\delta(1-\sigma)} & \frac{\rho(1-\alpha)}{\alpha(1-\sigma)} - \frac{\gamma\delta}{\alpha} & 0 \\ 0 & -\frac{\rho\gamma\delta}{\alpha^2(1-\sigma)} & \frac{\rho(\alpha-1)}{\alpha(1-\sigma)} \end{bmatrix}$$

and therefore

$$trJ = \frac{\rho(1-\alpha)}{\alpha(1-\sigma)} - \frac{\gamma\delta}{\alpha} < 0$$

$$DetJ = \frac{\gamma\delta(1-\sigma)}{\sigma}mxq > 0$$

$$BJ = -\frac{\rho^2(1-\alpha)^2}{\alpha^2(1-\sigma)^2} < 0$$

$$-BJ + \frac{DetJ}{trJ} = \frac{1}{trJ}\frac{\rho^2(1-\alpha)}{\sigma\alpha^3(1-\sigma)^3}\left[\rho(1-\alpha)-\gamma\delta(1-\sigma)\right](\sigma-\alpha)$$

whose values may be useful to check for stability of the system by means of the aforementioned Routh–Hurwitz criterion.

Notes

1 An extensive interpretation of the well-known Butler theory provides us with three different scenarios that may eventually occur. In an unexplored area, the tourists are initially few in number and their number grows very slowly (exploration). Following this discovery period, there is a phase of rapid growth, in general accompanied by concomitant capital development (and resource harvesting), and finally a stagnation phase with environmental degradation (see Butler, 1980: 5).

2 To avoid confusion in the terminology used in this chapter, we will alternatively consider the terms 'natural capital', 'stock of natural resources' or 'environmental quality' as possible synonymns to identify the same environmental variable *E*.

3 The so-called Schaefer harvesting production function basically states that $H = \alpha SLH$, where H is the harvest of the natural stock, S, supplied to production by the LH labour force used in resource harvesting, and α is a positive constant parameter, commonly referred to as the 'harvestability' coefficient, that hereafter we set to unity for the sake of simplicity (see Schaefer, 1957: 669).

4 The famous Verhulst logistic equation describing the evolution of an x-population commonly takes the form

$$\dot{x} = rx\left(1 - \frac{x}{K}\right)$$

where r is called the intrinsic growth rate, and K is referred to as the carrying capacity, or the saturation level, of the natural site being considered. In our case, we simply assume that $r = \delta$, and $v = 1/K$.

5 Some authors, such as Pittel (2003), either leave v out of the analysis or assume $f(\cdot)$ to be strictly concave in E ($fEE < 0$) and of an inverted U-shape, with a maximum at a certain point called E^* ($fE > 0$ for $E < E^*$ and $fE < 0$ for $E > E^*$). This type of regeneration function was originally adopted to describe the population dynamics of fish stocks and other renewable resources, and later applied to the analysis of aggregate stocks of natural resources too (Smith, 1968: 409). A broad justification for this application follows from physics and is provided by Bovenberg and Smulders (1996). Conversely, others, such as Musu (1995), propose a linear representation of the regeneration function in (9.4), even though Rosendahl (1996) argues that it could be reasonably useful for those analyses where only the positively sloped arm of the hump-shaped regeneration function is of interest. Following the same argument, Aghion and Howitt (1998) provide an approximation for the development of nature along the negatively sloped arm of the hump-shaped function.

6 Various interpretations of the externality parameter, γ, can be given. Let us think, for example, of the positive spillover effect coming to the Sardinian archipelago of La Maddalena thanks to the presence of the beautiful, though undisposable, site of the famous 'pink beach'. On the contrary, consider the negative impact accruing to a natural site as a result of a severe climate change (see, for example, Berritella *et al.*, 2006: 913; and Hamilton *et al.*, 2005: 253).

7 The use value is derived from the direct utilization of the resource being considered, while the non-use value is generally referred to as the existence, or bequest, value that people derive from the intergenerational availability of the same resource (see, for example, Turner *et al.*, 1994).

8 A sufficient condition for concavity of the optimization problem is fully provided in the appendix to this chapter.

9 Given the characteristic equation associated with system $S2$,

$$-\kappa^3 + trJ^*\kappa^2 - BJ^*\kappa + DetJ^* = 0$$

where κ is the eigenvalue of the system, the Routh–Hurwitz theorem states that *the number of roots of the characteristic polynomial with positive real parts is equal to the number of variations of sign in the scheme*

$$-1 \quad trJ^* \quad -BJ^* + \frac{DetJ^*}{trJ^*} DetJ^*$$

10 The plausibility of indeterminacy problems due to the presence of externalities has been investigated in the empirical literature (see, for example, Caballero and Lyons, 1992: 209; Domowitz *et al.*, 1988: 55; Harrison, 2003: 963).

11 The result comes by implicitly differentiating the function expressing the optimal value of tourist arrivals, q^*, previously derived in Lemma 2.

166   *G. Bella*

References

Aghion, P. and Howitt, P. (eds) (1998) *Endogenous Growth Theory*, 2nd ed., Cambridge, MA: MIT Press.

Asada, T., Semmler, W. and Novak, A. J. (1998) 'Endogenous growth and the balanced growth equilibrium', *Research in Economics*, 52: 189–212.

Barro, R. J. and Sala-i-Martin, X. (eds) (2004) *Economic Growth*, Cambridge, MA: MIT Press.

Benhabib, J. and Perli, R. (1994) 'Uniqueness and indeterminacy: on the dynamics of endogenous growth', *Journal of Economic Theory*, 63: 113–142.

Berritella, M., Bigano, A., Roson, R. and Tol, R. S. J. (2006) 'A general equilibrium analysis of climate change impacts on tourism', *Tourism Management*, 27 (5): 913–924.

Boldrin, M. and Rustichini, A. (1994) 'Growth and indeterminacy in dynamic models with externalities', *Econometrica*, 62: 323–342.

Boldrin, M., Nishimura, K., Shigoka, T. and Yano, M. (2001) 'Chaotic equilibrium dynamics in endogenous growth models', *Journal of Economic Theory*, 96 (1–2): 97–132.

Bovenberg, A. L. and Smulders, S. (1996) 'Transitional impacts of environmental policy in an endogenous growth model', *International Economic Review*, 37: 861–893.

Brau, R., Lanza, A. and Pigliaru, F. (2007) 'How fast are small tourism countries growing? Evidence for the data 1980–2003', *Tourism Economics*, 13 (4): 603–614.

Bretschger, L. and Smulders, S. (2007) 'Sustainable resource use and economic dynamics', *Environmental and Resource Economics*, 36 (1): 1–13.

Budowski, G. (1976) 'Tourism and environmental conversation: conflict, coexistence or symbiosis?', *Environmental Conversation*, 3 (1): 27–31.

Butler, R. (1980) 'The concept of a tourist area cycle of evolution', *Canadian Geographer*, 24: 5–12.

Caballero, R. J. and Lyons, R. K. (1992) 'External effects in US productivity', *Journal of Monetary Economics*, 29: 209–226.

Candela, G. and Cellini, R. (2006) 'Investment in tourism market: a dynamic model of differentiated oligopoly', *Environmental and Resource Economics*, 35: 41–58.

Casagrandi, R. and Rinaldi, S. (2002) 'A theoretical approach to tourism sustainability', *Conservation Ecology*, 6 (1): 13–27.

Cerina, F. (2007) 'Tourism specialization and environmental sustainability in a dynamic economy', *Tourism Economics*, 13 (4): 553–582.

Costa, P. and Manente, M. (eds) (2000) *Economia del turismo*, Milan: Touring University Press.

Domowitz, I. R., Hubbard, G. and Peterson, B. C. (1988) 'Market structure and cyclical fluctuations in US manufacturing', *Review of Economics and Statistics*, 70: 55–66.

Giannoni, S. and Maupertuis, M. A. (2005) 'Environmental quality and long run tourism development a cyclical perspective for small island tourist economies', FEEM Working Paper, 145.05.

Gómez, M. A. (2005) 'Transitional dynamics in an endogenous growth model with physical capital, human capital and R&D', *Studies in Nonlinear Dynamics and Econometrics*, 9 (1).

Hamilton, J. M., Maddison, D. J. and Tol, R. S. J. (2005) 'Climate change and international tourism: a simulation study', *Global Environmental Change*, 15: 253–266.

Hardin, G. (1968) 'The tragedy of the commons', *Science*, 162: 1243–1248.

Harrison, S. G. (2003) 'Returns to scale and externalities in the consumption and investment sectors', *Review of Economic Dynamics*, 6 (4): 963–976.

Hillary, M., Nancarrow, B., Griffin, G. and Syme, G. (2001) 'Tourist perception of environmental impact', *Annals of Tourism Research*, 28 (4): 853–867.

Hughes, G. (2002) 'Environmental indicators', *Annals of Tourism Research*, 29: 457–477.

Ladrón-de-Guevara, A., Ortigueira, S. and Santos, M. S. (1997) 'Equilibrium dynamics in two-sector models of endogenous growth', *Journal of Economic Dynamics and Control*, 21: 115–143.

Lanza, A. and Pigliaru, F. (1994) 'The tourism sector in the open economy', *Rivista Internazionale di Scienze Economiche e Commerciali*, 41: 15–28.

Lanza, A. and Pigliaru, F. (2000) 'Tourism and economic growth: does country's size matter?', *Rivista Internazionale di Scienze Economiche e Commerciali*, 47: 77–85.

Lozano, J., Gómez, C. and Rey-Maquieira, J. (2005) 'An analysis of the evolution of tourism destinations from the point of view of the economic growth theory', FEEM Working Paper, 146.2005.

McElroy, J. L. (2006) 'Small island tourist economies across the life cycle', *Asia Pacific Viewpoint*, 47 (1): 61–77.

Matsuyama, K. (1991) 'Increasing returns, industrialization, and indeterminacy of equilibrium', *Quarterly Journal of Economics*, 106: 587–597.

Mattana, P. (ed.) (2004) *The Uzawa–Lucas Endogenous Growth Model*, Aldershot, UK: Ashgate.

Musu, I. (1995) 'Transitional dynamics to optimal sustainable growth', FEEM Working Paper, 50.95.

Nishimura, K. and Shigoka, T. (2006) 'Sunspots and Hopf bifurcations in continuous time endogenous growth models', *International Journal of Economic Theory*, 2 (3–4): 199–216.

Papatheodoru, A. (2003) 'Modelling tourism development: a synthetic approach', *Tourism Economics*, 9: 407–430.

Pittel, K. (ed.) (2003) *Sustainability and Endogenous Growth*, Cheltenham, UK: Edward Elgar.

Restrepo-Ochoa, S. I. and Vázquez, J. (2004) 'Cyclical features of the Uzawa–Lucas endogenous growth model', *Economic Modelling*, 21: 285–322.

Rosendahl, K. E. (1996) 'Does improved environmental policy enhance economic growth?', *Environmental and Resource Economics*, 9: 341–364.

Sachs, J. D. and Warner, A. M. (2001) 'Natural resources and economic development: the curse of natural resources', *European Economic Review*, 45: 827–838.

Schaefer, M. B. (1957) 'Some considerations of population dynamics and economics in relation to the management of marine fishes', *Journal of the Fisheries Research Board of Canada*, 14: 669–681.

Smeral, E. (2003) 'A structural view of tourism growth', *Tourism Economics*, 9: 77–93.

Smith, V. L. (1968) 'Economics of production from natural resources', *American Economic Review*, 58: 409–431.

Smulders, S. (1995) 'Environmental policy and sustainable economic growth: an endogenous growth perspective', *De Economist*, 143: 163–195.

Swarbrooke, J. (1999) *Sustainable Tourism Management*, Wallingford, UK: CABI.

Turner, K. R., Pearce, D. and Bateman, I. (1994) *Environmental Economics: An Elementary Introduction*, Baltimore: Johns Hopkins University Press.

Verhulst, P. F. (1838) 'Notice sur la loi que la population suit dans son accroissement', *Correspondance Mathématique et Physique*, 10: 113–121.

Xie, D. (1994) 'Divergence in economic performance: transitional dynamics with multiple equilibria', *Journal of Economic Theory*, 63: 97–112.

10 How tourism can help preserve cultural heritage sites

Constructing optimal entrance fee schemes to collect visitors' WTP for the World Heritage Site My Son in Vietnam

Tran Huu Tuan, Nguyen Van Phat and Ståle Navrud

10.1 Introduction

The tourism potential of World Cultural Heritage Sites can be very large, and can be used to help preserve these global public goods if optimal revenue collection schemes are constructed and implemented. We apply the contingent valuation (CV) method to estimate the economic benefits that would be created by a proposed plan to preserve and restore the World Heritage Site (WHS) My Son sanctuary in Vietnam. The study focuses on the benefits derived from foreign visitors and Vietnamese visitors to My Son.[1] The design, development and administration of the two CV survey instruments for foreign visitors and Vietnamese visitors are described, and data for the two groups are analysed. The study then discusses policy implications of the results, and the implications for revenue collection schemes that maximize revenue for the site.

This study is of obvious interest given that the estimation of economic value of cultural heritage conservation has increasingly been recognized as a fundamental part of cultural policy (Mourato and Mazzanti, 2002; Navrud and Ready, 2002; eftec, 2005) – that is, a need to document the social benefits of conservation works in order to justify the costs of the conservation. Estimating and expressing in monetary terms the economic benefits of perserving My Son is important because these benefits could give insight into the magnitude of the benefits and to show the respondents' willingness to pay (WTP) to preserve and restore the site. The study can also be very useful in informing decisions on designing pricing strategies (i.e. entrance fees) for cultural tourist destinations like My Son. Working out the demand for cultural assets, and particularly the price elasticity of the WTP for this site with different visitor groups, can help policy-makers to form a pricing policy that can regulate visitor flows and maximize visitor revenues for this tourist destination.

The rest of this chapter is structured as follows. Section 10.2 describes the theoretical framework, study site and survey, and development of the CV questionnaire. Section 10.3 presents respondents' perceptions, knowledge and attitudes, socio-economic characteristics, and how these affect their WTP. We also estimate the income elasticity of WTP and analyse no-responses to pay and protest responses. WTP estimates are presented and aggregate WTP are calculated in order for us to assess the total social benefits. Section 10.4 estimates optimal entrance fees that maximize revenues from visitors. Section 10.5 concludes the study with a discussion of opportunities for future research in this area.

10.2 Methodology

10.2.1 Theoretical framework

The CV method (Mitchell and Carson, 1989) was used to elicit the economic benefits of the preservation and improvement of the My Son cultural heritage. The individual's compensating variation for the proposed improvement is given by:

$$U(Y, Q_0) = U(Y - WTP, Q_1) \tag{10.1}$$

where U represents the indirect utility function of an individual, Y is the income level, Q_0 is the current condition of the site, Q_1 is the improved condition, and WTP is interpreted as the maximum amount that the individual would be willing to pay to secure the improvement.

For empirical estimation, the WTP welfare measure is specified as:

$$WTP_i = X_i \beta' + \varepsilon_i \tag{10.2}$$

where X_i represents a vector of explanatory variables, β is a vector of parameters, and ε_i is the error term reflecting unobserved taste components. The parameters of this equation can be estimated by the maximum likelihood method (Cameron, 1988).

The total benefits can be calculated by summing up the aggregate benefit for each group of respondents. With each group, we aggregate using the sample mean WTP multiplied by the corresponding number of visitors. The sample of each group is randomly selected and is assumed to be representative of all visitors of that group to My Son in the year of study.

10.2.2 Study site and survey

The My Son sanctuary dates back to the fouth century and was a flourishing cultural centre until the thirteenth century (UNESCO, 1999). It is considered one of the main Hindu temple complexes in South-East Asia and is the sole example of its kind in Vietnam. Located in Quangnam province in central Vietnam, My Son represents the height of Cham architectural achievement. It is a large complex of temples and originally comprised more than 70 structures, 25 of which remain today (GHF, 2002). In December 1999, My Son was listed as a UNESCO World Cultural Heritage Site (WHS) for the following main reasons: (1) it is an exceptional example of cultural interchange, which exemplifies the introduction of the Hindu architecture of the Indian subcontinent into South-East Asia; and (2) the Champa Kingdom was an important phenomenon in the political and cultural history of South-East Asia, and is vividly illustrated by the ruins of My Son.

Immediately after UNESCO recognized My Son as a WHS, the number of visitors to the site soared by 40 per cent per year. It has now become a major tourist destination, attracting more than 100,000 Vietnamese and foreign visitors per year. The development of tourism in this area has helped to improve cultural exchange and to raise the living standards of local people (Weitzel, 2000; Tuan, 2006).

In spite of its cultural importance to society, My Son is severely threatened with degradation and loss (see Kinh, 2001; VNS, 2003). Natural factors that have damaged the site include soil erosion, landslides, floods and the unforgiving tropical climate. However, human activities are arguably the main cause of the site's degradation and destruction. These include wars, neglect and tourism pressure. As a result of all these problems, this unique site is now in a state of significant disrepair and urgently requires conservation.

In order to measure the potential benefits accruing to visitors to My Son, two CV surveys have been conducted with foreign visitors and Vietnamese visitors. For foreign visitors, the survey was conducted at My Son. Also, a number of interviews were carried out with foreign visitors to My Son on board tourist buses on the routes between My Son and Hue (a city 170 kilometres north of My Son) and Hoian (a town 60 kilometres east of My Son). Hue and Hoian are selected for this survey as they are two of the main tourist destinations in Vietnam and are where most visitors stay during their trips to My Son. The sample consisted of 243 interviews. For Vietnamese visitors, the survey was conducted at My Son with 245 interviews. These surveys were conducted in the summer of 2005.

10.2.3 Development of CV questionnaires

Two questionnaire instruments were used for the CV surveys with foreign visitors and Vietnamese visitors. For foreign visitors, the questionnaire had English and French versions. This questionnaire instrument was written in English and revised until it reached its final version. The final English version was then translated into French. The questionnaires used for the Vietnamese visitors were written in Vietnamese.

This subsection presents the questionnaire for foreign visitors and comments, where appropriate, on the other questionnaire used with the Vietnamese visitors. The questionnaire for foreign visitors was divided into six main sections.

Section I consisted of some questions that investigated the general perceptions of respondents towards the importance of cultural heritage preservation. Questions related to attitudes of foreign visitors to Vietnam and My Son, their reasons for visiting Vietnam and My Son, their knowledge of My Son before visiting, their travel experiences in Vietnam and their attitudes to My Son.

Section II consisted of a clear description of My Son using text, maps and photos. It described the good that the respondents were asked to value. The purpose of this section was to provide each respondent with the same set of information about the characteristics and the condition of My Son today. This current scenario was presented as the status quo, and it was explained that under this existing state of affairs the deterioration of My Son would continue because insufficient resources are available for its preservation. Then the proposed preservation plan was presented. It was explained that the plan would improve the condition of My Son and preserve the site for the future. Table 10.1 gives a detailed description of the information provided to respondents.

Section III described the information related to means of payment, elicitation methods, and bid amounts used in the questionnaire. For the means of payment, a one-time special fee (levied via an increase in the entrance fee) was used. The entrance fee was detailed as a mandatory (not voluntary) payment to give respondents an incentive to state truthfully their preferences for the preservation of My Son.

Details of the elicitation methods were posed as in Table 10.2. This was done because the standard referendum-type question would not be meaningful to non-residents. This way of framing the CV question reminded respondents that they could visit other, 'substitute' sites that were already on their itinerary or could be added to their itinerary. It forced them to consider whether My Son would still be worth visiting if the cost of a visit were increased by the stated amount. These bid amounts were stated in US dollars with four price points of $1, $5, $10 and $15. For Vietnamese visitors, bid amounts were stated in local currency, equivalent to $0.31, $1.26, $3.14 and $6.29.

Section IV of the questionnaires included debriefing questions to detect the prevalence of embedding or strategic behaviour. Section V collected socioeconomic data such as sex, age, educational attainment, employment status and income level. These data were used in a regression analysis. Section VI contained interview evaluation questions designed to provide feedback from all interviewers about the interview situation, how respondents attended to the interview and any difficulties the respondents may have had.

10.3 Results and discussions

10.3.1 Public perceptions towards the importance of preserving cultural heritage

A number of perceptional statements were included to seek respondents' underlying motives for supporting the preservation of WHSs in Vietnam. Respondents were asked to rate the relative importance of these statements (Table 10.3). The first question asked respondents how important it was to have these sites so that they could visit them now. This question was aimed at revealing whether respondents had any direct experience of these cultural heritage sites. Ninety-six per cent of foreign visitors and 90 per cent of Vietnamese visitors agreed with

Table 10.1 Description of the scenario provided to respondents

Text read by interviewer	Description of visual aids used
As you may know, My Son is the most important Cham temple complex in Vietnam. Because of its uniqueness it was listed by UNESCO as a World Heritage Site in 1999.	This card contains an aerial image of My Son and a number of pictures of the My Son temples that remain today.
Description of the My Son: My Son was inhabited from the 4th until the 15th centuries AD, far longer than any of the other Indian-influenced sites in South-East Asia. This complex of temples originally comprised more than 70 temples. The vestiges of 25 of these temples remain today.	
Current condition of My Son: My Son was once a veritable forest of temples, many of which were destroyed (as shown in photo card A) by the ravages of time, war and a lack of awareness.	Photo card A contains a number of pictures of the collapsed and ruined temples.
Unfortunately, government resources are too limited to keep up with the need for preservation and restoration. As a result, many temples continue to deteriorate year by year; many others collapse before they can be restored.	Photo card B shows a number of pictures of recently restored temples.
Despite the efforts of government and other agencies that have helped to maintain some of the temples, as seen in photo card B, many of the important temples have become run down, such as the temples in photo card C. Many other temples urgently need refurbishing to keep them from further degrading.	Photo card C contains pictures of temples that have already collapsed or are in danger of collapsing.
There is a concern that if a major effort is not undertaken, the My Son temples will rapidly degrade and many will soon collapse, losing their historical character for ever.	
A proposed preservation project: The Vietnamese government, in collaboration with experts from international agencies, has developed a plan to preserve the My Son sanctuary. If it is implemented, the plan will: • Stop any further degradation of the remaining temples and avoid any further irreversible loss. • Ensure that these temples will remain as part of the cultural heritage of future generations.	Photo card D shows the two things that the preservation plan will accomplish if the plan is implemented.

Table 10.2 The CV question for foreign visitors to My Son

1. Still visit My Son even though the entrance fee would <u>add</u> US$ – per adult to the cost of your visit
Or
2. Not to include My Son in your itinerary for this trip and use the money for other purposes.

this statement. Note that a lower percentage of Vietnamese visitors agreed with this statement (and the difference in this statement between the two groups is significant), which reflects use values of these sites.

The second question was asked in order to discover how important it was to have these sites so that other people can visit them at the present time. This statement would suggest that the sites had some non-use values in terms of option or/ and existence values. The majority of respondents agreed with this statement.

Bequest value is the other non-use value component; it refers to benefits from ensuring that cultural heritage sites will be preserved for future generations. Nearly all respondents in both surveys agreed with this statement, indicating that visitors believe that the preservation of WHSs benefited future generations.

Statements 4 and 5 were intended to discover whether respondents believed that the temples had 'existence value' and therefore they had a duty to protect them. A majority of respondents agreed with these statements.

It is worth noting that there were no significant differences in the statements 2, 3 and 4 between the two surveys. Further, as regards all the statements, the percentage of foreign visitors registering agreement was higher than that for Vietnamese visitors. This difference in respondents' perceptions may have an impact on the WTP of these two groups of respondents.

There are significant differences between the two groups regarding statements 5, 6 and 7. The difference for statements 6 and 7 implies that foreign visitors are more concerned with the loss to the sites and the benefits to local people than Vietnamese visitors are.

Socio-demographic characteristics, knowledge and attitude of respondents

Table 10.4 describes some socio-demographic characteristics of respondents. It is observed that fewer females were interviewed in the surveys. This could be explained by the fact that during field interviews, there were some couples for whom the task of answering questions was delegated to their husbands. Further, the rate of non-participation and incomplete interviews for females is higher than for male respondents.

Table 10.4 shows that the survey respondents are relatively young, averaging 33 and 37 years of age for foreign and Vietnamese visitors, respectively. The mean annual household income of foreign visitors is much higher than for

Table 10.3 Respondents' perceptions towards the importance of preserving World Heritage Sites

Variables	Description	Foreign visitors Mean (Std)	Vietnamese visitors Mean (Std)	T-test p-value
Attitude 1 (use value)	It is important to have these sites so that you can visit them now.	0.96 (0.189)	90 (0.292)	0.03
Attitude 2 (non-use)	It is important to have these temples so that other people can visit them now.	0.95 (0.208)	0.92 (0.268)	0.26
Attitude 3 (bequest)	It is important to have these sites so that future generations can visit them.	0.98 (0.110)	0.95 (0.198)	0.13
Attitude 4 (existence)	It is important to have these sites because they inspire pride in Vietnamese heritage.	0.95 (0.217)	0.95 (0.198)	0.47
Attitude 5 (existence)	It is important to have these sites to remember events in history.	0.98 (0.110)	0.94 (0.232)	0.02
Attitude 6	It is important to preserve these sites because they could be an irreversible loss.	0.97 (0.142)	0.93 (0.254)	0.02
Attitude 7	It is important to have these sites because local residents could benefit from them.	0.93 (0.248)	0.77 (0.415)	0.00

Table 10.4 Respondents' socio-demographic characteristics

	Foreign visitors Mean (Std)	Vietnamese visitors Mean (Std)
Sex (sex = 1 for female, 0 for male)	0.46 (0.50)	0.37 (0.48)
Age (age of respondents, years)	33.41 (10.91)	37.26 (12.13)
Income (household yearly income, US$)	57,075 (40,834)	1,328 (525)
Education (1 = primary; 2 = secondary; 3 = high school; 4 = college; and 5 = graduate)	3.63 (0.87)	3.64 (0.84)
Alone (= 1 if the visitor is travelling alone)	0.44 (0.50)	0.42 (0.49)
Number of respondents	243	245

Vietnamese visitors, as was expected. The education level of the two groups is fairly similar. Because trip costs can be influenced by the number of family members and the means of payment was in terms of entrance fee per adult, the variable *Alone* was introduced. Forty-four per cent and 42 per cent of foreign and Vietnamese visitors travelled alone, respectively.

Table 10.5 shows the mean values and standard deviations of respondents' knowledge and attitudes. Several variables measured the respondents' knowledge and attitudes towards My Son. The first variable was visitors' knowledge of My Son before they visited the site (*Know*). Overall, previous knowledge of My Son was very low. Most foreigners knew 'nothing' or 'only a little' about My Son before they visited it. For Vietnamese, most of them knew 'only a little' or 'a fair amount' about My Son.

The second variable concerned the respondents' views regarding the importance of the existence of WHSs in Vietnam (*Importance*). Sixty-seven per cent of the foreign and 73 per cent of Vietnamese visitors thought that the WHSs' existence in Vietnam was important.

The third variable sought the most important reason for the respondents' trip to Vietnam. If visitors wanted to visit historical cities, *Hcity* was coded as one. If visitors selected other possible reasons such as beaches, the countryside, modern cities and others, *Hcity* coded as zero. This variable was only used for foreign visitors; 41 per cent of them selected historical cities as the first reason to visit Vietnam.

The variables *Hue* and *Hoian* assessed whether respondents had visited either of these two 'competing' destinations (Hue and Hoian are both UNESCO World Cultural Heritage Sites). Hue is fairly distant from My Son while Hoian is fairly close by. Sixty per cent and 79 per cent of foreign and Vietnamese visitors, respectively, had previously visited Hue. Ninety per cent of foreign visitors had previously visited Hoian, while 83 per cent of Vietnamese visitors had visited Hoian.

Other variables used to explain the variation in respondents' WTP included *Visit*, *Satisfied*, *Ftrip* and *Before*. *Visit* was defined as whether a respondent had

Table 10.5 Respondent's knowledge and attitudes

Variable	Foreign visitors Mean (Std)	Vietnamese visitors Mean (Std)
Know (visitor's knowledge of My Son before visited the site, scale from 1 to 5, where 1 = nothing and 5 = very much)	1.82 (0.65)	2.78 (1.04)
Importance (1 if visitors regard the existence of WHSs in Vietnam as important, 0 otherwise)	0.67 (0.47)	0.73 (0.45)
Hcity (1 if visitors selected historical cities as the first reason for the visit to Vietnam)	0.41 (0.49)	–
Hue (1 if visitors had visited Hue before)	0.60 (0.49)	0.79 (0.41)
Hoian (1 if visitors had visited Hoian before)	0.90 (0.30)	0.83 (0.38)
Visit (1 if visitors had visited My Son before)	–	0.15 (0.36)
Satisfied (1 if visitors are satisfied with their experience of visiting My Son)	0.68 (0.47)	0.81 (0.39)
Ftrip (1 if respondents are considering visiting My Son again sometime in the future).	0.29 (0.45)	0.65 (0.49)
Before (1 if visitors were interviewed before visiting My Son and 0 otherwise)	0.36 (0.48)	0.26 (0.44)
Number of respondents	243	245

visited My Son before. Because most foreign visitors in the survey were visiting My Son for the first time, this variable was only used for the Vietnamese visitors, of whom 15 per cent had previously visited My Son.

Satisfied investigated the respondents' satisfaction with their visit to My Son. Sixty-eight per cent of foreign visitors were satisfied with their visit, while 81 per cent of Vietnamese visitors were satisfied.

Ftrip measured whether visitors were considering visiting My Son again sometime in the future. Twenty-nine per cent and 65 per cent of foreign and Vietnamese visitors, respectively, wished to visit My Son again. This result seems to us reasonable, since Vietnamese visitors are rather close to My Son; thus, a visit to the site may be more likely to feature in their choice of trips in the futuure. Foreigners have more substitute sites they could visit than Vietnamese visitors.

Finally, *Before* was defined as whether visitors were interviewed before they had visited My Son. Thirty-six per cent and 26 per cent of foreign and Vietnamese visitors, respectively, were interviewed before they visited My Son.

10.3.2 Determinants of the WTP

To examine the construct validity of the CV results, valuation functions are estimated. The dependent variable is the discrete yes/no response to the WTP question. The explanatory variables are the bid amount the respondent was asked, the respondent's socio-economic characteristics, and the knowledge and attitude variables described above. Two binary logit models, one for each group of respondents, are estimated and reported in Table 10.6.

Results show that valuation functions achieve relatively good fits. The coefficients of *bids* are statistically significant and negative, implying that the probability of a 'yes' response decreases as the bid increases, which is consistent with economic theory.

For foreign visitors, many variables in the model have the expected signs and are significant. The probability of a 'yes' response increases for a respondent who has higher income (*Income*), has attended college (*Ugo*), wants to visit historical cities (*Hcity*), is satisfied with his or her visit (*satisfied*) and wants to return to My Son (*Ftrip*). The probability of a 'yes' response decreases if the respondent is being asked about the preservation plan *before* visiting My Son. Thus, having experienced the site increases the probability of paying.

For Vietnamese visitors, the importance they attach to the existence of WHSs in Vietnam (*Importance*), the satisfied experience of visiting My Son (*Satisfied*) and the consideration of returning to My Son in the future (*Ftrip*) all have an expected positive and significant effect on the probability of a 'yes' response. Having attended college (*Ugo*) has a positive and significant (at 10 per cent level) effect on the probability of accepting a 'yes' response.

Table 10.6 Estimated parameters of the logit models

Variables	Foreign visitors (p-value)	Vietnamese visitors (p-value)
Constant	−1.23 (0.112)	−3.75 (0.020)**
Bids	−0.41 (0.000)***	−0.02 (0.000)***
Sex	0.0004 (0.654)	0.0001 (0.955)
Age	−0.003 (0.856)	−0.002 (0.501)
Income	0.002 (0.002)***	0.001 (0.582)
Ugo	1.47 (0.002)***	0.63 (0.076)*
Alone	−0.13 (0.759)	0.18 (0.608)
Hcity	1.56 (0.001)***	−
Hue	−0.61D−4 (0.935)	−0.003 (0.114)
Hoian	0.001 (0.582)	−0.005 (0.831)
Visit	−	−0.41 (0.383)
Importance	0.74 (0.118)	0.03 (0.000)***
Know	0.004 (0.938)	0.68 (0.148)
Satisfied	2.21 (0.000)***	2.31 (0.000)***
Ftrip	2.27 (0.000)***	2.30 (0.001)***
Before	−1.97 (0.000)***	0.59 (0.181)
Log-likelihood	−77.46	−111.99
Pseudo-R^2	0.54	0.33
Chi-squared	181.85	110.04
Number of observations	243	245

Notes
*** Significance level at 1 per cent or lower; ** significance level at 5 per cent; * significance level at 10 per cent.

Visiting Hue (*Hue*) and Hoian (*Hoian*) do not have a significant impact on WTP for My Son, either for foreign or for Vietnamese visitors.

Overall, this shows a high degree of construct validity of the valuation functions for both foreign and Vietnamese visitors as most determinants of WTP are significant and have a priori expected signs.

10.3.3 Analysis of the income elasticity of WTP

WTP for a discrete change in a public good (z) from an initial level z_0 to a higher level z_1 can be defined from indirect utility function as follows:

$$V(q, y - WTP, z_1) = V(q, y, z_0)$$

where q is an *n*-vector of market prices of private goods, p is the price of the public good, and y is income.

WTP is estimated from a valuation function. Income is included as an explanatory variable in the valuation function. Income elasticity of WTP (ε_{WTP}) is calculated as

$$\varepsilon_{WTP} = \frac{y}{WTP} * \frac{\partial WTP}{\partial y}.$$

The estimated results of income elasticity of the WTP (ε_{WTP}) are 0.04 and 0.02 for foreign and Vietnamese visitors, respectively. These are both greater than zero but smaller than unity, which means that the WTP is not very sensitive to changes in income. This suggests that improvements in cultural heritage would be relatively more beneficial to low-income visitors than to high-income visitors.

This result is consistent with results found in the literature. For instance, Kriström and Riera (1996) estimated the income elasticity of WTP for environmental improvements from a number of European data sets. They found that the income elasticity of WTP is consistently less than 1, with a few exceptions. Hokby and Soderqvist (2003) presented 21 estimates of the income elasticity of WTP for environmental services in Sweden ranging from −0.71 to 2.83, and the majority of the estimates were in the lower part of this range.

10.3.4 Analysis of 'no' responses and protest responses

Respondents refusing to pay were asked about the reasons for their reply. A series of reply options in the follow-up question were provided in order to determine whether those unwilling to pay represent a real 'no' or a protest about some aspect of the CV scenario.

A common approach the majority of CV practitioners apply in order to identify protest responses is to classify 'no' responses into: (1) those associated with a rejection of the payment vehicle; (2) 'no' responses related to other reasons than lack of current or future use benefits; and (3) 'no' responses linked to reasons other than ability to pay or budget constraints (see Sutherland and Walsh, 1985; Edwards and Anderson, 1987; Jorgensen *et al.*, 1999).

Our classification of genuine 'no' and protest responses is presented in Table 10.7. The debriefing question had 11 response categories plus an 'other reasons' category. The first two categories represent valid reasons for indicating that the respondent receives no benefits from the preservation programme or faces budget constraints. The remaining ten categories are classified as protest responses.

10.3.5 Mean WTP and WTP as a fraction of income

Table 10.8 reports mean WTP estimates from the two surveys. Mean WTP values are computed using the sample means of all variables in the logit models.

The results show that foreign visitors would be willing to pay much more than Vietnamese visitors: $8.78 and $2.27 for foreigners and Vietnamese, respectively. This result is in line with a general pattern found in the literature, e.g. Mourato *et al.* (2004) and Navrud and Vondolia (2005), and also in economic theory (i.e. foreign visitors have higher incomes and spend more for a visit to My Son than Vietnamese visitors do). However, if we look at the WTP as a fraction of household income, foreign visitors' WTP constitutes a much smaller part of annual household income than Vietnamese visitors' WTP.

Table 10.7 Reasons for respondents not being willing to pay

Respondent's reasons for not paying	Foreign visitors	Vietnamese visitors
1. I have no spare income*	8 (6.7)	34 (24.1)
2. I think the cost is too high*	67 (56.3)	34 (24.1)
3. If an acceptable method of paying is found	6 (5.0)	19 (13.5)
4. I would pay if other people agree to pay	2 (1.7)	13 (9.2)
5. I would pay if the payment period is extended	0	3 (2.1)
6. There are other sites that I prefer to visit	2 (1.7)	3 (2.1)
7. The preservation of My Son is unimportant	0	2 (1.4)
8. I do not believe paying will solve the problem	3 (2.5)	3 (2.1)
9. It is the government's responsibility	20 (16.8)	10 (7.1)
10. I do not trust the institutions that will handle the money for preservation work	3 (2.5)	5 (3.5)
11. I oppose the plan regardless of costs	0	1 (0.7)
12. Other reasons	6 (5.0)	9 (6.4)
13. Don't know/Not sure	2 (1.7)	5 (3.5)
Total respondents not WTP	119	141

Note
Number of respondents stating different reasons (percentages in parentheses); asterisked categories are classified as genuine 'no' responses.

Table 10.8 Mean WTP estimates

	Foreign visitors	Vietnamese visitors
Mean WTP (US$)	8.78	2.27
WTP as per centage of household income (per cent)	0.02	0.17

The next section presents mean WTP estimates for both including and excluding protest responses for each group of respondents. Table 10.9 presents the parametric estimates of the mean WTP for each group of respondents. The confidence intervals for the parametric estimates were obtained by using the Delta method (Greene, 2000).

Including protest responses in the WTP analysis, which means treating all 'no' responses as zero, the WTP estimates are lower for all groups of respondents (Table 10.9). On average, the WTP estimates with protest responses are 16 per cent lower than when protest responses are removed from the sample (to reflect the fact that their real WTP is positive). In the following sections, we will use the results from the sample where protest responses are included. This will provide a conservative estimate of the benefits.

10.3.6 Aggregation of WTP estimates

Table 10.10 describes the aggregate WTP estimates for each group of visitors. For both groups, the CV question asked for a one-time payment rather than annual payments. The issue is mainly to emphasize the idea that the preservation plan is a one-time project – that is, the temples could not be restored repeatedly over time. Therefore, in order to calculate the annual benefits over a period of time, the issue of repeat visits should be noted.

For foreign visitors, nevertheless, results of the survey show that most of them visited My Son just once (241 out of 243 foreigners were visiting My Son for the first time). Thus, in this particular case an aggregate estimate of the annual benefits can be obtained by multiplying the mean WTP by the number of foreign visitors to My Son (assuming that all foreigners visit My Son just once in their lifetime). According to the site management, the number of adult foreign visitors to My Son in 2005 is 86,461. This yields an estimate of $759,128.

Table 10.9 Mean WTP estimates (US$)

	Foreign visitors	Vietnamese visitors
Including protest responses	8.78 [7.53–10.02]	2.27 [1.47–3.08]
Excluding protest responses	9.80 [8.56–11.05]	2.72 [1.91–3.52]

Note
Numbers in square brackets are 95 per cent confidence intervals.

Table 10.10 Aggregate WTP estimates

Groups of respondents	Foreign visitors	Vietnamese visitors
Mean (US$)	8.78 [7.53–10.02]	2.27 [1.47–3.08]
Number of visitors	86,461	25,948
Aggregate WTP (US$)	759,128 [651,051–866,339]	58,930 [38,041–79,835]
Total	818,058 [689,092–946,174]	

Note
Numbers in square brackets are 95 per cent confidence intervals.

For Vietnamese visitors, results of the survey show that 15 per cent of them had visited My Son before; thus, we assume that 85 per cent of these visitors should be used in calculation of the annual benefits. This ad hoc adjustment provides a conservative estimate of the annual benefits for preserving My Son.

There were 30,527 adult Vietnamese visitors to My Son in 2005. With the above assumption, the adjusted number of Vietnamese visitors to My Son is 25,948, as shown in Table 10.10. This gives an estimate of $58,930. The aggregate benefits of the two groups are $818,058, with an interval ranging from $689,092 to $946,174.

10.4 Policy implications for maximizing revenues

From economic theory, given a demand curve for access to a given site, the economic value of access can be measured from the area under the curve. The entry price (entrance fee) chosen will divide this area into two parts, i.e. consumer surplus and revenue (Figure 10.1). The consumer surplus part is above the current price, which represents the value that accrues to visitors. In other words,

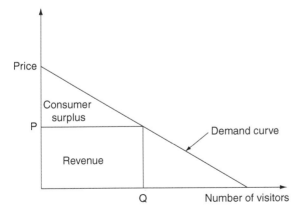

Figure 10.1 Demand curve for access to a given site.

consumer surplus is the value that visitors would have been prepared to pay for access to the site over and above the current entry price. The revenue part represents the value accrued to the site management and can be captured via entrance fees; for example, see Mourato *et al.* (2004).

In the next section, we estimate the optimal entrance fees that maximize revenues[2] for the site. The expected visitation rate and revenues at different entrance fees for foreign visitors and Vietnamese visitors are reported in Table 10.11.

For foreign visitors, with the current entrance fee of $4, 86,461 foreigners visited the site, yielding a total revenue of $345,844 in 2005. As the entrance fee increases, the percentage of those willing to visit decreases, as expected. However, the percentage decrease in visitation is less than the percentage increase in the entrance fee; thus, the expected revenue increases, reaching a maximimum at about $14. As the entrance fee exceeds $14, the expected revenue begins to decrease.

Note that this increase in entrance fees to maximize revenue would create side effects. This study shows that if entrance fees exceeded $14, the number of visitors would drop by 54 per cent compared to current numbers (because those whose WTP is less than the entrance charge would no longer visit the site). This would have an impact on the economy as the whole, depending on whether these people would visit other sites instead. Further, it is assumed that the marginal cost to the site of an additional visitor is constant.[3]

Table 10.11 also shows the expected visitation rate and revenue at different entrance fees for Vietnamese visitors to My Son. As the entrance fee increases, both the visitation rate and revenue decrease. The expected revenue is maximal at the current entrance fee of $1.89.

It is interesting to see that the expected revenue for foreign visitors is maximal at $14, which is 1.61 times higher than the current entrance fee, while the expected revenue of Vietnamese visitors is maximal at the current fee ($1.89). This suggests that in designing the pricing policy, more emphasis should be placed on foreign visitors than on Vietnamese visitors.

According to Table 10.11, if optimal entrance fees that maximize revenues were imposed, substantial annual revenues could be captured to finance the required preservation investments. For example, if the optimal entrance fees of

Table 10.11 Expected revenue at different entrance fees (optimal in bold)

Foreign visitors			Vietnamese visitors		
Entrance fee (US$)	*% visitors*	*Expected revenue (US$)*	*Entrance fee (US$)*	*% visitors*	*Expected revenue (US$)*
4	100	345,844	**1.89**	**100**	**57,598**
5	78	338,639	2.20	69	46,605
9	69	535,775	3.14	51	48,785
14	**46**	**555,618**	5.03	30	45,323
19	11	188,513	8.18	20	49,100

$14 for foreign visitors and $1.89 for Vietnamese visitors were imposed, the revenues generated would be $613,216 ($555,618 for foreign visitors and $57,598 for Vietnamese visitors). This would be 52 per cent higher than the current fee revenues. This policy recommendation would also reduce congestion[4] at My Son by reducing the number of foreign visitors by 54 per cent. For Vietnamese visitors, however, there is no decline in the visitation rate at the optimal entrance fee. Thus, overall, imposing the optimal charge for the Vietnamese visitors would not reduce the problem of congestion.

In order to deal with the congestion problem at My Son due to Vietnamese visitors, some possible solutions are discussed as follows. In the long term, one solution might be to enhance infrastructure and services at the site. Another solution is to limit the number of visitors to the site. However, this might exclude individuals with high values for visiting the site while including those attaching low values to these public goods. The other option is to use pricing to limit access. As discussed above, an increase in price would reduce both the visitation rate and revenue. Thus, this is an inefficient solution as regards Vietnamese visitors. There is room for a pricing structure that charges a higher price at specific times in the high season and a lower price during the low season to try to stop all domestic tourism from taking place in the summer, say, and spreading the visits more evenly across the year.

The current fee policy for cultural heritage sites in Vietnam is not properly based on the individual preferences of tourists (i.e. demand) or on the supply in tourism market; nor is it properly designed to maximize revenues or restrict tourism demand to meet the environmental carrying capacity of endangered sites. There is also a tendency to apply a uniform pricing policy for foreign and Vietnamese visitors to sites in Vietnam. For example, the entrance fee for visiting My Son before 2004 was VND 50,000 and VND 10,000 for foreign and Vietnamese visitors, respectively. This has now increased to VND 60,000 (US$4) and VND 30,000 (US$2), respectively. Thus, from entrance fees being five times as high for foreigners, the differential has now been reduced to twice as high. This pricing policy is generally imposed on an uninformed basis. Based on the calculated consumer surplus (and total WTP), our results suggest that an even larger price differentiation would increase revenues and facilitate preservation because there would be more money for preservation and reduced damage to the site from reduced congestion. This could possibly also secure social equity; see Laarman and Gregersen (1996) and Lindberg (1991), for example, for discussion of this point.

10.5 Conclusions

This chapter has estimated the economic benefits derived from a proposed preservation plan to preserve and restore the My Son sanctuary in Vietnam. The study focused on the benefits accruing to foreign visitors and domestic visitors to My Son. The economic benefits were measured using two CV surveys that were administered at the My Son site in 2005.

Results show that foreign visitors' WTP is much higher than that of Vietnamese visitors (about US$9 and US$2 for foreigners and Vietnamese, respectively). However, if we consider the WTP as a fraction of household income, foreign visitors' WTP constitutes a much smaller part of annual household income than that of Vietnamese visitors (0.02 per cent and 0.17 per cent for foreigners and Vietnamese, respectively). Implementing this entrance fee structure would increase revenues at the site by about half of the current revenues, and at the same time reduce half the number of foreign visitors,

Thus, the results imply that the adoption of an optimal price regime would both increase revenues and reduce congestion at the site. However, this pricing regime would not reduce the congestion problem due to Vietnamese visitors. The idea of imposing a pricing structure with seasonal differentiation to reduce the number of Vietnamese visitors in the high season is feasible.

The lack of data on the tourist carrying capacity of My Son shows the need for future research to fill this information gap. We need to know more about the impact of additional visitors on this site if a truly sustainable pricing policy is to be developed.

This study has shown how the field of environmental valuation can contribute to sustainable tourism in cultural heritage sites. There is, however, only limited empirical evidence in Vietnam on WTP in terms of increased fees and taxes and the income elasticity of WTP. Therefore, more studies should be conducted to ensure an informed basis for the development of optimal fee policies for tourists visiting cultural heritage sites.

Notes

1   The economic benefits of a preservation plan for My Son sanctuary could potentially accrue to many groups of beneficiaries, including visitors to My Son (both foreigners and Vietnamese), local residents, other Vietnamese, foreign visitors to Vietnam who do not visit My Son, and foreigners not visiting Vietnam (see Tuan, 2006, for detailed discussion). This chapter focuses on the benefits that accrue to foreign and Vietnamese visitors to My Son.

2   The entry price that would maximize revenue can be determined from the demand curve for visits to a site. Willis (2003) and Navrud and Vondolia (2005) specify a functional relationship between visits and price as $Q = \beta_0 e^{-\beta_1 P}$, where Q is number of visits, P represents the bid or WTP, and β_0 and β_1 are constants. The optimal price that achieves maximum revenues can be derived from estimating this demand function. Since this study used the closed-ended elicitation format of CV with four bid amounts, the levels of bids are few and give little variation in the demand curve if we apply the demand estimation approach. We therefore instead use a table to describe the bid amounts with corresponding visitation rates at each level of the entrance fees, and to show the optimal entrance fees that would maximize revenues.

3   While fixed costs per additional visitor could be expected to be low, marginal environmental costs could be high if visitor numbers exceed the carrying capacity of the site. Without information on the site's carrying capacity, however, it is hard to take this into account.

4   During the peak hours (from 11 a.m. to 1 p.m.), there is occasional congestion at My Son. In the summer – the high season for Vietnamese visitors – the congestion

problem occurs more often. With the current growth of visitors, this will be a big problem in the near future unless there is a great improvement in infrastructure and services at the site.

References

Cameron, T. (1988) 'A new paradigm for valuing non-market goods using referendum data: maximum likelihood estimation by censored logistic regression', *Journal of Environmental Economics and Management*, 15: 355–379.

Edwards, S. F. and Anderson, G. D. (1987) 'Overlooked biases in contingent valuation surveys: some considerations', *Land Economics*, 63: 168–178.

eftec (Economics for the Environment Consultancy) (2005) *Valuation of the Historic Environment: The Scope for Using Results of Valuation Studies in the Appraisal and Assessment of Heritage-Related Projects and Programs*, Final Report, London: eftec.

GHF (Global Heritage Fund) (2002) 'Global Heritage Fund 2002 Nominations'.

Greene, W. (2000) *Econometric Analysis*, Upper Saddle River, NJ: Prentice-Hall.

Hokby, S. and Soderqvist, T. (2003) 'Elasticities of demand and willingness to pay for environmental services in Sweden', *Environmental and Resource Economics*, 26: 361–383.

Jorgensen, B. S., Syme, G. J., Bishop, B. J. and Nancarrow, B. E. (1999) 'Protest responses in contingent valuation', *Environmental and Resource Economics*, 14: 131–150.

Kinh, H. D. (2001) 'Cultural monuments maintenance and restoration in Vietnam – choosing a strategy', paper presented at the conference 'Conserving – An Asian Perspective of Authenticity in the Consolidation, Restoration and Reconstruction of Historic Monuments and Sites', Hanoi.

Kriström, B. and Riera, P. (1996) 'Is the income elasticity of environmental improvements less than one?', *Environmental and Resource Economics*, 7: 45–55.

Laarman, J. G. and Gregersen, H. M. (1996) 'Pricing policy in nature-based tourism', *Tourism Management*, 17: 247–254.

Lindberg, K. (1991) 'Policies for maximizing nature tourism's ecological and economic benefits', International Conservation Financing Project Working Paper, World Resources Institute, Washington, DC.

Mitchell, R. and Carson, R. (1989) *Using Surveys to Value Public Goods: The Contingent Valuation Method*, Resources for the Future, Washington, DC.

Mourato, S. and Mazzanti, M. (2002) 'Economic valuation of cultural heritage: evidence and prospects', in M. de la Torre (ed.) *Assessing the Values of Cultural Heritage*, Research Report, Los Angeles: Getty Conservation Institute.

Mourato, S., Ozdemiroglu, E., Hett, T. and Atkinson, G. (2004) 'Pricing cultural heritage: a new approach to managing ancient resources', *World Economics*, 5 (3): 95–113.

Navrud, S. and Ready, R. (eds) (2002) *Valuing Cultural Heritage: Applying Environmental Valuation Techniques to Historic Buildings, Monuments and Artifacts*, Cheltenham, UK: Edward Elgar.

Navrud, S. and Vondolia, G. K. (2005) 'Using contingent valuation to price ecotourism sites in developing countries', *Tourism*, 52 (2): 115–125.

Sutherland, R. J. and Walsh, R. G. (1985) 'Effect of distance on the preservation value of water quality', *Land Economics*, 61: 281–291.

Tuan, T. H. (2006) Valuing the Economic Benefits of Preserving Cultural Heritage: The World Heritage Site, My Son Sanctuary in Vietnam', Research Report no. 2006-RR6, EEPSEA.

UNESCO (United Nations Educational, Scientific and Cultural Organization), My Son Sanctuary (1999). Online, available from http://whc.unesco.org/sites/949.htm.

VNS (Vietnam News) (2003) 'My Son's towers threatened by erosion', 10 November.

Weitzel, V. (2002) 'Vietnam to develop heritage site', VNForum Archive.

Whittington, D. (1998) 'Administering contingent valuation questions in developing countries', *World Development*, 26 (1): 21–30.

Willis, K. G. (2003) 'Pricing public parks', *Journal of Environmental Planning and Management*, 46: 3–17.

The economics of sustainable tourism

Summary and suggestions for future research

Fabio Cerina, Anil Markandya and Michael McAleer

The purpose of this concluding chapter is to summarize the primary issues raised in the ten main chapters, evaluate the main findings and messages, and discuss some future developments in this exciting area of research in tourism economics.

The book was divided into three parts, namely 'Tourism demand and the host community', 'Tourism and productivity' and 'Sustainable tourism: environment and cultural heritage conservation'. Part I presented four chapters that were concerned with the analysis of tourist satisfaction and the impacts of tourists on the host community, namely a rigorous analysis of the determinants of tourism demand and the effects of tourism demand on residents' attitudes and residential demand for water. Part II dealt with the productivity of the tourism sector. This issue was investigated, from both empirical and theoretical perspectives, by three chapters that analysed how different factors (environmental resources, trade relationships, rural areas and labour) may contribute to increasing the productivity of an economy that specializes in tourism. Part III focused on the sustainability of tourism development. Sustainable tourism was investigated from three different perspectives, namely: (1) methodological, through the construction of an index that is able to measure sustainability of tourist destinations; (2) theoretical, through a growth model that analyses the dynamic properties of an economy specializing in tourism based on environmental resources; and (3) empirical, by means of an analysis of the economic benefits derived from a proposal that is designed to preserve and restore a cultural heritage site.

The ten chapters comprised an interesting and vibrant combination of theory and applied research, time frequency and analysis of data (namely, annual and monthly time series, cross section, panels, surveys, contingent valuation), variety of countries (Italy, Japan, Spain, Thailand, the United Kingdom and Vietnam), different model specifications (ARMAX, cross section, panel, logit, factor analysis, dynamic optimization and causality analysis), and a wide range of numbers of observations (from hundreds to thousands). It is to be expected that these chapters will be invaluable to both researchers and tourism practitioners with a wide variety of interests.

The availability of panel data (to and from various countries, and for a variety of variables) and different time frequencies (monthly, weekly and daily), make it possible to consider a wide range of sophisticated models and techniques for empirical analysis. Dynamic panel data analysis, with seasonal, periodic and zero-frequency unit roots, and corresponding co-integration processes, will undoubtedly expand the horizons of research in tourism economics in the years ahead. Furthermore, the increasing availability of weekly and daily international tourist arrivals data, as well as daily observations on exchange rates (as a proxy for relative prices), will make it possible to estimate univariate and multivariate VARFIMA models containing measurement errors, fractionally integrated and long memory processes, and heterogeneous autoregressive processes.

The availability of high-frequency data, such as daily international tourist arrivals, has already enabled challenging analysis of international tourist arrivals data in the same light as financial time-series data. This leads to the requirement that appropriate models be chosen sensibly from among a wide variety of univariate conditional, stochastic and realized volatility models, with a concomitant emphasis on choosing models that can accommodate thresholds, asymmetry and leverage. In addition, the complexity of multivariate volatility models should not be underestimated. Finally, careful thought should be given to the choice of appropriate forecasting models and forecasting expertise, as well as the optimal combination of models using both formal models and the intuition of expert forecasters.

The careful analysis of data is also shown to be useful in determining preferences of tourists and local communities. Such analysis should aid in the design of facilities that better meet the needs of visitors while also recognizing those of local communities. Certainly there is scope for more efficient provision of key services that are in short supply, such as water, as Chapter 4 clearly demonstrates.

As far as sustainability is concerned, the question of the sustainability of current tourism practices remains only partly answered. Indices like the one developed in Chapter 8 are needed to track sustainability and to respond to changes that result in a lower recorded measure of this indicator. We also need to understand the trade-offs between increased tourism and its environmental footprint so that more informed choices can be made. Models like the one in Chapter 9 are helpful in that regard, as is Chapter 5. Finally, the protection of cultural assets is a sensitive issue where many see a conflict with tourism. Yet with care, such assets can be better protected and managed if revenues from tourist visitors are used for that purpose. The design of such schemes is a complex issue, but one that can be tackled, as has been well explained in the last chapter of the book.

Index

Note: Page numbers in **bold** denote figures, those done in *italic* denote tables.